Emerging Voices

Critical Social Research by European Group Postgraduate and Early Career Researchers

Co-ordinated and Edited by Samantha Fletcher and Holly White

For dear Sam

Let's stay critical together!

love, Maomao
May 2018 HK

Emerging Voices

Critical Social Research by European Group Postgraduate
and Early Career Researchers

Co-ordinated and Edited by
Samantha Fletcher and Holly White

Associate Editing by the Emerging Voices Collective
Preface by Steve Tombs

EG Press Limited
London
2017

Published by the EG Press Limited,
London, England

www.egpress.org/

ISBN 978-1-911439-09-7

The European Group for the Study of Deviance and Social Control held its first conference in Italy in 1973. Since then, annual conferences have been held at different venues throughout Europe with academics, researchers, activists and practitioners in criminology and related fields participating. While initially class and certain political hierarchies were the focus, the European Group gradually sought to address other national, linguistic, class, ethnic, sexual, and gender barriers in an effort to develop a critical, emancipatory, and innovative criminology. This was to be done through the topics of members' research and in the conduct of conferences, with the ultimate aim being to provide a forum for, and recognition of, emancipatory science and emancipatory politics as legitimate areas of study and activism. One goal of the group has been to highlight social problems in the field of deviance and social control which are under-exposed by criminologists in many other contexts; thus to create a forum not commonly provided at other conferences and international networks for academics, practitioners, and activists working towards the promotion of social justice, human rights and democratic accountability.

www.europeangroup.org/

© The *European Group for the Study of Deviance and Social Control* and Authors, 2017

All authors' royalties have been donated to the European Group

The Emerging Voices Collective

Maya Barak

Una Barr

Paul Betts

Jon Davies

Helen Elfleet

Natacha Filippi

Samantha Fletcher

Helena Gosling

Kirsty Greenwood

Nicola Harding

Laura Kelly

Claudia Mantovan

Agnieszka Martynowicz

Gillian McNaull

Michele Miravalle

Ashley S.F. Rogers

Alex Simpson

Maryja Šupa

Katie Tucker

Holly White

Hannah Wilkinson

Contributors

Maya Barak	University of Michigan-Dearborn, US
Una Barr	University of Central Lancashire, UK
Paul Betts	University of Birmingham, UK
Jon Davies	University of Manchester, UK
Helen Elfleet	Edge Hill University, UK
Natacha Filippi	University of Oxford, UK
Samantha Fletcher	The Open University, UK
Helena Gosling	Liverpool John Moores University, UK
Kirsty Greenwood	Liverpool John Moores University, UK
Nicola Harding	Manchester Metropolitan University, UK
Andrew Henley	Keele University, UK
Laura Kelly	University of Central Lancashire, UK
Claudia Mantovan	University of Padua, Italy
Agnieszka Martynowicz	Edge Hill University, UK
Gillian McNaull	Queen's University Belfast, UK
Ashley S.F. Rogers	University of Stirling, UK
Adam Scott	Liverpool John Moores University, UK
Katja Simončič	University of Ljubljana, Slovenia
Alex Simpson	University of Brighton, UK
Carly Speed	Liverpool John Moores University, UK
Luca Sterchele	University of Padova, Italy
Maryja Šupa	Vilnius University, Lithuania.
Katie Tucker	Liverpool John Moores University, UK
Holly White	Edge Hill University, UK
Hannah Wilkinson	Keele University, UK
Xiaoye Zhang	City University of Hong Kong, China

Contents

Preface **Steve Tombs**	ix
Introduction **Samantha Fletcher and Holly White**	1
1. Fairness and the Law: Central American Experiences in U.S. Immigration Court **Maya Barak**	3
2. Are Neoliberal, Patriarchal Societies Compatible with Desistance? A Consideration of the Experiences of a Group of English Women caught up in the Criminal Justice System **Una Barr**	15
3. Evidence-Based Policing or Policy-Based Evidence-Making? The Case of British Policing **Paul Betts**	27
4. Labour Exploitation and Migrant Workers in UK Food Supply Chains **Jon Davies**	37
5. Post-Release Experiences after Corston (2007): An Introduction to my Research **Helen Elfleet**	49
6. Prisons, Citizenship and Democratic Transitions: A Crossed Gaze between South Africa and Spain **Natacha Filippi**	61
7. 'It's not a protest, it's a process': Protest, Resistance and the War of Position in the Advanced Capitalist State **Samantha Fletcher**	71
8. Creating and Developing Inclusive Learning Environments Beyond the Prison Gates **Helena Gosling**	83

9. 'Social justice' in Women's Centres? Experiences and Impact of Gender-Specific Service Provision
Kirsty Greenwood

91

10. Why Feminist Criminology Must Pose a Methodological Challenge to Male-Centred Criminological Theory
Nicola Harding

105

11. Criminal Records and Conditional Citizenship: Towards a Critical Sociology of Post-Sentence Discrimination
Andrew Henley

119

12. Life in Prison through the Lens of Deafness: The Experiences of Deaf Prisoners in England and Wales
Laura Kelly

129

13. An Alternative to Zero-Tolerance Policies? The Project Implemented in the Multi-Ethnic 'Piave' Neighbourhood in Mestre, Venice
Claudia Mantovan

141

14. "...They Didn't Ask Us to Come Here, Did They?" The Pain of the Threat of Expulsion in a Contemporary Prison
Agnieszka Martynowicz

153

15. Critical Feminist Methodology: A Reflexive Account of Prison Research
Gillian McNaull

165

16. Women's Rights and Legal Consciousness in Bolivia: A Socio-Legal Ethnography
Ashley S. F. Rogers

179

17. Resistance From Within: Early Findings from a Study on Youth Justice Practitioner's Experiences of Policy
Adam Scott

193

18. Addressing the Collateral Damage of Fast Fashion: the Perception of Social Harm and the Possibility of Consumer Agency
Katja Simončič

203

19. Neutralising Deviance: The Legitimation of Harm and the Culture of Finance in the City of London
Alex Simpson

215

20. Deafening Attempts to Silence: Critically Exploring the Deaths of Patients Detained in Psychiatric Detention 225
Carly Speed

21. Subverting 'Crime Diagnosis': the Deconstruction of Social Dangerousness in Biographical Tales of 'Mentally Ill Offenders' 235
Luca Sterchele

22. Foucault and the City: Conceptualising Social Control Over Urban Space 247
Maryja Šupa

23. From *"Amused Tolerance to Outrage"*: A Critical Analysis of the Framing of Child Sexual Abuse within Institutional Sites 257
Katie Tucker

24. Westminster's Narration of the Neoliberal Crisis: Rationalising the Irrational? 271
Holly White

25. 'What Was it All For?' 21st Century Theatres of War and the Return to 'Post-Conflict' Life 283
Hannah Wilkinson

26. Prison Theatre as Method: Focused Ethnography and Auto-ethnography in a Chinese Prison 295
Xiaoye Zhang

Preface

The European Group for the Study of Deviance and Social Control was founded in Florence, Italy, in 1973, and since then has grown to some 1500 members drawn from six continents, a scale which supports its claim that it is the largest Critical Criminology forum in the world. It has held an annual conference each year since 1973, and outwith this there tends to be various country-specific events of more or less formality. Probably less, in fact, because one of the features that characterises this Group is that there is a relative spontaneity to it. It is an *organisation*, of course, so it has plans, processes and structures, but it retains a little of a Do-It-Yourself ethos that escapes many other professional organisations, at least those inhabited by academics.

A second characteristic is that the Group is avowedly committed to being non-hierarchical – and so, for example, at the Annual Conferences of the Group I have listened to plenaries given by PhD students as well as internationally acclaimed Professors (and will not disclose here which I have preferred!). Newcomers to the Group participate in the academic and social activities of our meetings with as much voice and legitimacy as those who have attended most of the 44 conferences. We attempt collectively to offer a space of mutual support, respect, friendship and, it should be emphasised, fun.

Third, the Group is diverse in our areas of focus, in our theoretical perspectives and philosophies, in the countries and languages in which we work, in our biographies and intellectual histories, and in our specific social and political commitments. But at the same time, we are all committed to engaging in genuinely dialogic conversations and to mutual learning from these, perhaps for the sake of learning but certainly for furthering various dimensions of social justice.

Finally, then, we are all engaged beyond the academy – whether we think of ourselves as activists, practitioners, volunteers, campaigners or something similar. In its own words, the European Group is "an international network for academics, practitioners, and activists working towards social justice, state accountability and decarceration. It is an open forum promoting critical analysis and connecting theory, politics and activism". We may not always live up to these lofty ideals, but we constantly strive towards them. Certainly, the Group is not merely a professional association of academics.

These four characteristics of the organisation are all in evidence in the twenty-six substantive contributions that constitute this volume, features which are skilfully and imaginatively woven throughout the chapters. They are, indeed, in evidence in the very initiative that has resulted in this book. The European Group has only got this far – in terms of longevity, reach and significance – through consistently and constantly welcoming 'emerging voices' – new colleagues and comrades, who in turn have become established within and around the Group – and then welcomed successive 'emerging voices'. This text is testament to that process of renewal and commitment to vitality.

Focusing on a diverse range of empirical areas within and beyond 'crime', Criminology and Criminal Justice, the chapters here, taken together, combine a variety of forms of structural analyses with consistently insightful observations on the micro-realities of peoples' lives, lives which traverse Africa, the Americas, Asia, and Europe. What is more, each chapter takes time to reveal the biography that has led its author to the words that they have committed to the page – as we too learn of the various disciplinary trajectories the authors have taken towards, and which must necessarily comprise, a critical 'criminology'.

Across forty-four years our Group has waned at times as well as waxed. But in its best moments – and there have been and will be very many of these – it is a meeting point for and a melting pot of conversations between new and old friends. With no little blood, sweat and tears, Samantha Fletcher and Holly White have assembled a collection of essays which stands as a significant and original contribution to critical social science in its own right, but which simultaneously captures so many of the commitments of the European Group. So, I would like to express my thanks to Samantha, Holly, the Emerging Voices Collective and all of the contributors on behalf of some of the, shall we say, 'longer-established' voices. My and our trust that the organisation is in excellent hands is completely confirmed by what is to come in the following pages.

A bearded philosopher once said that the point of our work is to change the world – although to do so requires that we first interpret it accurately. These emerging voices contribute to this necessary, accurate interpretation.

Steve Tombs, June 2017

Introduction

The idea for this collection emerged at the European Group for the Study of Deviance and Social Control's 44th annual conference at the University of Minho in Braga in September 2016. Reflecting the Group's commitment to supporting and encouraging the development of newer members, as postgraduate researchers ourselves we were invited by the EG Press to co-ordinate and edit a collection to disseminate the work of postgraduate and early career researchers. We were delighted to accept the invitation and have sought to share the opportunity for gaining experience in the process of creating an edited collection by inviting other postgraduate and early career researchers to take part in peer review, and those who took part formed the Emerging Voices Collective.

This collection of twenty-six short chapters introduces the scholarly and activist work currently being undertaken by emerging voices in the European Group. What unites this diverse collection is a commitment to the founding principles and the ethos of the Group: the promotion of critical analysis, speaking truth to power, direct engagement, challenging dominant narratives that marginalise, and seeking out social justice.

To give an insight into the wide range of subject matters, the book includes chapters that explore: experiences of immigration court; the relationship between researchers and the state; the specific experiences of women in prison and the wider criminal (in)justice system; corporate crime regulation across different nation states; routine harms in migrant labour exploitation; protest in the advanced capitalist state; integrated education; participatory action research; discrimination pertaining to criminal records; the experience of incarcerated Deaf persons; social exclusion and marginalisation; community alternatives to zero tolerance policies; deportation; theatre in prisons; research methods for Critical Criminology; resistance within youth justice paradigms; consumer agency and harms in the fashion industry; neutralisation strategies in the finance industry; socio-legal ethnography in Bolivia; social constructions of the 'dangerous'; critical examinations of the narration of the neoliberal crisis; post conflict experiences; and deaths in custody. All chapters are accompanied by extended biographies that detail the wider research, activism, and other endeavours of the contributors.

As ever a project such as this is far from completed in isolation. As a result, we have an extensive list of acknowledgements in order to recognise the wider contributions to the book's production and all who have made its publication possible. Firstly, we wish to thank John Moore for all his dedication to EG Press, and particularly for his advice and support at every stage of editing this book. We wish to thank Kym Atkinson, Emma Bell, Kris Cardosa, James Heydon, Agnieszka Martynowicz, Lindsey Metcalf, Adam Scott, David Scott, Steve Tombs, Azrini Wahidin and Richard Wild for undertaking the proof reading of this collection.

A special thank you to Steve Tombs for his genuine enthusiasm and constant support for emerging voices in the European Group, reflected in his contribution of the preface to this book. In addition to this we thank Thaiquan Lieu for support with translation. Perhaps most of all we extend the biggest thank you to all our comrades in the Emerging Voices Collective who took the time to engage roundly in the peer review process, generously sharing their knowledge and providing valuable constructive feedback. We were overwhelmed by how many persons volunteered their time, especially given the pressures we all face in our work lives at this current conjuncture in our careers.

The support and involvement of the wider Emerging Voices Collective firmly endows this collection with the ethos, spirit, and comradeship we have come to expect from the Group and will always value. Another thank you is extended to the research participants who importantly share their stories with us. Our final thank you goes to all members of the European Group who over the years have welcomed, encouraged, and supported us and so many of the contributors to this book.

We hope that this collection is a platform for dialogue between all members of the Group. The collection is inclusive of works that are in the early stages of their development, and contributors in the early stages of their endeavours. All contributors welcome feedback and we anticipate this book being a catalyst for conversations and collaborations, and a mechanism for further building a supportive network. We also hope this is the start of a series that will continuously provide an inclusive place for members to share their ideas in their early stages and develop their skills in editing and peer review. We dedicate this volume to all those in the pursuit of critical and emancipatory knowledge.

In solidarity,
Sam and Holly

1

Fairness and the Law: Central American Experiences in U.S. Immigration Court

Maya Barak

Introduction

Sara came to the United States out of necessity. As she explained, "life is very different [in Central America]." Not only were Sara and her family living a life of poverty, but, not long before she migrated, her son was targeted by a criminal gang. Harassment quickly escalated from verbal to physical—Sara's son was nearly beaten to death just outside his school. She felt helpless. Unable to turn to the local authorities, whom she viewed as incapable, Sara sent her son—illegally—to the United States. She followed soon after. Caught at the border and placed in removal, Sara's hearing has been postponed multiple times. Meanwhile, Sara does not have permission to work and is subject to immigration supervision, requiring her to wear an electronic monitoring device and check in with an immigration officer regularly. Frustrated with what she considered to be a lack of options, Sara broke down crying: "one doesn't come here to do damage or to hurt anyone [...] we only came here to try to help our families. People here don't know what it's like there".

Sara's story captures the desperation driving many Central American people to migrate to the United States. Confronted with poverty, violence, and the state's inability to provide even a semblance of protection, Sara chose to violate immigration law and move her family to the United States without permission. Although she had little knowledge of immigration law or the American legal system, Sara was convinced that the United States was a country governed by the 'rule of law'. Ultimately, the search for security and opportunity, appreciation of 'law and order' and belief in the government's legitimacy is what attracted Sara to the United States.

Based upon 40 in-depth interviews with Central American immigrants and U.S. attorneys, as well as observations of two strategically chosen immigration courts over an 18-month period, this study captures the ways culture, experience, and positionality toward the law shape assessments of legal encounters. Sara's experience with the immigration system is not unique. Hundreds of thousands of immigrants are processed through U.S. immigration court each year (Executive Office for Immigration Review, 2015). These individuals and their families experience the immigration system through the lens of removal, or deportation. Most will be ordered to be removed (deported). For many, this is a defining experience with the American legal system, shaping understandings of and compliance with the law.

Procedural Justice Expectations

Immigrants generally expect to be treated poorly in immigration court and quickly removed from the United States. Many study participants were afraid of immigration judges and attorneys prior to their hearings. They were often unsure if they would be provided with court interpretation, or how much, if any, of the removal hearing process would be explained to them. Most, especially undocumented immigrants, expected to have very few, if any, legal rights (see: Abrego, 2011, 2016; Coutin, 2000, 2007; Menjívar, 2006, 2011, 2012).

Given expectations, immigrants generally found their hearings procedurally fair. Most viewed court attorneys, judges, and interpreters as polite, professional, and unbiased. Even when an aspect of the removal hearing process was deemed problematic, participants did not necessarily find the removal process, itself, unfair. For many, the experience of being treated with even a semblance of procedural fairness in immigration court was appreciated. Despite assessments of fair process, however, most immigrants were dissatisfied with outcomes of removal.

While this may not be surprising—who would be happy with deportation? —such findings are perplexing when viewed through the lens of procedural justice theory. Over three decades of research demonstrates that procedural justice, or process fairness, is crucial to broader assessments of legal encounters, such as removal hearings. Evaluations of fair process are associated with increased outcome satisfaction (even when the outcome is not desired), enhanced beliefs in state legitimacy, and increased compliance, and have even been shown to outweigh outcome desirability and the equitable distribution of processes and outcomes (Gau and Brunson, 2009; Hinds, 2007; Hollander-Blumoff and Tyler, 2008; Paternoster *et al*, 1997; Sunshine and Tyler, 2003; Tyler,

2003). Yet, immigration appears to defy the standard rules of procedural justice.

Why do traditional understandings of procedural justice break down in the immigration context? The answer is simple: immigrant legal consciousness, or the ways in which immigrants think about and relate to the law. Immigrants are a distinct group. Their understandings of the law are deeply influenced by the immigrant experience and legal cultures in their home countries. Most immigrants' legal knowledge is derived from informal sources, such as the stories of family, friends, and the media. This legal 'knowledge', accurate or inaccurate, shapes how immigrants think about the law. It also forms the backdrop against which immigrants compare their experiences. Thus, the way immigrants think about the law is integrally connected to how they assess legal encounters.

Compliance, Fairness, and Legitimacy

Again, participants were surprised by their experiences of the removal process, which often exceeded their procedural justice expectations. Such assessments, however, did not translate to outcome satisfaction, as procedural justice theory would predict. Instead, distributive justice assessments—or comparisons of one's own outcome and treatment to that of others—appeared to be as, if not more, important than assessments of process fairness when predicting outcome satisfaction.

In a classic article on assessments of procedural justice, Tyler (1988) unknowingly forecasts the relationship described here. Finding that consistency with past experiences and prior expectations have no effect on procedural justice assessments or outcome satisfaction, he proposes a link between population characteristics, legal knowledge acquisition, and procedural justice:

> In this study citizens are not basing their judgements on a comparison of their outcomes or treatment with other experiences, either their own or of others' [...] Citizens may thus lack the knowledge necessary for judging whether their outcomes or treatment were better or worse than those of others [...] It may be that the lack of awareness of others' experiences is characteristic of only some populations. Special groups may have greater knowledge about others and rely more on other's experiences when evaluating their own (Tyler, 1988: 131-132).

As Tyler explains, some populations may lack the information needed to make consistency judgements pertaining to treatment or outcome. These populations rely on information they do have, like officials' behaviour and formal legal knowledge including standards of conduct (Tyler, 1988). The findings of this study are indicative of the alternative Tyler presents. Lacking the formal knowledge needed to assess the fairness of removal hearings on their legal merits, and in the context of relative isolation within immigrant communities, immigrants rely heavily upon past experiences and prior expectations. Through experiences and stories, notions of possible immigration treatment and outcomes crystallise. This information is compiled alongside stories about, and experiences with, the law in immigrants' home countries. Together, it is used to assess the procedural and distributive fairness of removal hearings and plays a central role in assessments of outcome satisfaction.

In yet another divergence from procedural justice theory, immigrants' assessments of the substantive fairness of immigration law weighed heavier on their satisfaction with removal hearing outcomes than distributive or procedural justice. Substantive fairness is typically overlooked in procedural justice research. While 'substantive fairness' is subjective, those interviewed agreed that 'substantively fair' immigration law should entail the ability to live and work legally in the United States. For most, anything other than relief from removal was considered unsatisfactory, regardless of procedural or distributive fairness.

This, too, may appear unsurprising as it is hard to imagine immigrants who would be happy if deported. Certainly, removal conflicts with individual desires to reside in the United States, but, for many, assessing the substantive fairness of immigration law was about more than this. Irrespective of procedural or distributive fairness, many immigrants held that removal ignores their ethical, moral, and necessity-based claims to U.S. residence. Substantively fair immigration law, they explained, would acknowledge the equality of all, as well as the right to migrate, to live a life free from violence, and to provide for one's family, implicitly grounding arguments in principles of human rights not unlike those set forth by the United Nations.

Perceptions of the substantive fairness of immigration law—or lack thereof—not only impacted outcome satisfaction, but greatly influenced immigrants' compliance with the law. Most non-detained immigrants in this study who were ordered removed chose to remain in the United States. Those who were forcibly removed while in immigration custody had either already returned to the United States illegally or had plans to do so. Those awaiting case outcomes planned to remain in the United States or return illegally if removed. In fact, the majority of immigrants who participated in this study were in violation of a number of immigration-related civil and/or criminal offences. As most explained, it would be wonderful to be able to comply with U.S. law, but existing law is often incompatible with immigrant needs.

It appears that compliance with immigration law is not a question of distributive or procedural justice. Fair treatment does not make the realities of removal more tolerable. Equitable distribution of removal only makes it slightly more palatable. The fairness of immigration law matters, first and foremost, to immigrants when evaluating their experiences with removal, not how one is treated in court or how one's hearing compares to that of another. Removal is removal regardless of equity, impartiality, or pleasantries.

At the same time, immigrants in this study expressed strong beliefs in the legitimacy of the U.S. government, as well as its enforcement powers. They noted a great appreciation for the "rule of law" in the U.S., stressing that an absence of law and order in their home countries makes life difficult. Most applauded strict enforcement of the law against those who commit crimes. Moreover, many immigrants felt the United States has the authority and *obligation* to enforce immigration law. Immigrants held these opinions even when faced with removal. Yet, perceptions of state legitimacy did not result in compliance.

These findings, again, contradict procedural justice theory (Gau and Brunson, 2009; Hinds, 2007; Hollander-Blumoff and Tyler, 2008; Paternoster *et al*, 1997; Sunshine and Tyler, 2003; Tyler, 2003). Contrary to prior literature, fair process and legitimacy were not associated with outcome satisfaction or compliance. Legal consciousness offers one explanation. Just as immigrants' understandings of law influence assessments of procedural and distributive justice, as well as legitimacy, they influence compliance. Immigrants interviewed for this study come from countries with high levels of corruption, criminality, and impunity. They often characterised judges, lawyers, and police in their home countries as corrupt and untrustworthy. Many had experienced direct and indirect criminal victimisation. Some came to the U.S. fleeing violence at home. They frequently cited the absence of law in their home countries when explaining why they felt unable to return.

Such negative experiences with the law are not unique to the study participants, but instead characterise the most recent wave of Central American migration to the United States (Stinchcomb and Hershberg,

2014). In this context, immigrants place a high value on 'law and order' and, perhaps ironically, are willing to violate the law in order to live in a society where the law has meaning. Belief in state legitimacy thus drives immigrants to come to—and remain in—the United States illegally. In the same vein, immigrants 'downplay' the severity of their own immigration violations as nonviolent, victimless, and necessary to escape violent victimisation at home.

Discussion

Study findings present a number of challenges to procedural justice theory. In the immigration context, positive process fairness assessments are not indicative of outcome satisfaction; dissatisfaction with outcomes does not imply disbelief in state legitimacy; and neither positive process fairness assessments nor a belief in state legitimacy are correlated with compliance. Perhaps individuals with low procedural justice expectations, like immigrants, may be more concerned with matters of substantive fairness than process fairness when assessing legal encounters. More likely, still, is the possibility that process fairness matters less than substantive fairness when the stakes are high. The consequences of removal are devastating and long-lasting. Immigrants may find process fairness irrelevant in the 'bigger picture' of removal. Ultimately, in some contexts, fairness and legitimacy may be irrelevant to fostering satisfaction and legal compliance.

These findings also highlight the role legal consciousness plays in assessments of procedural and distributive justice, outcome satisfaction and compliance, and legitimacy. Legal consciousness helps explain why procedural justice operates differently in the immigration context than in U.S. studies of American-born citizens. It also addresses a major shortcoming of procedural justice theory: a tendency to overlook the impacts of culture and context on assessments of legal encounters (see: Murphey and Cherney, 2011; Pillai et al, 2001; Tankebe, 2009, 2013). This understanding of procedural justice provides a plausible explanation for group and individual-level variations in process fairness assessments, explicitly tying them to personal experiences and views of the law.

This study also implies the emergence of a broader theory of legal consciousness and justice. While procedural justice may have a significant impact on outcome satisfaction, state legitimacy, and compliance in some contexts, this and other 'second wave' procedural justice studies demonstrate this is not always the case (Murphey and Cherney, 2011;

Pillai *et al*, 2001; Tankebe, 2009, 2013). Distributive, procedural, and substantive justice influence outcome satisfaction, state legitimacy, and compliance—which type of justice matters most in evaluations of legal encounters likely depends upon one's legal consciousness, or one's understanding of and positionality toward the law. Individuals with formal legal knowledge may prioritise procedural justice when assessing legal encounters, while individuals possessing more informal legal knowledge— like immigrants—may prioritise distributive and substantive justice. Lacking both formal and informal legal knowledge, individuals may rely most heavily upon understandings of justice derived from outside the legal realm, such as when immigrants draw upon morality and rights discourses to make sense of removal.

Policy Implications

As stated at the outset of this chapter, hundreds of thousands of immigrants are processed through immigration court each year, making this a defining experience with the American legal system. How these individuals experience and make sense of the U.S. immigration system has serious implications for how they interact with the legal system. Much attention has been given to the shortcomings of the U.S. immigration system. Activists and attorneys have pushed for enhanced due process within immigration courts, such as addressing indigent defense and the elimination of mandatory detention. These changes could enhance immigrants' perceptions of removal process fairness, but policy implications of this study are clear: fostering compliance with immigration law cannot rest solely upon fair procedure—it must be rooted in substantive fairness. For the immigrants in this study, removal hearing outcomes far outweigh questions of fair process.

Moreover, immigrants greatly appreciate the 'rule of law' in the United States—in fact, it is partially responsible for drawing them here. Regardless of a desire to comply with the law, and aside from whether or not immigration court is procedurally just, desperate conditions at home overpower inclinations to obey the law. Unless country conditions in Central America improve, Central Americans will be inclined to come to the United States illegally, refuse to self-deport, and return illegally if removed. This stark reality evidences the need for comprehensive immigration reform that creates viable pathways to legalisation and citizenship for all.

Acknowledgements

I would like to thank my Chair, Jon Gould, as well as the rest of my dissertation committee, Eric Hershberg, Marjorie Zatz, Jayesh Rathod, and Raymond Michalowski, along with the attorneys, court staff, immigrants, interpreters, judges, and security guards with whom I spoke over the course of this project. I am also grateful to the supportive faculty and staff of the Department of Justice, Law and Criminology in the School of Public Affairs at American University, as well as to the Tinker Foundation for awarding me the Tinker Field Research Grant, and the School of Public Affairs for awarding me the Neil and Ann Kerwin Doctoral Fellowship, which supported my data collection efforts.

References

Abrego, L. (2011) 'Legal consciousness of undocumented Latinos: Fear and stigma as barriers to claims-making for first-and 1.5-generation immigrants' *Law & Society Review* Volume 45, No. 2 pp 337-370

Abrego, L. (2016) 'Illegality as a source of solidarity and tension in Latino families' *Journal of Latino/Latin American Studies* Volume 8, No.2 pp 5-21

Coutin, S.B. (2000) *Legalizing Moves: Salvadoran Immigrants' Struggle for U.S. Residency* Michigan: The University of Michigan Press

Coutin, S.B. (2007) *Nation of Emigrants: Shifting Boundaries of Citizenship in El Salvador and the United States* New York: Cornell University Press

Executive Office for Immigration Review (2015) *FY 2014 Statistical Year Book*. U.S. Department of Justice

Gau, J.M. and Brunson, R.K. (2009) 'Procedural justice and order maintenance policing: A study of inner-city young men's perceptions of police legitimacy' *Justice Quarterly* Volume 27, No. 2 pp 255-279

Hinds, L. (2007) 'Building police-youth relationships: The importance of procedural justice' *Youth Justice* Volume 7, No. 3 pp 195-209

Hollander-Blumoff, R. and Tyler, T.R. (2008) 'Procedural justice in negotiation: Procedural fairness, outcome acceptance, and integrative potential' *Law & Social Inquiry* Volume 33, No.2 pp 473-500

Menjívar, C. (2006) 'Liminal legality: Salvadoran and Guatemalan immigrants' lives in the United States' *American Journal of Sociology* Volume 111, No. 4 pp 999-1037

Menjívar, C. (2011) 'The power of the law: Central Americans' legality and everyday life in Phoenix, Arizona' *Latino Studies* Volume 9, No.4 pp 377-395

Menjívar, C. (2012) 'Transnational parenting and immigration law: Central Americans in the United States' *Journal of Ethnic and Migration Studies* Volume 38, No.2 pp 301-322

Murphey, K. and Cherney, A. (2011) 'Fostering cooperation with the police: How do ethnic minorities in Australia respond to procedural justice-based policing?' *Australian & New Zealand Journal of Criminology* Volume 44, No. 2 pp 235-257

Paternoster, R., Brame, R., Bachman, R., and Sherman, L.W. (1997) 'Do fair procedures matter? The effect of procedural justice on spouse assault' *Law & Society Review,* Volume 31, No. 1 pp 163-204

Pillai, R., Williams, E.S., and Tan, J.J. (2001) 'Are the scales tipped in favor of procedural or distributive justice? An investigation of the U.S., India, Germany, and Hong Kong (China)' *The International Journal of Conflict Management* Volume 12, No.4 pp 312-332

Stinchcomb, D. and Hershberg, E. (2014) 'Unaccompanied migrant children from Central America: Context, causes, and responses' Center for Latin American and Latino Studies, American University

Sunshine, J. and Tyler, T.R. (2003) 'The role of procedural justice and legitimacy in shaping public support for policing' *Law & Society Review* Volume 37, No.3 pp 513-548

Tankebe, J. (2009) 'Public cooperation with the police in Ghana: Does procedural fairness matter?' *Criminology* Volume 47, No.4 pp 1265-1293

Tankebe, J. (2013) 'Viewing things differently: The dimensions of public perceptions of police legitimacy' *Criminology* Volume 51, No.1 pp 103-135

Tyler, T.R. (1988) 'What is procedural justice?: Criteria used by citizens to assess the fairness of legal procedures' *Law & Society Review* Volume 22, No. 1 pp 103-136

Tyler, T.R. (2003) 'Procedural justice, legitimacy, and the effective rule of law' *Crime and Justice* Volume 30, pp 283-357

Extended Biography

Research

I am an Assistant Professor of Criminology and Criminal Justice at the University of Michigan-Dearborn. I hold a PhD in Justice, Law and Criminology from American University (2016), an MA in Criminology and Criminal Justice from Eastern Michigan University (2011), and a BA in Social Anthropology and Peace and Social Justice from the University of Michigan (2009). My research brings together the areas of law, deviance, immigration, and power, utilising interdisciplinary approaches that span the fields of Criminology, Law and Society, and Anthropology.

My dissertation, in which I examine the relationship between legal consciousness and procedural justice in immigration court *vis a vis* the experiences of Central American immigrants, exemplifies this. This research was greatly influenced by my experiences as a labour and immigrant rights community organiser, as well as volunteer work with a number of immigrant rights organisations, in the United States. Using in-depth interviews with immigrants and attorneys, as well as systematic social observation of court proceedings, I uncover the ways legal orientations shape evaluations of process fairness, distributive justice, outcome satisfaction, legitimacy, and compliance.

In "Motherhood and Immigration Policy: How Immigration Law Shapes Central Americans' Experiences of Family," (*forthcoming*), I explore gendered themes found in the dissertation through the reexamination of a single deportation case. I argue that immigration law produces 'legal' and 'illegal' immigrants and redefines the meaning—and experience—of denizenship. Of equal importance, I note how immigration law produces 'good' and 'bad' mothers and, ultimately, has the power to redefine the meaning and experience of motherhood altogether. Overall, this research makes important contributions to the fields of Criminology and Criminal Justice, Legal Sociology, and Latin American Studies, linking disparate bodies of theory, capturing the immigration court experience, and extending procedural justice research into the immigration realm.

Like my dissertation work, much of my scholarship engages multiple disciplines and diverse research methods, including surveys, interviews, social observation, ethnography, and content analysis. For example, in "Popular Media and the Death Penalty: A Critical Discourse Analysis of the Death Penalty in Film" (*forthcoming*), I use linguistic analysis to examine death penalty discourse and messaging in popular film. I argue that American death penalty films construct messages that reaffirm or contest the death penalty by strategically avoiding or emphasising execution. It is through this strategic positioning of execution within death penalty films that death penalty discourse and, indeed, discourse about the American criminal justice system itself, is created, translated, and produced for consumption by audiences. In "Collaborative State and Corporate Crime: Fraud, Unions and Elite Power in Mexico," (2015) I draw upon archival work, along with fieldwork in Northern Mexico, to introduce the concept of 'collaborative state and corporate crime', highlighting the ways in which governments and corporations collaboratively commit harm in the interest of shared goals and ideology.

I have also carried out theory-rich scholarship, as evidenced in "Re-Imagining Punishment: An Exercise in 'Intersectional Criminal Justice,'" (2014) which draws upon alternative Criminologies to present a new model of 'intersectional' criminal justice that combines aspects of adversarial, restorative, social, and transformative justice frameworks. Some of my favorite research endeavors have been collaborative projects utilising mixed methods, such as a study of the Occupy Movement protestors' attitudes toward use of violence against the police in Washington, DC, and New York City. Ultimately, while varied, my work is united by a constant exploration of structural inequalities in the American criminal justice and immigration systems, as well as attention to the ways in which criminal justice actors and laypeople understand their subjective experiences with crime, crime control, and the law.

Future Aspirations

I am currently collaborating on several projects including a comprehensive national survey of immigration attorneys' perceptions of justice, a binational study of the criminal MS-13 gang drawing upon surveys and interviews with gang members and law enforcement experts in El Salvador and the United States, as well as an exploration of denizenship, legitimacy, and compliance in the U.S. immigration context. I am also coauthoring a book on the lives and work of capital defense attorneys (*forthcoming*, NYU Press). In the future, I plan to extend my existing research into a comparative analysis of the lives and work of immigration lawyers and capital defense attorneys, the legal consciousness of transnational "MS-13" gang members, and examinations of the parallels between marginalised and hyper-surveilled immigrant and inner-city minority communities.

Selected Works

Barak, M. (2014) 'Re-imagining punishment: An exercise in 'intersectional criminal justice'' *Laws* Volume 3, No 4 pp 693-705

Barak, M. (2015) 'Collaborative state and corporate crime: Fraud, unions and elite power in Mexico' pp 373-385 in Barak, G. (ed) *Routledge International Handbook on the Crimes of the Powerful* Pennsylvania: Taylor and Francis

Barak, M. (forthcoming), 'Motherhood and immigration policy: How immigration law shapes Central Americans' experience of family' in Golash-Boza, T. (ed)

(forthcoming) *Forced Out and Fenced In: Immigration Tales from the Field* New York: Oxford University Press

Barak, M. (forthcoming) 'Popular media and the death penalty: A critical discourse analysis of the death penalty in film" in Lee, G. and Bohm, R. (eds) (forthcoming), *Routledge Handbook on Capital Punishment*, Taylor and Francis

Gould, J. B. and Barak, M. (forthcoming) *Capital Defense: The Lives and Work of Capital Defenders* New York: NYU Press

Contact Details

www.mayabarak.com

2

Are Neoliberal, Patriarchal Societies Compatible with Desistance? A Consideration of the Experiences of a Group of English Women Caught up in the Criminal Justice System

Una Barr

Introduction

> You know what, I'm not being funny, the only thing I can turn round and tell ya is this government that are in now [...] I can tell you I've never felt so strongly about it in my life, this government that are in now have made such a fucking mess of this country, honest to God, they've made such a fucking mess of it. 'Cause I'm telling you now, they've taken away [...] I'm telling you, I mean look what's happening with this bedroom tax and everything. Before you know it how many people are going to be homeless? How many families are going to be homeless on the streets? And that's 'cause of this government. And then you've got to look at it this way; whatever, even if we get them out when we next vote, are you listening to me? How long is it going to take the next ones that get in to clean up the mess they made? 'Cause I think it's disgusting, food banks and everything? It's disgusting! That's something that doesn't happen in our country, that's something that happens in the Third World, that shouldn't be happening here, what's that about? It just makes me so angry. And taking all that money off students to pay tuition fees every year, what's that about? [...] It just makes me so angry because they're doing it to their own people. They really are. No wonder people are committing crime you know [...] and you know I don't agree with people selling death, I don't agree with people selling heroin and shit like that, but you know what? I'm not being nasty or nothing but I can understand why they do it, because how the fuck do you live when you want to make money? (Shelly, Age 53)

The above quote comes from an interview with a woman who had 'lost count' of the number of times she had been in prison since becoming a heroin addict at the age of 28. After entering into a romantic relationship a few years later however, Shelly began a methadone prescription. This relationship became abusive and, the end, resulted in a period of homelessness and a subsequent return to prison following an assault on a police officer. Yet, when we met, Shelly was living at the Housing for Northshire Project (HfN). She was in a stable relationship with her partner Michaela, whom she met in prison whilst on remand for a burglary for which she was subsequently deemed innocent. Shelly could certainly be described as travelling a desistance journey, encouraged both by Michaela and the Housing for Northshire manager, Rebecca. Yet the above quotation highlights the difficulty of negotiating desistance in an unequal world. The structural inequalities created by patriarchy and neoliberalism are intimately linked. My research contends that these inequalities are not adequately explored in the desistance literature. This chapter very briefly examines three themes—motherhood, volunteering, and shame—which were pervasive in both the desistance narratives studied herein, as well as in the existing desistance literature. I argue that although desistance appears to be incompatible with neoliberal and patriarchal constructs, female desistance narratives can challenge these constructs, much in the same way that their law-breaking often does.

The Current Study

In order to consider desistance as a gendered process, I spent a year observing weekly group work sessions aimed at encouraging desistance in a range of Northshire Women's Centres (WCs) where women had been referred from various parts of the Criminal Justice System (CJS). Following this I conducted narrative, life-course interviews (Maruna, 2001; McAdams, 2008) with 12 women attending the groups as part of specified activity orders. Additionally, I interviewed four women, Shelly among them, at the Housing for Northshire Project, a housing-based community project offered to women following imprisonment, including the project manager. I also interviewed a volunteer at the HfN Project and four staff members at the WCs. Additionally, I carried out 2 6-month follow up interviews with 2 of the original WC-attending women. Observation notes and interviews were transcribed, coded and analysed using N-Vivo software. Analysis consisted of monitoring for prominent themes from the desistance literature, as well as themes from feminist analysis and any emerging points of interest. This chapter examines three of these themes emerging from the 'social bonds' (Sampson and Laub, 1993; 2003) and the 'cognitive/narrative' (Maruna, 2001; LeBel *et al*, 2008) literature. In particular the social bonds of motherhood and voluntary employment, alongside the cognitive-level theme of shame, are explored in the structural context of neoliberalism, patriarchy and the intersection with desistance. All people and place names, including those of the community projects, have been given pseudonyms.

Desistance, Gender and the Absence of the Macro

Carlen (1992) noted that there are three major features of women's lawbreaking and imprisonment: women's crimes are, in the main, crimes of the powerless, women in prison are disproportionately from ethnic minority groups and a majority of women in prison have been in poverty for the greater part of their life. The *feminisation of poverty* (Carlen, 1988) is particularly pertinent, with charity and activist groups 'A Fair Deal for Women'[1] and 'Sisters Uncut'[2] highlighting the disproportionate effects of austerity measures on women through fractional employment, zero-hours contracts, and cuts to women's services. Additionally, the 'double deviance' thesis argues that women in the CJS are 'doubly damned' for not only breaking the social contract, but breaking the gender contract that frames women as passive, meek caregivers (Heidensohn and Silvestri, 2012; Worrall, 1990; Leverentz, 2014). Desistance theories that do not account for difference, therefore, reinforce the inequalities and repressions that difference—including gendered difference—creates (Weaver and McNeill, 2010). Although women's criminal justice experiences have received attention elsewhere, women's voices within desistance literature are still marginalised, particularly in England.

My research suggests that by locating women's desistance journeys as parallel to men's, we replicate the substantive inequalities which result in women entering the CJS in the first place, in addition to the substantive inequalities that they then face in a system built by men, for men. Whilst desistance theory has been an illuminating, progressive light within

---

[1] A group of 13 organisations campaigning to bridge the economic gap between men and women

[2] A feminist direct-action collective acting to highlight and challenge the disproportionate effect of austerity on women, particularly concerned with cuts to domestic violence services

criminological research and practice, it has largely (with a few exceptions: Jamieson *et al*, 1999; Giordano *et al*, 2002; Rumgay, 2004; Barry, 2006; Rodermond *et al*, 2016) neglected its sisters. It is generally considered that desistance theories fall into three overlapping categories: maturational (Glueck and Glueck, 1950; Gottfredson and Hirschi, 1990), social bonds, and narrative theories (discussed above). None of these fully consider the structural, macro-level contexts in which desistance occurs. Yet critical theorists have argued that inequality is discordant with social justice (Pickett and Wilkinson, 2010; Dorling, 2014). By considering women's desistance narratives, I argue that whilst desistance journeys are occurring in these contexts, they are all the more arduous because of the environment of travel.

Motherhood

Within the desistance literature that includes women there appears to be a consensus that motherhood is a strong indication of a move towards non-offending (Bersani *et al*, 2009; Giordano *et al*, 2002; Graham and Bowling, 1995; Uggen and Kruttschnitt, 1998; Rutter *et al*, 1998; McIvor *et al*, 2011). The current study included 13 women affected by the CJS who were mothers, including 2 who were grandmothers. All 13 committed their varied offences after becoming a mother, and 8 of these individuals had lost full custody or completely lost their children to social services or family members due to issues surrounding their offending, alcohol or drug use or, in one case, homelessness. For some women, offending was related to being able to provide a life for their children. Marie connected offending to being able to "put food on the table," whilst Grace linked the money she was getting for growing marijuana to being able to provide her daughter with a happy Christmas. For a second group of women, deviance was not something which was related to their role as mothers nor their relationship with their children. Paula, for example, noted that neither the threat of nor loss of her sons encouraged her to stop drinking.

In line with cognitive/narrative theory, many of the women linked their identities as mothers and their desire to become law-abiding to their relationship with their children. It was again not the act of becoming a mother that provided the impetus for change, but the identity of motherhood which helped maintain change. Motherhood provided the 'script' (Rumgay, 2004) for change in these women's lives. Yet expectations around motherhood tended to blur the narrative; women frequently talked about the expectations of others – their families, friends and criminal justice agencies and what it was to be a 'good mother'. These notions often conflicted with providing for their children or, in one case, taking the blame for their children's deviance. Unlike most desistance studies, this research did not find that becoming a mother—nor grandmother—automatically created a social bond leading to desistance. 'Good mother' identities are not necessarily as straightforward as they appear. Without addressing poverty and gendered expectations of parenthood, desistance is unlikely to take hold; where it does, it is all the more difficult to navigate.

Volunteering

In concordance with what is known about female convictions more generally (Prison Reform Trust, 2014), the majority of women I studied had been convicted of non-violent, acquisitive crimes. Paradoxically, many of the women were encouraged to become involved in volunteering work post-sentencing. Under the Conservative/Liberal-Democrat coalition government, which was in power when the interviews took place, the 'Big Society' rhetoric of voluntarism as linked to social solidarity was pervasive. Yet so too was the idea of working for free as encouraged by the government's 'Help to Work' programme. Volunteering can have many benefits for those emerging from the criminal justice system; the mental health benefits alongside access to alternative social groups and improving skills and gaps in CVs are well known in the literature (Edgar *et al*, 2011) and both the WCs and HfN Projects advocated such work. Additionally, volunteering offers a restorative element that can be part of identity change (Maruna, 2001). Many of the women involved in this research extolled the virtues of volunteering from their own personal experience. Yet, volunteering does not provide the economic benefits of paid employment. Sue, for example, noted her own 'luck' in inheriting money from her father, creating the conditions for her volunteering, which has provided not only mental health benefits, but enabled her to attend the courses and training that have been part of her desistance journey. It must also be noted that Sue was one of only two women involved in the project who had never been convicted of an acquisitive offence. Julie meanwhile lamented the lack of paid opportunities for females in the criminal justice system.

It appears that women with convictions are often encouraged to adopt hyper-moral roles (Matthews *et al*, 2014), perhaps as both an individual and societal reaction to their supposed 'double deviance'. Yet, there is a concern that promoting volunteering specifically for women will reinforce their gender specific roles, further entrenching the feminisation of poverty (Carlen, 1988) and patriarchal ideas around what it is to be a 'good woman'.

Shame

I argue that shame, remorse, and stigma are important cognitive level themes that emerge in women's desistance narratives just as they do in men's (LeBel *et al*, 2008). Yet even in the absence of offending pasts, women's narratives may also contain these themes. Shame can surround motherhood, abuse, or poverty for example. Women involved in the criminal justice system are often 'doubly demonised' (Heidensohn and Silvestri, 2012; Worrall, 1990; Leverentz, 2014) as a result of their imagined moral transgressions in the eyes of the CJS and wider society in general, related in particular to their positions as mothers, daughters, and partners. On top of this, women experience levels of shame and stigma attached to other 'deviant' behaviour particularly related to these roles (for example in perceptions of their own parenting), or even engulfing shame related to the deviant behaviour of others. Challenging neoliberal constructs surrounding benefit fraud and the myth of the 'scrounger', patriarchal constructs of 'ideal victimhood' *alongside* the shame and stigma that women caught up in the criminal justice system face, are essential elements of advocating for women attempting to maintain desistance.

Conclusion

By considering three key themes taken from the desistance literature - motherhood, volunteering and shame - this chapter has highlighted the importance of structural considerations in any discussion of desistance. I argue that women's pathways out of offending can be situated in their desire for independence, just as much as their pathways into offending can turn on their desires to be a 'good mother'. Women's apparent desire to seek conventional, pro-social roles can actually mask a patriarchal system which promotes women as gentle, caring and 'feminine'. Perry (2013) for example found that discourses used by criminal justice practitioners continue to situate rehabilitation of female law-breakers in conformity to traditional 'feminine' gender norms. Desistance practice should not just replicate social and structural inequalities. Women should be offered alternative roles to mother or partner. Voluntary work, whilst not without its merits, is often put forward as a panacea for women caught up in the criminal justice system. Yet, this notion stems from a patriarchal construct of what it is to be a woman. My research has highlighted that shame—particularly around poverty and abuse, but also around the 'double deviance' of women as lawbreakers and their relational identities as mothers, daughters, and partners—is pervasive following conviction. However, Skeggs (1997) has argued that although white, working-class women are inscribed and marked with the symbolic systems of denigration and degeneracy, they manage to create systems of value and attribute respectability and high-moral standing to themselves. Similarly, as Rebecca's quote below shows, desistance can mean resistance to patriarchal and neoliberal constructs about what it is to be an '(ex)-offender':

> But you know, my morals had gone, all my moral fibre, but my values never changed; I always knew deep down that I have got values and they never changed. I was still a mother, I was still a daughter, I was still a sister; I was still a friend. And you know, I was still the same person I was that had been loved and had a successful career before I went down that road [...] (Rebecca, Age 46)

Shelly's introductory quote highlights something that desistance theorists tend to gloss over: the kind of society into which one desists. As Farrall (2002: 208) noted "just as seeds thrown on stony ground will not take root", the current system of advanced capitalism with remnants of previous patriarchal control alongside new elements of gendered inequality is far from the ideal ground from which desistance can grow. Yet Shelly's case study, alongside the narratives of the other women involved in this research, also show that desistance is possible and, where it happens, any moves towards desistance must be celebrated. The closer we move to equality the better these journeys will be supported.

Acknowledgements

Thank you to my doctoral supervision team, Dr Maria Sapouna, Dr Martin O'Brien and Dr Megan Todd, and to everyone who has supported me during this PhD. I would also like to thank the editor of this chapter for all their help.

References

Bersani, B.E. Laub, J.H. and Nieuwbeerta, P. (2009) "Marriage and Desistance from Crime in the Netherlands: Do Gender and Socio-Historical Context Matter?" *Journal of Quantitative Criminology* Volume 25, No.1 pp 3-24

Barry, M. (2006) *Youth Offending in Transition: The Search for Social Recognition* London: Routledge

Carlen, P. (1992) "Criminal Women and Criminal Justice: The Limits to, and Potential of, Feminist and Left Realist Perspectives", in Matthews, R. and J.Young, (eds.) *Issues in Realist Criminology* London: Sage

Carlen, P. (1988) *Women, Crime and Poverty* Milton Keynes: Open University Press

Dorling, D. (2014) *Inequality and the 1%* London: Verso

Edgar, K. Jacobsin, J. and Biggar, K. (2011) *Time Well Spent: A Practical Guide to Active Citizenship and Volunteering in Prison* London: Prison Reform Trust.

Farrall, S. (2002) *Rethinking What Works with Offenders* Cullompton, Devon: Willan Publishing

Glueck, S. and Glueck, E. (1950) *Unravelling Juvenile Delinquency* New York: Harvard University Press

Giordano, P.C. Cernokovich, S.A. and Rudolph, J.L. (2002) "Gender, Crime and Desistance: Toward a Theory of Cognitive Transformation" *American Journal of Sociology,* Volume 107, No. 4 pp 990-1064

Gottfredson, M. and Hirschi, T. (1990) *A General Theory of Crime* Stanford, California: Stanford University Press

Graham, J. and Bowling, B. (1995) *Young People and Crime* Research Study No. 145, London: HMRSO

Heidensohn, F. and Silvestri, M. (2012) "Gender and Crime" pp 226 – 369 in Maguire, M. Morgan, R. and Reiner, R. (eds) *The Oxford Handbook of Criminology* Oxford: Oxford University Press

Jamieson, J. McIvor, G. and Murray, C. (1999). *Understanding Offending Amongst Young People* Edinburgh: The Scottish Executive

LeBel, T.P. Burnett, R. Maruna, S. and Bushway, S. (2008) "The 'Chicken and Egg' of Subjective and Social Factors in Desistance from Crime" in *European Journal of Criminology* Volume 5, No.11 pp 131-159

Leverntz, A. (2014) *The Ex-Prisoner's Dilemma: How Women Negotiate Competing Narratives of Re-entry and Desistance* London: Rutgers University Press

Maruna, S. (2001), *Making Good – How Ex-Convicts Reform and Rebuild their Lives* Washington DC: American Psychological Association Books.

Matthews, R. Easton, H. Reynolds, L. Bindel, J. and Young, L. (2014) *Exiting Prostitution* Basingstoke: Palgrave Macmillan

McAdams, D.P. (2008) "The Life Story Interview" Available from: www.sesp.northwestern.edu/docs/Interviewrevised95.pdf [accessed on 7th June, 2016]

McIvor, G. Murray, C. and Jamieson, J. (2011) "Desistance from Crime: Is it Different for Women and Girls?" pp 181 – 200 in Maruna, S. and Immarigeon, R. (eds) *After Crime and Punishment: Pathways to Offender reintegration* Devon: Willan Publishing

Perry, E. (2013) "'She's Alpha Male': Transgressive Gender Performances in the Probation 'Classroom'" *Gender and Education* Volume 25, No.4 pp 396-412

Pickett, K. and Wilkinson, R. (2010) *The Spirit Level: Why Equality is better for Everyone* London: Penguin

Prison Reform Trust (2014) *Transforming Lives: Reducing Women's Imprisonment* Stockport: Soroptimist International

Rodermond, E. Kruttschnitt, C. Slotboom, A.M. and Bijleveld C.C.J.H. (2016) Female Desistance: A Review of the Literature *European Journal of Criminology* Volume 13, No.1 pp 3-28

Rumgay, J. (2004) "Scripts for Safer Survival: Pathways Out of Female Crime" *The Howard Journal of Crime and Justice* Volume 43, No.4 pp 405-419

Rutter, M., Giller, H., & Hagell, A. (1998). *Antisocial behavior by young people*. New York: Cambridge University Press.

Sampson, R.J. and Laub, J.H. (1993) *Crime in the Making: Pathways and Turning Points through Life* London: Harvard University Press

Sampson, R.J. and Laub, J.H. (2003) *Shared Beginnings, Divergent Lives: Delinquent Boys to Age 70* London: Harvard University Press

Skeggs, B. (1997) *Formations of Class and Gender: Becoming Respectable* London: Sage

Uggen, C. and Kruttschnitt, C. (1998) "Crime in the Breaking: Gender Differences in Desistance" *Law and Society Review* Volume 32, No.2 pp 339-366

Weaver, B. and McNeill, F. (2010) *Changing Lives? Desistance Research and Offender Management* Glasgow: The Scottish Centre for Crime and Research

Worrall, A. (1990) *Offending Women: Female Lawbreakers and the CJS* London: Routledge

Extended Biography

Research

Criminology is my life's passion. As a young person growing up in Northern Ireland in the aftermath of The Troubles and the wake of the Good Friday Agreement, criminal, political and social justice matters were extremely close to home. During my LLB at Queen's University, Belfast, I became interested in criminological subjects, particularly Critical Criminology. For these reasons, I chose to study an MRes in Criminology and Socio-Legal Studies at the University of Manchester. My Master's thesis was a study of the experiences of female republican former prisoners in Northern Ireland and my fieldwork included interviews with republican ex-prisoners. In the period after my Masters, my love for Criminology did not falter and I completed voluntary work at the Policy Evaluation and Research Unit at Manchester Metropolitan University on a project considering the use of legal highs. In 2012, I applied for a PhD in Criminology at the University of Central Lancashire. The studentship through which this PhD was funded originally bore the title: *Young Offenders on the Road to Desistance*. It was not, initially, intended as an exploration of the gendered desistance journey. However, upon beginning the literature review, it quickly became apparent that women's experiences were largely side-lined, marginalised, and incorporated within the male-focused explorations of desistance, echoing women's positions within the male-dominated criminal justice system. For example, one of the first texts I considered was Farrall and Calverley's (2006) *Understanding Desistance from Crime: Theoretical Directions in Resettlement and Rehabilitation*. This book dedicates three pages—of 209—to women; two of these are dedicated to limitations of the study. A book published in 2013 by Sam King, *Desistance Transitions and the Impact of Probation,* contained only a single short paragraph about women. Although women's experiences have had some focus elsewhere, women's voices within desistance literature are still marginalised, particularly in England. Therefore, my thesis examined desistance journeys as travelled by a small group of Northshire-based (pseudonym) women as a challenge to this marginalisation. I found that their desistance narratives contained clear resistance to patriarchal and neoliberal ideas.

Whilst I was completing my PhD, I worked in a variety of roles including in market research. Throughout this time, I taught as an Associate Lecturer at Manchester Metropolitan University and in 2016 at the University of

Manchester. I am passionate about teaching and am currently working towards a PGCert in Teaching and Learning in Higher Education. I worked as a Research Assistant at the University of Manchester in summer 2016, working on the School of Law's Athena SWAN application. I passed my viva examination in October 2016. Since January 2017 I have been employed as a Lecturer in Criminology at Liverpool John Moore's University. I am currently working on funding bids for a project exploring a local women's service, alongside disseminating my research findings. I will be submitting a book proposal related to my PhD. My main passion continues to be social justice and challenging inequality and injustice in all its forms.

Future Aspirations
I intend to publish my thesis as a monograph. I would like to continue to work with women who have been affected by the criminal justice system, continue to teach Critical Criminology whilst questioning patriarchal and neoliberal assumptions in all my work.

Selected Works
Barr, U. (2016), "Ontological Theory and Women's Desistance: Is it Simply a Case of 'Growing Up'?" *The Howard League for Penal Reform Early Career Academics Network Bulletin*, Volume 30, pp 3-30
Peer reviewer for Diffusion: The UCLan Journal of Undergraduate Research
Additional work currently in draft format or under review

Contact Details
Email: unabarr@hotmail.com
Twitter: @unamaireadbarr

3

Evidence-Based Policing or Policy-Based Evidence-Making? The Case of British Policing

Paul Betts

Introduction

My current research aims to examine the rise of evidence-based policy in British policing. The research seeks to investigate the growth of evidence-based policing as a hegemonic strategy to deliver more efficient and effective policing within the context of, and in response to, austerity. This chapter is set out in four parts. First, I discuss the rise of evidence-based policing as a hegemonic project. Second, I present the themes and issues in the evidence-based policy-making literature in general, to begin to open the space to explore how these issues might apply to evidence-based policing in the UK. Third, I briefly address why this is an important issue worthy of further critical review. Finally, I suggest methodological approaches for exploring the phenomenon.

The Rise and Rise of Evidence-Based Policing

Evidence-based policing is championed by powerful forces within the political and operational leadership of British policing as 'the answer' to deliver 'more for less' as austerity grips. The rise of evidence-based policing as the way forward in policy making to date, has been met with limited challenge, despite extensive academic and practitioner critique following its growth in other public policy fields such as health. It is being developed in parallel with an attempt to 'professionalise' policing through the development of a professional 'college': The College of Policing. The College is seeking to achieve "Royal" status in line with the medical profession. Proponents of evidence-based policing draw on the language of the medical profession seeking to harness the status conferred on medico-scientific knowledge to their own scholarly and professional endeavours. It seems that any current analysis of rhetoric about change in

UK policing emanating from the College, the National Police Chiefs' Council, Police and Crime Commissioners, or the Home Office is incomplete without reference to the 'evidence-base' or 'what works'. For example:

> A fundamental element of the College's role as a professional body is to be a catalyst for the *development and use of knowledge and research* by and for those working in policing. This will ensure that the *best available evidence of what works* is accessible for practitioners when making decisions. To achieve this aim, the College works with police forces, policing and crime commissioners, national policing leads and academic partners (College of Policing, 2017, emphasis added).

Numerous 'administrative criminologists' contribute to the 'what works' agenda of the evidence-based policing project. For example, Professor Sherman champions experimental criminology as Director of the Institute of Criminology at the University of Cambridge, provides consultation for the Home Office, and is Chair of the Police Executive Programme which delivers courses on evidence-based policing to senior police officers. Professor Sherman also sits on the Board of the College of Policing.

> This body (the UK College of Policing) has tremendous potential to follow the pathway to innovation Jonhson (2010) associates with such major advances as the printing press, which was inspired by the wine press: a lateral-thinking style of adaption of an idea used in one setting (evidence-based medicine) to another (such as evidence-based policing) (Sherman, 2013: 3).

The 'tremendous potential' described in Sherman's sentence above is not clearly defined, but from a broader reading of his chapter it seems that 'evidence-based policing' offers potential to improve public safety and policing legitimacy. Wider than this, Professor Sherman notes that the drop in crime in the UK and the US in fact correlates to the rise in the evidence-based policing movement in those countries. Without being as bold as to suggest the rise of the evidence-based policing has *caused* the drop in crime, Sherman (2013) advocates that this hypothesis is impossible to rule out scientifically without further robust testing.

There is also a weighty 'critical' literature debating the emergence of the evidence-based policy agenda, some of which calls for evidence-based policy-making to be challenged (Marston and Watts, 2003), others suggesting it should be more modest in its claims (Solesbury, 2001). There is also academic critique of variants of 'administrative criminology' and its close relationship to the state that delimits critical perspectives and research (Squires, 2013). Professor Sherman's claim that deployment of research 'evidence' into policing shares a similar potential for human flourishing as the invention of the printing press feels like a very bold assertion indeed. Certainly, it is a claim worthy of further examination.

Themes and Issues in Evidence-Based Policy

There are three key troublesome themes in the literature on evidence-based policy-making. First, the ever-increasing alliance of neoliberal strategic objectives between policy makers, politicians, think-tanks, and universities: 'knowledge-commissioners' and 'knowledge-producers'. Second, so-called 'policy-based evidence-making', which the political selection of evidence for use in policy-making, which supports pre-determined ideological policy or party political positions. Third, the academic selection of 'evidence' for use in policy through the increasing deployment of 'experts' and 'knowledge hierarchies'.

i. Neoliberal Coalitions
This alliance of policy makers, politicians, officers, and academics trying to deliver shared neoliberal strategic objectives might help to explain the remarkable absence of critical scholars in the evidence-based policing project. All sides gain considerably from the development of evidence-based policing. Evidence-based policing rests on delivering 'new', 'robust', 'objective', 'value-free', 'scientific' knowledge neatly packaged and 'authorised' in independent and non-ideological frames for policing and politicians to base policy upon. Concurrently, academia is furnished with an inexhaustible supply of willing collaborators to chase grant funds, access data, demonstrate 'impact' and 'knowledge transfer' to move their way up league tables. Evidence-based policing therefore is a mutually beneficial match made in neoliberal hegemonic heaven for its participants and followers.

I suggest this (un)holy alliance of strategic objectives, determined and shaped by neoliberal hegemony, serves to function as a 'disciplinary governmental technology' such that it is increasingly difficult to attain funding for alternative or critical research and there is a paucity of independent scholarly critique (see: Foucault, 1977, 1975). There are identifiable overlapping complicities in the criminology/policy 'industry' which see universities, funders and policy makers join together in "policy-led evidence-chasing" which operates in a mutually reciprocal beneficial relationship, leading to *"research prevention"* (Squires, 2013).

Sanderson (2002) and Pawson *et al* (2005) note what Solesbury (2001: 4) describes as *"the utilitarian turn in research"*. Combined with Slater's (2012) observations on the narratives surrounding the funding of academic research, "'REF returnable' and 'the impact agenda' – usually used alongside 'income generation'", suggests a notable coming together of the political and the research academic. This raises serious concerns over the degree to which the 'evidence' on which policy is increasingly based may be becoming ever more tainted, or lack the much-vaunted independence and objectivity associated with Enlightenment ideas of scientific knowledge on which evidence-based policing is predicated.

ii. Political Selection of 'Evidence'
There is literature that suggests that evidence-based policy is not as 'independent', 'objective' and 'robust' as the narratives surrounding it might suggest. This literature speaks to a theme of 'policy-based evidence-making', which can be adapted to critique evidence-based policing. Marston and Watts (2003) critique the spread of bio-medical evidence-led approaches to social policy in Australia. They provide a case study of juvenile crime research and note "a risk that 'evidence-based policy' will become a means for policy elites (to) increase their strategic control over what constitutes knowledge" (ibid: 158).

Learmonth and Harding (2006) point to a growing body of work which suggests that increasingly government sponsored research finds 'evidence' that supports government reform agendas and managerialism in general. In effect, the commissioning agents of much of the research are public officials who have a vested interest in research evidence that supports their own positions and the reform programmes of the political elite:

> This debate is not simply obscured by evidence-based management (in the NHS) – it is necessarily written out [...], radical understandings of 'the evidence' cannot be included in the project of evidence-based management for it to remain coherent (2006: 251).

Hope (2004) suggests that where politics and research overlap the political imperatives of those commissioning the study may skew the 'evidence' produced. Hope considers the network of governance surrounding the Reducing Burglary Initiative projects. All had a keen interest in ensuring they were 'a success' and he highlights resource dependency in the Treasury, tying funding to 'evidence' of success. Hope asserts that results were manipulated to 'prove' 'success'. He concludes that research should be independent of politics, and politics needs to maintain its autonomy to provide scrutiny over research. Similarly, Stevens (2010), who undertook an ethnographic study of the use of evidence-based policy in the UK civil service, reports civil servants selected 'evidence' to favour particular policy agendas.

iii. Academic Selection of 'Evidence'

There is pre-determination of what counts as evidence, what knowledge is included and excluded, funded or commissioned, based on the methodological and epistemological preferences of the 'experts' selected. These questions are addressed in the literature as a concern for those who expound the use and development of evidence-based policy from realist positions (see Nutley *et al*, 2012; Nutley *et al*, 2002; Thomas, 2014; Ellefsen, 2011; Bullock and Tilley, 2009). Even the most ardent advocates are aware, and have responded to, the debate within evidence-based policing about 'what counts' as evidence for inclusion. There is a shared narrative about the need for the evidence to be 'scientifically robust', 'independent' and 'objective'. The narratives found here are on the reverence to evidence produced by the methods deployed in the natural sciences, following Enlightenment ideas about pursuit of objective truths and development of 'knowledge hierarchies' to assess quality of knowledge and potential for policy inclusion.

Professor Sherman recommends the use of the 'Maryland Scale' of scientific methods, which promotes the Randomised Control Trial, as a basis for assessment – in line with evidence-based medicine - as the 'gold standard' of research evidence. The College of Policing's 'What Works Centre for Crime Reduction' (WWCCR), has its own hierarchies. There is much to say about this in terms of methodological critique but for now, I shall simply say that the nature or ontological status of 'crime' is unconsidered, and policy outcomes which are broader on health, human flourishing, social harm, economic, social, or political inequalities are not a consideration of 'effective' policy initiatives or interventions for evidence-based policing. This is despite the considerable critical criminological, political and sociological literature that calls for stronger ontological debate on 'crime', 'policing' and 'justice' (see Pemberton, 2015 for an example).

As noted by Beck (1992: 173), "[i]t is not uncommon for political programmes to be decided in advance simply by the choice of what expert representatives are included". It seems possible therefore that we are likely to see a (re)production of status quo in policy and outcomes from application of evidence-based policing, rather than the prospect of radical social or political change.

The Impact of 'Evidence-based Policing' 'Research'

Acceptance of 'evidence-based policing' as the *only* or *best* way of 'doing policy' raises significant questions about the sources of evidence used, what counts as evidence, whose evidence is used and who decides, how is evidence interpreted, how is evidence production funded and commissioned, and, who manages the evidence (for examples, see: Solesbury, 2001; Learmonth and Harding, 2006). Given the literature summarised here it seems probable that the expansion of the evidence-based policing project will reinforce current neoliberal policy positions and the inequalities they generate. The introduction of radical critique and thought promoting real change will, out of necessity, be silenced.

Given the impact policing has on the disenfranchised and marginalised through processes of criminalisation, policing's deployment as a (re)enforcer of state power, incarceration, surveillance and the negative social outcomes those deployments can create, it is concerning that there is not a louder and more coherent critical voice on the side of the oppressed challenging the neoliberal rise of the evidence-based policing project in the UK in recent years. There is a gap however in the critique of evidence-based policy-making as it is being applied to policing, and a particularly acute gap in literature informed by political, philosophical, and theoretical perspectives. My research aims to contribute to filling this gap.

Methodology and Research Design

I am currently re-examining evidence-based policing, using a different lens to explore its hegemonic rise. I am using key concepts from Foucault's work to create a history of evidence-based policing revealing its problematisation, which "is *genealogical* in its design and *archaeological* in its method" (Foucault, 1997: 125 emphasis added). Through exploring genealogical aspects of the application of power-knowledge, and how this application can operate as a technology of discipline through governmentality on different subjects I hope to demonstrate how evidence-based policing serves to delimit radical perspectives and so leads to the (re)production of the social status quo and works to prevent the emergence of alternatives.

To undertake this archaeology, I will use discourse analysis techniques drawing on key concepts from Argumentative Discourse Analysis (Hajer, 2002), and Post-Structural Discourse Theory (Howarth, Glynos, and Griggs, 2016). These key concepts include: hegemonic discourses; shared statements and narratives which articulate and come to signify truths; subject positionality; 'truth regimes' and 'authorisation'; and, institutional modifications. I am collecting data from 'texts' within the criminal justice system and academy, and anticipate revealing an alternative narrative about evidence-based policing in which the current hegemony can be critically challenged.

References

Beck, U. (1992) *Risk Society* London: Sage

Bullock, K. and Tilley, N. (2009) 'Evidence-Based Policing and Crime Reduction' *Policing* Volume 3, No. 4 pp 381-387

College of Policing (2017) What Works Centre for Crime Reduction Available from: http://whatworks.college.police.uk/Research/Pages/default.aspx (accessed 29th January, 2017)

Ellefsen, B. (2011) 'Evaluating Crime Prevention – Scientific Rationality or Governmentality?' *Journal of Scandinavian Studies in Criminology and Crime Prevention* Volume 12, No. 2 pp 103-127

Foucault, M. (1977) *Discipline & Punish: The Birth of the Prison* London: Penguin

Foucault, M. (1975) *Madness and Civilisation: A History of Insanity in the Age of Reason* London: Random House

Foucault, M. (1997) *The Politics of Truth* Los Angeles: Semiotext(e)

Hajer, M. (2002) *'Discourse Analysis and the Study of Policy Making'* European Political Science Volume 2, No. 1 pp 61-65

Hope, T. (2004) *'Pretend it Works: Evidence & Governance in the Evaluation of the Reducing Burglary Initiative'* Criminal Justice Volume 4, pp 287-308

Howarth, D., Glynos, J. and Griggs, S. (2016) 'Discourse, Explanation and Critique' *Critical Policy Studies Volume* 10, No. 1 pp 99-104

Learmouth, M. and Harding, N. (2006) 'Evidence-based Management: The Very Idea' *Public Administration* Volume 84, No. 2 pp 245-266

Marston, G. and Watts, R. (2003) 'Tampering with the Evidence: A Critical Appraisal of Evidence-based Policy-making' *The Drawing Board: An Australian Review of Public Affairs* Volume 3, No. 3 pp 143-163

Nutley, S., Davies, H. and Walter, I. (2002) *Evidence Based Policy and Practice: Cross Sector Lessons From the UK* ESRC UK Centre for Evidence Based Policy & Practice: Working Paper 9

Nutley, S. Powell, A. and Davies, H. (2012) *What Counts As Good Evidence?* Research Unit for Research Utilisation, School of Management, University of St. Andrews

Pawson, R. Greenhlagh, T. Harvey, G. and Walshe, K. (2005) 'Realist Review – A New Method of Systematic Review Designed for Complex Policy Interventions' *Journal of Health Services, Research and Policy* Volume 10, No. 1 pp 21-34

Pemberton, S. (2015) *Harmful Societies: Understanding Social Harm* Bristol: Policy Press

Sanderson, I. (2002) *'Evaluation, Policy Learning and Evidence-based Policy Making' Public Administration* Volume 80, No. 1 pp 1-22

Slater, T. (2012) 'Impacted Geographers: a Response to Pain, Kesby and Askins' *Area* Volume 44, No. 1 pp 117-119

Sherman, L.W. (2013) 'The Rise of Evidence-Based Policing: Targeting, Testing and Tracking' *Crime and Justice* Volume 42, No. 1 pp 377-451

Solesbury, W. (2001) *Evidence-based Policy: Whence it Came and Where its Going* ESRC Centre for Evidence Based Policy & Practice, London

Squires, P. (2013) 'Research Prevention and the Zombie University' *Criminal Justice Matters* Volume 91, No. 1 pp 4-5

Stevens, A. (2010) 'Telling Policy Stories: An Ethonographic Study of the Use of Evidence in Policy-making in the UK' *Journal of Social Policy* Volume 40, No. 2, pp 237-255

Thomas, G. (2014) 'Research on Policing: Insights from the Literature' *Police Journal: Theory, Practice and Principles* Volume 87, No. 1 pp 5-16

Extended Biography

Research

I have a first degree in Politics and Modern History from the University of Manchester (1994), where I completed research into independence movements in post-colonial Africa. I graduated with 'Distinction' from a Masters in Public Administration (MPA) at the University of Birmingham in 2011. My Master's research used Foucault's ideas to explore discourse in UK Anti-Social Behaviour policy, re-positioning this as a disciplinary technology serving to extend the neoliberal political project. I am presently redrafting this research following legislative changes and hope to publish it in the near future.

Currently, I am exploring the rise of evidence-based policing in the UK under the supervision of Dr Emma Foster. The growth of evidence-based policing has been swift and all-consuming and has seen alliances form between politicians, policy makers, professionals and academics on an unprecedented scale. There is burgeoning hegemony over evidence-based policing as 'the way' to improve policing in modern Britain and there are considerable truth claims made about the research this produces and its potential for social improvements. There is a lack of debate on the rise of evidence-based policing. I am interested in the disciplinary processes that marginalise critique and therefore I am exploring this using discourse analysis. I am also troubled by the lack of concern shown by those engaged in the criminology-policy industry in the broader problems and issues associated with policing, crime, and justice and so seek to illuminate this in my research.

Activism, Organisational Work and /or Professional Membership

I have raised funding and led significant projects in the UK aimed to improve social outcomes for those encountering the criminal justice system, and have been invited to present this work across the UK, Europe and Australia. Principally, these projects have focused on experiences of children and vulnerable women, and involved working with statutory agencies and charitable organisations.

In recent years I have worked as a visiting lecturer at the University of Birmingham, supported undergraduate careers advice and mentoring, and presented papers in Athens for the European Union and at the ESRC Festival of Social Sciences. I also help to coordinate the Centre for Crime, Justice and Policing at the University of Birmingham; co-leading the 'critical perspectives' work stream with Dr Simon Pemberton.

Future Aspirations

On completion of my PhD and retiring from my criminal justice career I hope to continue my research and teaching in an academic position, using both my experiences and research to move forward the debate about policies which produce poor outcomes for those encountering the criminal justice system. I will produce theoretically informed research to challenge hegemonic thinking about crime and policing to support policy makers and practitioners to think differently and inspire change. I also hope to provide insights into theory to improve methodological and theoretical approaches, adding to developing post-structuralist philosophy.

4

Labour Exploitation and Migrant Workers in UK Food Supply Chains

Jon Davies

Introduction

Exploitative and other harmful labour practices against migrant workers in low-skilled occupations have been discussed in previous research (Allain *et al,* 2013; Malloch and Rigby, 2016; Potter and Hamilton, 2014; Scott *et al,* 2012). However, a significant amount of this research tends to discuss the most 'newsworthy' and extreme exploitative labour abuses; namely modern slavery, human trafficking, and forced labour. This chapter argues that when labour exploitation is viewed as a continuum of harmful practices, a stronger emphasis is needed on the routine, repetitive, and embedded labour abuses that fall between 'decent work' and modern slavery. Routine labour abuses occur not just due to rogue employers or criminal organisations, but can be understood within legitimate socio-economic processes such as supply chain dynamics, labour market regulation and immigration policies. Based on the research themes of the author's current work, this chapter is structured as follows: first, there is an overview of theoretical issues including harm and labour exploitation, and how these relate to migrant workers' experiences. Second, migrant labourers' experiences are understood in the context of harmful food supply chain dynamics, including the demand for products and labour. The regulatory context is examined as part of these supply chain dynamics. This chapter cannot examine all these wide-ranging issues with the rigour they deserve, but it intends to provide a snapshot of critical issues concerning migrant labour exploitation in UK food production.

Harm and Migrant Labour Exploitation

The concept of harm has received increasing attention from within and beyond Criminology in recent years (Greenfield and Paoli, 2013; Hillyard *et al*, 2004; Tombs and Whyte, 2015; Pemberton, 2015). Paoli and Greenfield (2015) have called for researchers to "start at the end" by placing a greater emphasis on the consequences and harms of crimes. Their harm assessment framework allows researchers to begin empirically identifying, assessing and comparing the harms of crimes, while providing a means to prioritise harms based on their severity and incidence (Greenfield and Paoli, 2013). Therefore, researchers can focus on extreme harms while not neglecting less extreme harms, or "low hanging fruit" (Paoli and Greenfield, 2015: 94).

From a social harm perspective, Pemberton (2015: 14) notes that Greenfield and Paoli's (2013) work is a "distinct criminological enterprise to remedy the neglect of harm within discussions of 'crime'". Indeed, initial applications of their framework were on 'criminal harms' in the fields of drug trafficking (Paoli *et al*, 2013) and human trafficking (Greenfield *et al*, 2016). However, the framework could be extended to incorporate legitimate activities if they are suspected of generating harms in addition to their intended economic benefits (Greenfield and Paoli, 2013: 882). Regardless of whether the study of harm is better approached from a criminological or social harm perspective, the concept has significant implications for (migrant) labour exploitation.

The notion of "low-hanging fruit" used by Paoli and Greenfield (2015: 94) seems to imply that less extreme harms may be a lower priority for policy makers than extreme harms. This metaphor can be problematic when applied to labour exploitation, since previous research tends to focus on the most extreme practices, including modern slavery, human trafficking, and forced labour (Allain *et al*, 2013; Malloch and Rigby, 2016). In contrast, 'less extreme' or 'routine' labour harms that fall under the threshold of modern slavery are unlikely to receive the same attention, either from the media, policy makers, or researchers – with some notable exceptions (see: Ollus, 2016; Shamir, 2012).

Others have conceptualised migrant labour exploitation as a category of corporate crime (Alvesalo *et al*, 2014). A well-grounded point in corporate criminology is that the criminal justice system is unlikely to prosecute companies where harmful practices have occurred (Tombs and Whyte, 2015: 35-36). In the context of migrant labour exploitation, this point is illustrated by the DJ Houghton case. Between 2008 and 2012, a group of Lithuanian migrant workers were severely mistreated while working for DJ Houghton, a gangmaster[1] that supplied workers to UK

---

[1] Gangmaster is a colloquial term that refers to labour intermediaries who provide

farms (Lawrence, 2016). In 2012 the police arrested the Houghtons, and the Gangmasters Licensing Authority (GLA) called the company "the worst gangmaster ever" (ibid). Subsequently, the National Referral Mechanism (NRM) identified the Lithuanian workers as victims of human trafficking, yet the criminal investigation was dropped, seemingly due to a lack of evidence. This development led the workers to pursue a claim through the civil courts, whereby *Galdikas and Ors vs DJ Houghton QBD* became the first civil case against a British company for claims related to modern slavery. In 2016, the court found in favour of the claimants, who were later awarded over £1m compensation in lost earnings and redress for abuse. Since this was a civil case, 'slavery' was not demonstrated; however, the claimants demonstrated breaches of the Agricultural Wages Act 1948 regarding deductions from salary, as well as a lack of facilities to wash, rest, eat and drink.

In cases of corporate harm such as DJ Houghton, others have discussed whether trying to secure criminal or civil liability is more pragmatic (Wells, 2014). However, if the criminal justice system does not prosecute extreme labour harms, then routine harms are unlikely to be acknowledged, let alone be considered criminal. Instead, harmful labour practices tend to be addressed through civil or regulatory means (Skrivankova, 2014) – if they are even reported. Therefore, grasping the "low hanging fruit" may be harder to achieve in many labour exploitation cases.

Despite appearing to be 'less extreme', routine labour exploitation can collectively be just as harmful as extreme labour exploitation. Feinberg (1984: 190-191) argues that "the greater the probability of harm, the less grave the harm needs to be … the greater the severity of harm, the less likely it needs to be" in order to justify intervention. Greenfield and Paoli (2013) apply this principle to their harm assessment framework, whereby a 'severe' harm occurring less frequently may justify the same prioritisation when compared to 'less severe' harms that occur more frequently. Since routine labour abuses seem to occur more frequently than extreme exploitation (France, 2016; Haynes, 2009), this suggests that researchers are neglecting a significant number of exploitative practices.

Labour exploitation can be degrading and coercive to migrant workers, but does not have to be, since many enter employment in the absence of coercion and deception (Zwolinski and Wertheimer, 2016). When contrasted to most street crimes such as burglary, where victims suffer absolute losses, victims of labour exploitation usually make relative gains

---

companies with temporary workers for roles within the agricultural and food sectors.

from their work, despite being unfairly compensated (Mayer, 2007). In other words, migrant workers may consider themselves to be better off being exploited than having no work at all, or when compared to alternative work opportunities in their home countries (Waldinger and Lichter, 2003). Therefore, labour exploitation can be non-coercive and mutually advantageous, which is problematic from a law enforcement perspective, since migrants may appear to consent to harmful work conditions, which risks delegitimising victims (Alvesalo *et al*, 2014: 132).

While exploitative and harmful labour conditions should not be tolerated, this issue of 'consent' begins to explain why some migrants seem willing to tolerate mistreatment from their employers. Some migrants view exploitative work as a 'stepping stone' that they hope will lead on to better prospects (Kosny *et al*, 2016). Others tolerate mistreatment for fear of job dismissal, and where there appear to be limited alternative options (EHRC, 2012; Ruhs and Martin, 2008). Unfamiliarity with the UK 'system' such as employment rights and welfare provisions is a significant issue (TUC, 2008). When coupled with the possibilities of language barriers, irregular immigration status, and a lack of social networks, migrants may be unwilling or unable to complain about exploitative work conditions.

Harmful Food Supply Chain Dynamics

In recent years, research has progressed from regarding labour exploitation as an issue caused mainly by human traffickers and rogue or 'criminal' employers. Instead, researchers across disciplines are increasingly recognising the role of legal supply chain dynamics and immigration policy in facilitating harmful labour practices (Anderson, 2015; LeBaron, 2015). As Anderson (2010: 313) notes, researchers should not regard migrants' experiences solely as an issue of abusive employers, but should consider wider labour market processes. Although most research examines extreme labour harms, routine harms occur in similar contexts, including fields, processing factories, and food outlets. Food supply chains, whether local, national or global, are characterised by a feed-forward flow of products from raw materials to consumer outlets, and a feed-back flow of information concerning demand for products and labour (Mena and Stevens, 2010). The UK agri-food sector is dominated by a small number of multi-national retailers or 'buyers', who have significant purchasing influence, especially over smaller suppliers and growers, whereby competition is intense and profit margins are small

(Pollard, 2006). Migrants comprise approximately 40% of the UK agri-food sector workforce (Rienzo, 2016: 5), which is characterised by flexible employment contracts, low trade unionisation rates, and a high turnover of staff. The UK agri-food sectors have amongst the poorest health and safety records when compared to other sectors (HSE, 2016: 7).

The tension inherent to most food supply chains is found in the relationships between buyers and their suppliers or growers. Robinson (2010) summarises this tension, by asserting that fierce price competition between dominant retailers results in them pressuring their suppliers. Buyers tend to apply this pressure by transferring costs and risks down their supply chains; for instance, they demand high quality, low cost, 'just in time' products. Since their profit margins tend to be relatively small, suppliers may respond to cost pressures in a variety of ways. For instance, suppliers may manipulate the quality of their food, which begins to link with the challenges of food fraud (see: Lord *et al*, 2017). Alternatively, they may outsource their costs to labour intermediaries (Barrientos, 2013). These intermediaries, consisting of gangmasters and work agencies, provide labour to supply chain firms on a casual basis, in order to respond to daily or even hourly fluctuating levels of demand for products. Workers may experience these cost-cutting measures in the form of insecure work, low pay, poor safety practices, and other abuse (EHRC, 2012; Potter and Hamilton, 2014). When coupled with potential language barriers and poor understanding of employment rights, migrants can be particularly vulnerable to a range of labour harms, especially in the agri-food sector, whereby heavy manual work, long working hours, and night shifts are common.

For instance, zero-hours contracts[2] are a standard practice with some companies (Ollus, 2016: 33). Since labour intermediaries are under no obligation to guarantee any work under zero-hours contracts, some workers travel to their workplace and are sent home because there is no work for them that day (EHRC, 2012: 26). Flexible work in the long term is associated not just with job insecurity and low pay, but health problems in relation to stress and depression (TUC, 2008: 13). While labour intermediaries and flexible employment contracts are legal elements of supply chains and business practices, the consequences of these

---

[2] Zero-hours contracts are a type of casual employment contract that some employers advocate as a flexible means to meet fluctuating levels of demand. Employees are on call when needed, but employers do not have to guarantee a fixed number of weekly working hours. Therefore, employees may go from one week to the next not knowing how many work hours, if any, they will have.

corporate practices can be harmful, or "lawful but awful" (Passas, 2005). Common issues include underpayment of wages, physical and verbal abuse from employers, physically demanding work in the absence of adequate health and safety protections, and in the case of gangmasters, substandard accommodation (Pollard, 2006). As isolated incidents, these harms may not constitute modern slavery, but cumulatively feed into a diverse range of practices that can amount to labour exploitation (Ollus, 2016: 37).

As noted, routine labour harms that do not meet the threshold of modern slavery seem to occur more frequently than extreme harms (France, 2016; Haynes, 2012). In the longer term, routine harms can underpin the existence of more extreme practices. For instance, workers may not complain about underpayment or bullying from their employers if they fear dismissal, which could encourage employers to worsen conditions in the absence of any reprisals. Routine labour harms can therefore become normalised and accepted as part of legal, repetitive and standard business activities. The intention here is not to draw a superficial boundary between extreme and routine labour harms, since this "continuum of exploitation" (Skrivankova, 2014) is arguably a matter of degree, not kind (Shamir, 2012: 110).

The UK has a somewhat fragmented regulatory context when considering different forms of labour abuse. For instance, the newly formed Gangmasters and Labour Abuse Authority (GLAA) is extending its current remit from the agri-food sector to unregulated sectors such as construction. However, there are concerns that the UK government will not match this expanded remit with additional resources, which questions the future efficacy of the GLAA. The self-regulation of companies, or corporate social responsibility (CSR), has been criticised on the basis that CSR and ethical trading policies are "buzzwords in the boardroom" (Tombs and Whyte, 2007: xvi) that companies may disregard if behaving responsibly conflicts with maximising profits. Collective regulation in the form of trade unions can be limited, since union membership has been declining since the 1970s, and migrants are less likely than non-migrants to be unionised (Turner *et al*, 2014).

In terms of recent legislative developments, the Modern Slavery Act 2015 has implications for labour exploitation. Section 54 of The Modern Slavery Act requires large organisations[3] to publish individual annual statements on steps they are taking to identify and address 'slavery' in

---

[3] Defined in the legislation as organisations with an annual turnover of £36m or more.

their supply chains (HM Government, 2015). Since the statements are a relatively new development, there has been little analysis of them in the UK, but there are examples from comparable legislation in the US state of California, i.e. the California Transparency in Supply Chains Act 2011. A statement from Krispy Kreme Doughnuts includes wording such as "we do not engage in verification of product supply chains […] we do not maintain internal accountability standards" for the prevention of slavery-like practices (New, 2015: 700-701). Krispy Kreme appear to have suffered little reputational damage from this wording, which suggests that such statements are little more than extensions of companies' CSR policies, whereby wording can be vague or even nonchalant.

In any event, the Modern Slavery Act focuses on the most extreme exploitation, with no mention of harmful, less extreme practices. The Immigration Act 2016 claims to cover the full spectrum of labour non-compliance by establishing a new Director of Labour Market Enforcement (Davies, 2016), and allowing the new GLAA to extend its remit beyond the agri-food sector. However, organisations such as the TUC (2016) have criticised this legislation for conflating labour market oversight with immigration enforcement, since it criminalises irregular migrants by treating their earnings as proceeds of crime (Davies 2016: 8). While these regulatory and legislative developments appear to suggest stronger labour market oversight, they remain limited and are targeted at specific aspects of exploitation.

Concluding Thoughts

Migrant workers in low-skilled occupations are exposed to a range of exploitative and harmful labour practices in UK food supply chains. These problems include underpayment, abuse from employers, poor safety training, and substandard accommodation. While these practices can be considered harmful, they are unlikely to be treated as crimes such as modern slavery. Even the most extreme cases of 'criminal' exploitation are not necessarily criminally prosecuted, which suggests that routine labour harms are unlikely to be acknowledged or reported. Despite evidence that routine labour exploitation is more frequent when compared to extreme exploitation (France, 2016), most research continues to focus on extreme practices. Labour exploitation usually occurs in the context of legal processes such as supply chain dynamics, rather than being an exclusive problem of individual 'criminals' and exploiters. Therefore, a significant element of labour exploitation is routine, repetitive, normalised, and structural to supply chain dynamics and legitimate markets. Extreme labour exploitation undoubtedly deserves attention from researchers and policy makers. However, routine labour exploitation should not be neglected when contrasted with these more brutal and 'newsworthy' cases.

Acknowledgements

I have received a significant amount of support during this research, and there are too many people to name here individually. The research would not have been possible without the migrant workers and supply chain stakeholders who gave up their time to talk to me. I also wish to thank the colleagues and friends I have made in the School of Law, University of Manchester; the European Society of Criminology; and the European Group for the Study of Deviance and Social Control. They have made the last three years a truly enjoyable and rewarding experience. I would especially like to thank Jon Spencer, who has encouraged me since before this research started.

References

Allain, J. Crane, A. LeBaron, G. and Behbahani, L. (2013) *Forced Labour's Business Models and Supply Chains* York: Joseph Rowntree Foundation

Alvesalo, A. Jokinen, A. and Ollus, N. (2014) 'The Exploitation of Migrant Labour and the Problems of Control in Finland' pp 121-138 in Van Aerschot, P. and Daenzer, P. (eds) (2014) *The Integration and Protection of Immigrants: Canadian and Scandinavian Critiques* Surrey: Ashgate Publishing Limited

Anderson, B. (2015) 'Migrant Domestic Workers: Good Workers, Poor Slaves, New Connections' *Social Politics* Volume 22, No. 4 pp 636-652

Anderson, B. (2010) 'Migration, Immigration Controls and the Fashioning of Precarious Workers' *Work, Employment and Society* Volume 24, No. 2, pp 300-317

Barrientos, S. (2013) '"Labour Chains": Analysing the Role of Labour Contractors in Global Production Networks' in *The Journal of Development Studies* Volume 49, No. 8 pp 1058-1071

Davies, A.C.L. (2016) 'Legislation Note: the Immigration Act 2016' *Industrial Law Journal* Volume 45, No. 3 pp 431-442

EHRC (2012) *Meat and Poultry Processing Inquiry Review* London: Equality and Human Rights Commission

Feinberg, J. (1984) *Harm to Others* New York: Oxford University Press

France, B. (2016) *Labour Compliance to Exploitation and the Abuses In-Between* Labour Exploitation Advisory Group (FLEX): London

Greenfield, V. A. Paoli, L. and Zoutendijk, A. (2016) 'The Harms of Human Trafficking: Demonstrating the Applicability and Value of a New Framework for Systematic, Empirical Analysis' *Global Crime* Volume 17, No. 2 pp 152-180

Greenfield, V.A. and Paoli, L. (2013) 'A Framework to Assess the Harms of Crimes' *British Journal of Criminology* Volume 53, No. 5, pp 864-885

Haynes, D.F. (2009) 'Exploitation Nation: The Thin and Grey Legal Lines Between Trafficked Persons and Abused Migrant Labourers' in *Notre Dame Journal of Law, Ethics and Public Policy* Volume 23, No. 1, pp 1-71

Hillyard, P. Pantazis, C. Tombs, S. and Gordon, G. (eds) (2004) *Beyond Criminology: Taking Harm Seriously* London: Pluto Press

HM Government (2015) *Transparency in Supply Chains* London: HM Government

HSE (2016) *Health and Safety at Work: Summary Statistics for Great Britain 2016* London: Health and Safety Executive

Kosny, A. Santos, I. and Reid, A. (2016) 'Employment in a "Land of Opportunity?" Immigrants' Experiences of Racism and Discrimination in the Australian Workplace' in *International Migration and Integration*. Epub ahead of print 6 March 2016. DOI: 10.1007/s12134-016-0482-0

Lawrence, F. (2016) 'Gangmasters Agree to Pay More than £1m to Settle Modern Slavery Claim' *The Guardian* [online] 1st December Available from: https://www.theguardian.com/uknews/2016/dec/20/gangmasters-agree-1m-payout-to-settle-modern-slavery-claim (accessed 1st February 2017)

LeBaron, G. (2015) 'Unfree Labour Beyond Binaries: Insecurity, Social Hierarchy and Labour Market Restructuring' in *International Feminist Journal of Politics* Volume 17, No. 1 pp 1-19

Lord, N. Flores Elizondo, C. and Spencer, J. (2017) 'The Dynamics of Food Fraud: the Interactions Between Criminal Opportunity and Market (Dys)functionality in Legitimate Business' *Criminology and Criminal Justice*. Epub ahead of print 6 January 2017. DOI: 10.1177/1748895816684539

Malloch, M. and Rigby, P. (eds) (2016) *Human Trafficking: The Complexities of Exploitation* Edinburgh: Edinburgh University Press

Mayer, R. (2007) 'What's Wrong with Exploitation?' *Journal of Applied Philosophy* Volume 24, No.2 pp 137-150

Mena, C. and Stevens, G. (eds) (2010) *Delivering Performance in Food Supply Chains* Cambridge: Woodhead Publishing Limited

New, S. J. (2015) 'Modern Slavery and the Supply Chain: the Limits of Corporate Social Responsibility' *Supply Chain Management* Volume 20, No.6 pp 697-707

Ollus, N. (2016) 'Forced Flexibility and Exploitation: Experiences of Migrant Workers in the Cleaning Industry' *Nordic Journal of Working Life Studies* Volume 6, No.1 pp 25-45

Paoli, L. and Greenfield, V. A. (2015) 'Starting From the End: A Plea for Focusing on the Consequences of Crime' *European Journal of Crime, Criminal Law and Criminal Justice* Volume 23, No.2 pp 87-100

Paoli, L. Greenfield, V.A. and Zoutendijk, A. (2013) 'The Harms of Cocaine Trafficking: Applying a New Framework for Assessment' *Journal of Drug Issues* Volume 43, No. 4 pp 407-436

Passas, N. (2005) 'Lawful but Awful: "Legal Corporate Crimes"' in *The Journal of Socio-Economics* Volume 34, No.6 pp 771-786

Pemberton, S. (2015) *Harmful Societies: Understanding Social Harm* Bristol: Policy Press

Pollard, D. (2006) 'The Gangmaster System in the UK: Perspective of a Trade Unionist' pp 115-128 in Barrientos, S. and Dolan, C. (eds) (2006) *Ethical Sourcing in the Global Food System* London: Earthscan

Potter, M. and Hamilton, J. (2014) 'Picking on Vulnerable Migrants: Precarity and the Mushroom Industry in Northern Ireland' *Work, Employment and Society* Volume 28, No. 3 pp 390-406

Rienzo, C. (2016) *Migrants in the UK Labour Market: An Overview* Oxford: COMPAS

Robinson, P.K. (2010) 'Do Voluntary Labour Initiatives Make a Difference for the Conditions of Workers in Global Supply Chains?' in *Journal of Industrial Relations* Volume 52, No.5 pp 561-573

Ruhs, M. and Martin, P. (2008) 'Numbers vs. Rights: Trade-offs and Guest Worker Programs' *International Migration Review* Volume 42, No.1 pp 249-265

Scott, S. Craig, G. and Geddes, A. (2012) *Experiences of Forced Labour in the UK Food Industry* York: Joseph Rowntree Foundation

Shamir, H. (2012) 'A Labor Paradigm for Human Trafficking' *UCLA Law Review* Volume 60, No.1 pp 76-136

Skrivankova, K. (2014) *Forced Labour in the United Kingdom* York: Joseph Rowntree Foundation

Tombs, S. and Whyte, D. (2015) *The Corporate Criminal: Why Corporations Must be Abolished* Abingdon: Routledge

Tombs, S. and Whyte, D. (2007) *Safety Crimes* Cullompton: Willan Publishing

TUC (2016) *Tackling Exploitation in the Labour Market* London: Trades Union Congress

TUC (2008) *Hard Work, Hidden Lives* London: Trades Union Congress Commission on Vulnerable Employment

Turner, T. Cross, C. and O'Sullivan, M. (2014) 'Does Union Membership Benefit Immigrant Workers in "Hard Times"?' *Journal of Industrial Relations* Volume 56, No.5 pp 611-630

Waldinger, R. and Lichter, M.I. (2003) *How the Other Half Works: Immigration and the Social Organization of Labor* Los Angeles, CA: University of California Press

Wells, C. (2014) 'Containing Corporate Crime: civil or Criminal Controls?' pp 13-32 in Gobert, J. and Pascal, A. (eds) *European Developments in Corporate Criminal Liability* Abingdon: Routledge

Zwolinski, M. and Wertheimer, A. (2016) 'Exploitation' [online] 16th August Available from: https://plato.stanford.edu/archives/fall2016/entries/exploitation (accessed 18th February, 2017)

Extended Biography

Research

I first stumbled across the issue of labour exploitation during my Master's degree in Criminology, which I completed at Coventry University in 2012. My Master's dissertation focused on law enforcement responses to human trafficking cases. An issue that emerged from this work was that the criminal law and criminal justice system represent a fraction of the enforcement framework when considering the full spectrum of exploitative labour practices. Aside from the literature on corporate crime, researchers outside Criminology were starting to conceptualise labour exploitation as a problem of legitimate businesses, supply chains and labour markets, rather than solely a problem of migration and organised crime groups. These ideas laid the foundations for my current doctoral research at the University of Manchester, which examines how the dynamics of some food supply chains result in harmful employment practices for migrant workers in the UK agri-food sector. For future research, I am particularly interested in how the newly established Gangmasters and Labour Abuse Authority (GLAA) will help to address exploitation in the labour market. My general research interests include white-collar and corporate crime, labour exploitation, as well as the topic of harm.

Activism, Organisational Work and/or Professional Membership
I have engaged in extensive voluntary work during my time in Higher Education, most recently with a migrant support organisation in the West Midlands region of the UK. Having supported migrants who face a range of problems with their asylum claims, workplace problems and housing/welfare/healthcare, I am reminded of the daily challenges that some in society face, which continues to fuel my interest in Criminology. I am a member of the European Society of Criminology, within which I am involved in the European Working Group on Organisational and Corporate Crime (EUROC).

Contact Details
LinkedIn: https://www.linkedin.com/in/jondavies-criminology
Twitter: @jon_criminology

5

Post-Release Experiences after Corston (2007): An Introduction to my Research

Helen Elfleet

Introduction

The chapter outlines the author's on-going PhD research, which analyses the role of one women's centre in the lives of women with mental health problems, after their release from prison in a post-Corston Report (2007) context. The research has involved 16 interviews with members of staff at The Women's Centre (TWC),[1] 14 clients who accessed TWC services after their release from prison, and an on-going[2] period of participant observation on the premises of TWC. Drawing on the work of gender responsivity scholars (Hannah-Moffat, 2001; Kendall, 2013; Carlton and Seagrave, 2016), and utilising a Foucauldian feminist perspective, the research adopts a case study approach, examining the role of TWC in the lives of formerly imprisoned women with mental health problems. The research thus aims to contribute to a small body of literature in this field.

The Corston Report (2007)

In 2006 Baroness Corston was commissioned to carry out a *Review of Women with Particular Vulnerabilities in the Criminal Justice System*, in response to a number of self-inflicted deaths of women in prisons in England and Wales. In her report, Corston acknowledged that women's prisons were comprised of highly vulnerable individuals who were poorly served by a system designed with men in mind. She reiterated what researchers and activists have been arguing for many years, that women in prison are socially and economically disadvantaged (Carlen, 1983; Heidensohn, 1985; Worrall, 1990; Moore and Scraton, 2014). She further

---

[1] The name of the charity has been anonymised for confidentiality purposes.
[2] Fifteen months at the time of writing.

repeated the concern that the experiences of prison for women are different to the experiences of men, and stated that there was a clear lack of penal policy specifically designed with women in mind (Dunbabin, 2013; Elfleet, 2017). Corston (2007), in response to these concerns, suggested that the governance of women would be better conducted *by* women. She argued that this would be part of a woman centred, gender responsive approach; an approach that would be tailored to the needs of the individual (Corston, 2007).

In discussing her terms of reference, Corston argued that she sought not to provide a definition of vulnerable, but instead would include all women she considered to be inappropriately placed in prison:

> I consider these women in terms of their "vulnerabilities", which fall into three categories. First, domestic circumstances and problems such as domestic violence, child-care issues, being a single-parent; second, personal circumstances such as mental illness, low self-esteem, eating disorders, substance misuse; and third, socio-economic factors such as poverty, isolation and unemployment (Corston, 2007: 2, para 1).

Corston made 43 recommendations for change, which she argued would address these vulnerability factors. She described these proposals as "a blueprint for a distinct, radically different, visibly-led, strategic, proportionate, holistic, woman-centred, integrated approach" (Corston, 2007: 79). She further noted that this approach would acknowledge the differences between men and women, but that equality did not equate to equivalence of treatment. Her recommendations further included the acceleration and priority of the gender equality duty across all public bodies within the criminal justice system; the establishment of an Inter-Departmental Ministerial Group for women; a mainstreaming of services for women, which she proposed would reduce their risk of reoffending; and the establishment of a network of women's community centres (Dunbabin, 2013; Elfleet, 2017).

In what was clearly her most radical recommendation, Corston suggested that women's prisons (within a 10 year period) should be replaced by smaller custodial units staffed by women. Corston suggested that these units should deploy woman-centred strategies that were endorsed by existing women's centres, citing Asha in Worchester, and Calderdale in Halifax, as pioneers of this approach: "their broad approach is to treat each woman as an *individual* with her own set of *needs and problems* and to increase their *capacity* to take *responsibility for their lives*

(Corston, 2007:10, para 18, emphases added). Thus, in setting out her recommendations for change, Corston considers individual responsibility as key to addressing women's vulnerability factors (Dunbabin, 2013; Elfleet, 2017).

Gender Responsive Justice Models: Governing From a Distance

For over twenty years many countries have considered gender responsivity issues, incorporating health and childcare within penal policies.[3] They have however done so with very little critical discussion on what constitutes gender (Hannah-Moffat, 2010). Critics of gender responsive approaches have argued that they are reliant on a uniform definition of femininity, one which incorporates the stereotypical assumptions of normal feminine behavioural traits (Cruikshank, 1991; Goodkind, 2009). Whilst these assumptions are typically drawn from the experiences of white middle-class women and girls, gender responsive strategies drawing on these assumptions are predominantly directed at working class girls and women, and those from black and minority ethnic (BME) groups (Goodkind, 2009). In addition, they are argued to be reliant on feminist theory, which can be thought of as commercialised. Goodkind (2009: 397) describes commercialised feminism as a branch of feminist thought that has surfaced from the merging of feminist principles with neoliberalism. This mode of feminist thought deems self-esteem as integral to the empowerment of women and girls. It is thus assumed that low self-esteem acts as a barrier to a successful, independent, and fulfilling life (Goodkind, 2009; Rottenberg, 2013). The concerns therefore are that gender responsive strategies, operating in neoliberal political economies, endorse confidence and self-esteem building programmes as strategies that enable women to live self-sufficient lives, free from state dependency (Hannah-Moffat, 2000; 2001; 2010). As Hannah-Moffat (2001) has noted, for women in conflict with the law, this has resulted in the conflation of their needs with risk, through the assessment of their life histories, needs and experiences as criminogenic risk factors (Hannah-Moffat, 1999; Hannah-Moffat et al., 2009). Self-injury, victimisation and mental health difficulties are thus likely to be deemed factors contributing to dependency, and criminality (Hannah-Moffat, 2010).

---

[3] See Haney (2010) for a consideration of gender responsive approaches in the USA, and Hannah-Moffat (2001) for an analysis of such strategies in Canada.

A key concern, therefore, for the use of gender responsive correctional models is that they may incorporate training programmes designed to enable women to manage their *risky* needs, through an emphasis on individual responsibility (Hannah-Moffat, 2010). Empowerment based strategies are thus likely to incorporate self-esteem and confidence based training, in order to 'empower' women to take charge of their lives (Goodkind, 2009; Rottenberg, 2013). Gender responsive methods can thus be viewed as a 'feminized arm of the penal system' (Haney, 2010: 3). These methods are a unique means of governing female subjects, reinforcing gendered, racial and class based expectations (Goodkind, 2009). They are furthermore noted to be strategies that obscure the role of structural and economic factors, through an overwhelming emphasis on self-care and individual responsibility as solutions to hardship (Hannah-Moffat, 2001; Haney, 2010; Rottenberg, 2013).

In her influential report, Corston outlined three key vulnerability categories that were likely to result in the imprisonment of women: domestic, personal and socio-economic factors. In order to address these key vulnerabilities she proposed that women should be aided in developing a particular set of skills: "it is these underlying issues that must be addressed by helping women develop *resilience, life skills* and *emotional literacy* (Corston, 2007: 2, para 1, emphases added).

Corston envisaged a woman centred approach as one that restructures individual subjectivities into neoliberal subjectivities; those which internalise neoliberal aspirations of self-reliance, resilience, and adaptability (Elfleet, 2017). It is furthermore apparent that her report prioritises domestic and personal problems, since little attention is paid to socio-economic factors (Kendall, 2013). For Corston, individual responsibility is an integral feature in addressing women's particular vulnerabilities. This undoubtedly marginalises the role of the state in the creation and exacerbation of social and economic exclusion.[4] This disappointing feature of the Corston Report is perhaps unsurprising given her endorsement of resilience as a viable woman-centred strategy, an evidently neoliberal approach (Elfleet, 2017). As Joseph (2013) has noted, resilience as a concept is easily aligned with neoliberal aspirations, since it can be associated with notions of adaptability in uncertain climates, whether they are social or economic.

---

[4] See Dunbabin (2013) and Elfleet (2017) for further consideration of these issues.

Gender Responsive Post-Release Services: 'Empowerment' in a Women's Centre?

Increasing privatisation under the conditions of neoliberalism has resulted in the outsourcing of public services and assets to private 'for-profit' agencies and companies. As Haney (2010:16) has noted, whilst this has sometimes been perceived as a loss of sovereignty, governing from a distance has alternatively created "an environment of state hybridity". The creation of partnerships with a myriad of agencies has rapidly increased the numbers of individuals involved in offender governance. She further notes that these actors are frequently described as "community members, therapists, or non-governmental organisation (NGO) activists". Despite the appearance of a fracture from traditional methods of governance, they remain incorporated within the state arena through legal mandates, staffing, budgets, and contractual requirements. These agencies are, as Haney (2010:16) argues:

> akin to satellite states – they circle and hover around the centralized "mothership", relying on her for material survival, legitimacy and authority. Yet on a day-to-day level, they claim autonomy from her and the ability to set their own agendas.

Since one of the main achievements of the Corston Report is stated to be the establishment of women's centres in the community, for those at risk of offending/re-offending (Justice Committee, 2015; APPG, 2016), a consideration of their role in the lives of formerly incarcerated women is therefore important. They are frequently hailed as a superior form of support, which is more likely to reduce serial incarceration (Corston, 2007; APPG, 2016; Roberts, 2017).

Feminist contributions to women's experiences of imprisonment have drawn attention to the ways in which women's backgrounds and needs have contributed towards a differential experience of these institutions (Carlen, 1983; Worrall, 1990). However, as Carlton and Seagrave (2011a) have noted, they have resulted in two particular limitations. Firstly, they have led to the appropriation of (feminist) scholarship into policy development which has facilitated gender responsive governance strategies,[5] and secondly they have neglected women's post-release experiences; specifically the long lasting impacts of incarceration. For

---

[5] Such as the Corston Report (2007).

Carlton and Segrave (2016) imprisonment should not be viewed as a separate event from life experiences involving state intervention, including child welfare services and offender management services. Furthermore, release from imprisonment should not be viewed as the beginning of a new life, but should instead be viewed as a destructive event that exacerbates pre-existing social and economic marginalisation (Carlton and Seagrave 2011a; 2011b; 2016). Following Carlton and Seagrave (2011a; 2011b; 2016), this PhD research aims to add to a body of literature on women's post-release experiences, and analyses the role of one women's centre (which was opened in response to the Corston Report) in the lives of formerly imprisoned women with mental health problems.[6]

The Women's Centre (TWC) is a charity for women over the age of 18 years, and states that it provides a women only environment which facilitates the empowerment of its clients. Its overarching aims are focused on reducing reoffending and the prevention of initial offending, through the provision of support and assistance to women who have not yet entered the criminal justice system. TWC is the only women's charity in the local area that works with the criminal justice system, hosting privatised probation services, which supervise women subject to Community Orders and Licence Conditions. The centre is therefore acknowledged to be a semi-penal site; one which straddles the divide between both formal and informal modes of governance (Barton, 2004; 2005).

Whilst the number of women's centres established since the Corston Report is deemed to be modest (APPG, 2016), they are argued to be essential for ex-offenders and those at risk of offending. The All Parliamentary Group on Women in The Penal System (APPG) states that they have a 'positive impact on service users lives' (APPG, 2016: 2). Whilst this may indeed be the case, the APPG places an emphasis on the reduction in reoffending, noting that women's centres have a statistically significant impact on reducing reoffending. Despite this acknowledgement they state that women's centres may be rendered a relic of the past if serious commitments to funding are not made. They further argue that funding priorities should be awarded to those centres adhering to the

---

[6] All adult female ex-prisoners interviewed acknowledged that they had experienced mental health difficulties prior to their incarceration. The importance of mental health, in their pre-prison, in-prison and after prison experiences is undoubtedly important and is explored in the thesis.

principles and recommendations set out in the Corston Report, whereby women 'are treated as individuals and their needs can be addressed holistically' (APPG, 2016: 2).

It is therefore assumed that gender responsive services for women will result in successful outcomes for women by helping them 'lead happy, safe and successful lives' (APPG, 2016: 1). However, for Carlton and Seagrave (2016), gender responsive approaches are frequently unable to address the discrimination, marginalisation and disadvantage that formerly imprisoned women experience. Indeed, for centres endorsing the principles of the Corston report, their function is likely to enable women 'to take responsibility for their lives' (Corston, 2007: 10, para 18). They further note that success is frequently aligned with a reduction in recidivism, thus reintegration success is likely to be measured in terms of a woman's ability to engage with gender responsive programmes. Abstinence from drug use and alcohol consumption, leaving abusive relationships, or re-establishing relationships with children, are thus likely to be deemed integral factors in minimising criminogenic need (Carlton and Seagrave, 2016). They are therefore services that may be reliant on psychological reprogramming techniques designed to reduce a woman's risk of reoffending (Kendall, 2002). The potential implications of women centres endorsing the principles of the Corston Report, such as TWC, are therefore important.

Acknowledgements

My thanks go to my PhD supervisors Dr Alana Barton, Dr Eleanor Peters and Professor Alyson Brown for their continued support and guidance, and to my family for their constant encouragement.

References

All Parliamentary Group on Women in the Penal System (2016) *Is This the End of Women's Centres'* London: Howard League for Penal Reform

Barton, A. (2004) 'Women and Community Punishment: the Probation Hostel as a Semi-Penal Institution for Female Offenders' *The Howard Journal of Crime and Justice* Volume 43, No. 2 pp 149-163

Barton, A. (2005) *Fragile Moralities and Dangerous Sexualities: Two centuries of Semi Penal Institutionalisation for Women* Hampshire: Ashgate

Carlen, P. (1983) *Women's Imprison*ment London: Routledge

Carlton, B. and Seagrave, M. (2011a) 'Women's Survival Post-Imprisonment: Connecting Imprisonment with Pains Past and Present' *Punishment and Society* Volume 13, No. 5 pp 551-570

Carlton, B. and Seagrave, M. (2011b) 'Counting the Costs of Imprisonment: Researching Women's Post-Release Deaths in Victoria' *Australian and New Zealand Journal of Criminology* Volume 44, No. 1 pp 41-55

Carlton, B. and Seagrave, M. (2016) 'Rethinking Women's Post-release Reintergration and 'Success'' *Australian & New Zealand Journal of Criminology* Volume 49, No. 2 pp 281-299

Corston, J. (2007) *The Corston Report: A Report by Baroness Jean Corston of a Review of Women with Particular Vulnerabilities in the Criminal Justice System* London: Home Office

Dunbabin, H. (2013) *Gender Responsive Penality: A Feminist Abolitionist Analysis of Official Penal Discourse on Women's Imprisonment Post Corston Report (2007)* Unpublished Master's thesis, University of Central Lancashire. Available at: http://clok.uclan.ac.uk/9801/2/Dunbabin%20Helen%20Final%20e-Thesis%20(Master%20Copy).pdf

Elfleet, H. (2017) 'Empowered to be Resilient: Neo-liberal Penal Rhetoric and the Corston Report' *Prison Service Journal* No. 230 pp 33-38

Feeley, M. and Simon, J. (1994), 'Actuarial justice: the Emerging New Criminal Law' pp173-201 in Nelken, D. (1994) *The Futures of Criminology* London: SAGE

Goodkind, S. (2009) 'You Can Be Anything You Want, But You Have to Believe It: Commercialised Feminism in Gender Specific Programmes for Girls' *Signs* Volume 34, No. 3 pp 397-422

Haney, L. (2010) *Offending Women: Power, Punishment, and the Regulation of Desire* California: University of California Press

Hannah-Moffat, K. (1999) 'Moral Agent or Actuarial Subject: Risk and Canadian Women's Imprisonment' *Theoretical Criminology* Volume 3, No. 1 pp 71-94

Hannah-Moffat, K. (2000) 'Prisons That Empower: Neo-Liberal Governance in Canadian Women's Prisons' *British Journal of Criminology* Volume 40, No. 3 pp 510-531

Hannah-Moffat, K. (2001) *Punishment in Disguise* Toronto: University of Toronto Press

Hannah-Moffat,K. (2010) 'Sacrosanct or Flawed: Risk, Accountability and Gender Responsive Penal Politics' *Current Issues in Criminal Justice* Volume, 22, No. 2 pp 1 93-215

Hannah-Moffat, K. Maurutto, P. and Turnball, S. (2009) 'Negotiated Risk: Actuarial Illusions and Discretion in Probation' *Canadian Journal of Law and Society* Volume 24, No. 3, pp 391-409

Heidensohn, F. (1985) *Women and Crime* London: Macmillan

Joseph, J.(2013) 'Resilience as Embedded Neoliberalism: A Governmentality Approach' *Resilience: International Policies, Practices and Discourses* Volume 1, No. 1 pp 38-52

Justice Committee (2015) *Women Offenders: Follow-up: Thirteenth Report of Session 2014-15* London: House of Commons

Kendall, K. (2002) 'Time to Think Again about Cognitive Behavioural Programmes' pp182-198 in Carlen, P. (2002) (ed) *Women and Punishment: The Struggle for Justice* Devon: Willan

Kendall, K. (2013) 'Post-Release Support for Women in England and Wales: the Big Picture' pp 34-55 in Carlton, B and Seagrave, M. (eds) (2013) *Women Exiting Prison: Critical Essays on Gender, Post-release Support and Survival* London: Routledge

Moore, L. and Scraton, P. (2014) *The Incarceration of Women: Punishing Bodies, Breaking Spirits* Hampshire: Palgrave Macmillan.

Roberts, Y. (2017) 'I Always Say to a Woman Who May be in a Dark Place- If I Can Make It, So Can You' *The Guardian* [online] 17th February Available at: https://www.theguardian.com/society/2017/feb/19/jean-corston-women-prison-reform-if-i-can-make-it-so-can-you (accessed on 12th April, 2017)

Rottenberg, C. (2013) 'The Rise of Neoliberal Feminism' *Cultural Studies* Volume 28, No. 3 pp 418-437

Worrall, A. (1990) *Offending Women: Female Law Breakers and the Criminal Justice System* London: Routledge.

Extended Biography

Research

I completed a BA (hons) in Criminology and Criminal Justice at the University of Central Lancashire (UCLan) in 2011, achieving a first class honours degree. I remained with UCLan as a post-graduate student, completing a Master of Arts by Research without corrections in 2013.

My Master's research[7] was completed under the supervision of Dr David Scott at the University of Central Lancashire, in 2013. The research sought to find evidence for, and to critically analyse, the deployment of strategies of responsibilisation for women prisoners in official penal discourse. This was achieved through a critical investigation of the

---

[7] Titled, *Gender Responsive Penality: A Feminist Abolitionist Analysis of Official Penal Discourse on Women's Imprisonment Post Corston Report (2007).*

publication, reception and influence of the 2007 report by Baroness Jean Corston, on women in prison in England and Wales. The research utilised the ideas of Canadian feminist penologist Kelly Hannah-Moffat (2001), who has argued that feminist rhetoric of woman centeredness, when utilised by the state, can serve to promote the notion that women's prisons are 'healthy' places that can 'care' for women. As the Corston Report (2007) was put forward as a 'woman-centred' approach, consideration and analysis of the report formed the distinctive element of my research.

Key findings of the research highlighted that whilst the Corston Report (2007) presented itself as a real opportunity for change, it nonetheless subscribed to discourses of responsibilisation that were present in official discourse prior to its publication (Dunbabin, 2013). Corston (2007), whilst making her recommendations for change, stated that women in conflict with the law lacked 'resilience' and 'emotional literacy'. She advocated life-skills training as a means of helping women to become emotionally literate beings, which she purported would reduce their 'risk' of reoffending. She therefore envisaged a gender-responsive approach that was fused with neoliberal aspirations of self-care and individual responsibility.

My Master's research thus advocated the adoption of abolitionist perspectives, through a consideration and application of the work of Pat Carlen,[8] and David Scott.[9] I argued that gender responsive penal reform attempts were flawed, since they were all too easily co-opted by the state to form a 'feminized technology of penal governance' (Hannah-Moffat, 2001:198). It was therefore argued that these penal reform endeavours were unlikely to significantly reduce the women's prison population. The findings of this research were presented at the 43rd Annual Conference of the European Group 2015, in Tallinn, and formed the basis of my most recent publication (see selected works).

I am currently undertaking a full time PhD at Edge Hill University, under the Supervision of Dr Alana Barton, Dr Eleanor Peters, and Professor Alyson Brown. The research aims to add to a small body of literature on women's post release experiences, in a post-Corston Report (2007) context. The research utilises Foucauldian feminist and abolitionist

---

[8] Carlen, P.(1990). Alternatives to Women's Imprisonment, Buckingham: Open University Press.

[9] Scott, D.(2009). Ghosts Beyond Our Realm: A Neo-abolitionist Analysis of Prisoner Human Rights and Prison Officer Culture, Saarbrücken: VDM

perspectives, to analyse the role of one women's centre, in the North-West of England, in the lives of formerly incarcerated women with mental health problems.

The origins of the research idea were rooted in the findings of my M.Res. Having acknowledged the limitations of the Corston Report (2007), as a commercial/neoliberal feminist approach, I then became concerned with how gender responsive approaches function for women after leaving prison. Since one of the main stated achievements of this report is the further development of women's centres in the community for offenders, and those at risk of offending (APPG, 2016), the potential implications of these centres are important. The preliminary findings of this research were presented at the 44th Annual Conference of the European Group 2016, in Braga.

Activism, Organisation work, and/or Professional Membership

I am a member of Edge Hill University's Criminology Research Group, a Fellow of the Higher Education Academy, and a member of the organising committee for Edge Hill University's 2017 multi-disciplinary annual postgraduate conference, Cutting Edge. I am also a member of the European Group for the Study of Deviance and Social Control, the Postgraduate Prison Research Network, and the Common Study Programme in Critical Criminology.

Future Aspirations

Further research aims to build on the issues raised in my PhD research, exploring the role of community-based alternatives to women's imprisonment. Furthermore, a broader consideration of the impact of neoliberal political economies on mental health is of particular interest.

Selected Works

Dunbabin, H. (2013) *Gender Responsive Penality: A Feminist Abolitionist Analysis of Official Penal Discourse on Women's Imprisonment Post Corston Report (2007)* Unpublished Master's thesis, University of Central Lancashire. Available at: http://clok.uclan.ac.uk/9801/2/Dunbabin%20Helen%20Final%20e-Thesis%20(Master%20Copy).pdf

Elfleet, H. (2015) 'Responsibilising the 'Emotionally Illiterate': Critiquing the Corston Report (2007)' The European Group for the Study of Deviance and Social Control, 43rd Annual Conference, University of Tartu in Tallinn, September 2015

Elfleet, H. (2015) 'Gender Responsive Penal Reform: A Critical Analysis of The Corston Report (2007)' Cutting Edge: Answers to the Great Questions of Life, the Universe and Everything, Edge Hill University, April 2015

Elfleet, H. (2016) Un-silencing the Silenced: Narratives of Adult Female Ex-prisoners with pre-existing Mental Health Problems. The European Group for the Study of Deviance and Social Control, 44th Annual Conference, University of Minho in Braga, September 2016

Elfleet, H. (2017) 'Empowered to be Resilient: Neo-liberal Penal Rhetoric and the Corston Report (2007)' *Prison Service Journal* No. 230 pp 33-38

Contact Details

Email: hselfleet@gmail.com

ResearchGate profile: www.researchgate.net/profile/Helen_Elfleet

Twitter: HelenElfleet

6

Prisons, Citizenship and Democratic Transitions: A Crossed Gaze between South Africa and Spain

Natacha Filippi

Introduction

The democratic transitions that took place in South Africa from 1990 to 1994 and in Spain from 1975 to 1982 share several common features. Both marked the end of long-lasting authoritarian regimes characterised, among others, by a rapid development of capitalism, heightened social conflicts, a state rhetoric based on the construction of an 'inside enemy', resistance movements led by trade and student unions, as well as an intense police repression. Both democratic transitions also witnessed violent social confrontations and an increase in bomb attacks and murders organised by different political groups, sometimes instrumentalised by state security forces. In Spain, like in South Africa, those events challenged the official discourses on national reconciliation and on the construction of a new democratic society.

By shifting the level of this macro comparative analysis to a micro level, like the one of the prison institution, this diachronic comparison becomes even more interesting. During democratic transitions and following the end of armed conflicts, the issue of political prisoners' amnesty is often problematic (Keightley, 1993). It is usually linked to a more profound undermining of the judicial and penal system and a reflection on the values they are supposed to embody. In the South African and Spanish contexts, the crossed analysis of prison institutions reveals a striking similitude between the two historical configurations: the existence of large-scale revolts led by common-law prisoners, both men and women (Kriegler, 1995; Steinberg, 2004; Galván García, 2007; Lorenzo Rubio, 2013; Filippi, 2014). Prisoners involved in these movements asserted their will to participate in the construction of a new society based on a critical reorganisation of the judicial, penal, and prison system.

My current research project focuses on the similarities and differences between the prisoners' requests, modalities of action and processes of subjectification during these two transitions. By shifting between different frameworks and scales of analysis, this study will be centred on, without restricting itself to, two symbolic 'carceral complexes': Pollsmoor Prison, situated some 40km south of Cape Town, and 'La Modelo', located in a central district of Barcelona. Examples drawn from other contexts, such as the 1970s and 1990s France or the 1970s United States will also complement this study (Weiss, 1991; Artières *et al.*, 2003). The aim is to generate new interrogations, on how marginalised and invisibilised historical actors expressed their requests of citizenship, in the longevity of some authoritarian regimes and on the role played by the penal institution in the transition towards new political systems. The research pays specific attention to the way populations were governed during the last decade of the Francoist and apartheid regimes through the use of psychological and physical repression (Foster *et al.*, 2005; Gonzalez Cortés, 2008). Both states created and implemented categories aiming at classifying racial and social deviances and indexed these categories on population groups, rather than on the actual acts of individuals. This feature partly derived from an increased involvement of the psychiatric discipline within the judicial and penal system (Colman, 1991; Vinyes, 2001). As a result of these historical evolutions in the fields of criminal and political punishment, by the 1980s in South Africa and the 1970s in Spain, a large part of the society considered their regime's judicial system as illegitimate.

Prisons and Democratic Transitions, Between Revolts and Citizenship

In South Africa, from 1990 to the beginning of 1994, prisons witnessed a great number of protest movements led by men and women common-law prisoners. The latter had numerous claims. Most targeted the living and work conditions within prisons, the amnesty of all prisoners considered as victims of the apartheid laws, how the parole system was implemented, the challenging of a judicial system seen as biased and criminal, and the participation in the first democratic elections in April 1994. In March, April, June and July 1994, these protest movements evolved into large-scale revolts which shook the entire country's prisons. The issue of the penal and judicial system's renewal received front page coverage. In order to denounce the violence of the state, prisoners adopted modalities of protest that often induced the exercise of violence against oneself through hunger strikes, self-mutilations, and immolations. They highlighted the imperative necessity to redefine the limits of citizenship in the context of democratic transitions. If one takes into account the scale of these revolts and the way they were received by the public, there is no doubt they constituted an exceptional event in the South African history.

The study of the Spanish democratic transition reveals that the Francoist prisons witnessed a very similar phenomenon from 1976 to 1980. Despite different material conditions between the penal institutions of the two countries, the prisoners' requests were analogous. The modalities of action adopted by common-law prisoners were often drawn from the ones developed by political prisoners. The illegal creation of a prisoners' union (in South Africa) and of a prisoners' coordinating group (in Spain), the illegal formation of a warders' trade union in both countries and the participation of prisoners deprived of the right to vote in the making of electoral ballots to be used during the new democratic elections all constitute incredible resemblances that call for a deeper study of the connections between these two historical configurations. While the South African and Spanish governments attempted to establish more or less successful paradigms of national reconciliation, prisoners tried to constitute themselves as political subjects deserving the right to take part in the transition negotiations. By doing so, they shed light on the flaws of a reconciliation that did not take into account those silenced, excluded, and left on the margins of society.

Historiography and Sources within the Comparative Framework

The comparative method is a powerful and complex heuristic tool. Thanks to this method, it is possible to avoid rigid historiographical frameworks whilst making appear new structural bases of analysis. Combined with games of scale, it enables one to project new interrogations on different historical configurations and to explore in a distinct way individual gestures and collective trajectories, local actors, and institutional structures. Despite the fact that there are striking parallels between the South African and Spanish authoritarian regimes and democratic transitions, the historiography of the comparison between the two countries during the second half of the twentieth century is nearly non-existent. The few studies that there are on the topic focus on the social movements of resistance against the repressive regimes, and the issues of reconciliatory justice and political prisoners' amnesty during the democratic transitions (Bundy, 1987; Gormally and McEvoy, 1995). In addition, this project positions itself in the line of renewed historiographies such as the imperial history and the global history, which call for shedding new light and a gaze on the connections and commensurable categories between 'peripheral' territories and former 'metropoles', and between colonial and postcolonial chronologies, without undermining the significance of colonialism as a historical milestone (Cooper and Stoler, 1997; Green, 1990; Stoler, 2001; Ruggiu, 2010).

The comparative method forces one to engage with numerous historiographies, such as the ones of protest movements in prison, democratic transitions in Spain and South Africa and the logics of repression, resistance and collaboration under authoritarian regimes. This work also questions the commensurability of the concepts and archives used to realise it. For instance, reference to the same concept, like the 'right to vote', can echo diverging experiences in South Africa and Spain, while different terms such as *preso social, bandiet* or *freedom fighter* can share more connotations that it would seem. Indeed, as César Lorenzo Rubio stated on the Spanish prison movements, and which is easily applicable to the South African context, prisoners '*reinterpreted* their marginal condition' and considered themselves as 'presos *sociales* [*social* prisoners], victims of the dictatorship and of the capitalist society' (Lorenzo Rubio, 2013: 22). This blurred frontier between common-law prisoner, political prisoner, *preso social, bandiet* or *freedom fighter* is fundamental to understand the inmates' requests and modalities of action during prison riots.

In addition, the nature of the consulted archives must be deconstructed in order to analyse their specificities, their biases, and their silences. As the unity of comparison targets a sole institution, the prison one, the archives of the two historical contexts would seem quite similar at first sight: commissions of inquiry, prisoners' letters – some smuggled out and others sent through official channels of communication – institutional reports, circulars, newspapers, letters and pamphlets written by organisations of support and government statistics, among others. A detailed investigation of these sources should enable the extent to which they are comparable to be checked. At the same time, it will shed a new light on their texture, which is often quite complex to scrutinise. In the achievement of this project, the use of interviews led in South Africa with prisoners, warders, lawyers and judges, and the future realisation of similar interviews in Spain, should prove to be crucial. Indeed, it facilitates the study of how collective memories are built and complements institutional archives, which often convey a smoothed out version of history.

Governance and Repression under Apartheid and Francoism

One of the many interests stemming from connecting two historiographies is how they can benefit from this new dialogue and break away from exceptionalist and binary hypotheses. There is a tendency to portray the apartheid regime as a singular anachronism at a time when processes of national liberation were occurring in the rest of the African continent. Similarly, Francoism is often viewed as a conservative-style autarchic regime isolated from the rest of post-war Europe. Though these hypotheses are partly founded, they do not enable us to wholly grasp the stakes at play during the dying years of these regimes. Notwithstanding, part of the international pressure placed on each regime during its last decade was linked to this perceived anachronism and strongly influenced how each democratic transition took place. The introduction of the comparative tool reassesses these hypotheses and attempts to offer another understanding of the regimes' longevity. It also provides a broader, more nuanced account of specific phenomena such as police repression, torture and imprisonment under those regimes, in order to grasp their impact on the daily life of different social groups. It can indeed prove extremely useful to compare the available statistics on state violence, detentions and judicial sentences in the two countries, using categories of age, gender, class, and race, all the while being cautious to take into account the conditions of the production of these statistics.

The game of scales between micro and macro levels also aims at contributing to the academic and social debate on the role of racial and gender categories in the production of discourses, and the implementation of specific models of governance (Davis, 2003). On the one hand, legal and judicial mechanisms based on 'the struggle against terror', the myth of the 'communist threat' and the discursive construction of the 'Other' as an inside enemy share common characteristics in South Africa and Spain. On the other hand however, the exact role played by racial and gender categories in the two countries has diverged on many occasions, especially if taking into account such characteristics as the scientific racism displayed in South Africa, or the Francoist regime's focus on 'homosexual deviance' in Spain (Dubow, 1995; Pérez-Sánchez, 2007). This comparative work will hopefully bring new light to the precise function played by these categories in each authoritarian regime. More broadly, the study of these categories and their intersectionality in two different contexts highlights what social margins can teach us, even more so during democratic transitions, as to the creation of nations and the management of bodies through classification, exclusion, and imprisonment.

Conclusion

The prisoners' protest movements that took place during the South African and Spanish transitions reveal extremely interesting analogies, and dissemblances, between the two contexts. The slowing down of these movements, when each democratic transition was officially ending, also shared common characteristics. Reforms of the penal and judicial system were limited and partly delegitimised by the absence of real staff renewal. Within prisons, more individual actions gradually replaced collective forms of solidarity. This change coincided with the massive arrival of 'hard' drugs and easier access to parole, though this was indexed on the inmate's behaviour. The global prison problematically shifted towards punitive populism and the instrumentalisation of the phenomena of social alarm. As a consequence, prisoners' conditions of survival and requests rapidly disappeared from the public sphere.

Through this comparative approach, the investigation of prisons during democratic transitions is used as a magnifying glass revealing the difficult transformation of penal and judiciary systems inherited from authoritarian regimes. These difficulties were exacerbated in the case of Spain which, in difference to South Africa, did not put in place a commission of truth and reconciliation and chose silence as a form of collective memory (Rozenberg, 2006). In both historical configurations, the continuities with an authoritarian legacy give rise to interrogations on the links during democratic transitions, between the renewal of judiciary and penal paradigms, reconciliatory justice, social exclusion through imprisonment, and the creation of new collective identities.

Acknowledgements

Engaging with this new field of research would not have been possible without the support of the History Workshop at the Witwatersrand University. I would also like to express my posthumous acknowledgement to Jan-Georg Deutsch, my former supervisor, who offered incredible support and sharp advices in relation with my PhD and my later comparative research between the Spanish and South African transitions.

References

Artières, P., Quero, L. and Zancarini-Fournel, M. (2003) *Le Groupe d'information sur les prisons : archives d'une lutte : 1970-1972* Paris: IMEC

Bundy, C. (1987) 'Street Sociology and Pavement Politics: Aspects of Youth and Student Resistance in Cape Town, 1985' *Journal of Southern African Studies*, Volume 13, No. 3 pp 303-330

Colman, A.M. (1991) 'Crowd Psychology in South African Murder Trials' *American Psychologist* Volume 46, pp 1071-1179

Cooper, F. and Stoler, A.L., eds. (1997) *Tensions of Empire: Colonial Cultures in a Bourgeois World* Berkeley: University of California Press

Davis, A. (2003) *Are Prisons Obsolete?* New York: Seven Stories Press

Dubow, S. (1995) *Scientific Racism in Modern South Africa* Cambridge: Cambridge University Press

Foster, D., Haupt, P. and De Beer, M. (2005) *The Theatre of Violence. Narratives of Protagonists in the South African Conflict* Cape Town: HSRC Press, James Currey

Galván García, V. (2007) 'Sobre la abolición de las cárceles en la transición española' *Historia Actual Online* Volume 14, pp 127-131

González Cortés, J.R. (2008) 'Represión, esclavitud y exclusión. Un análisis a escala de la violencia franquista' *Entelequia. Revista Interdisciplinar: Monográfico* Volume 7, pp 153-171

Gormally, B. and McEvoy, K., eds. (1995) *Release and Reintegration of Politically Motivated Prisoners in Northern Ireland, A Comparative Study of South Africa, Israel/Palestine, Italy, Spain, the Republic of Ireland and Northern Ireland* Belfast: NIACRO

Green, N. (1990) 'L'histoire comparative et le champ des études migratoires' *Annales Économies, Sociétés, Civilisations* Volume 45, No. 6 pp 1335-1350

Keightley, R. (1993) 'Political Offences and Indemnity in South Africa' *South African Journal on Human Rights* Volume 9, No. 3 pp 334-357

Kriegler, J. (1995) *Unrest in Prisons: Final Report of the Commission of Inquiry into Unrest in Prisons Appointed by the President on 27 June 1994* Pretoria, sn

Lorenzo Rubio, C. (2013). *Cárceles en llamas. El movimiento de presos sociales en la transición* Barcelona: Virus Editorial

Pérez-Sánchez, G. (2007) *Queer Transitions in Contemporary Spanish Culture, From Franco to la Movida* Albany: State University of New York Press

Rozenberg, D. (2006) 'Le 'pacte d'oubli' de la transition démocratique en Espagne. Retours sur un choix politique controversé' *Politix* Volume 2, No. 74 pp 173-188

Ruggiu, F.-J. (2010) 'L'histoire comparée, méthode historique, pratique d'écriture' EHESS, Paris, Unpublished communication, Journée d'études sur l'histoire comparée et l'histoire croisée

Steinberg, J. (2004) *The Number. One Man's Search for Identity in the Cape Underworld and Prison Gangs* Johannesburg: Jonathan Ball Publishers

Stoler, A.L. (2001) 'Tense and Tender Ties: The Politics of Comparison in North American History and (Post)Colonial Studies' *The Journal of American History* Volume 88, No. 3 pp 829-865

Vinyes, R. (2001) 'Construyendo a Caín. Diagnosis y terapia del disidente: las investigaciones psiquiátricas militares de Antonio Vallejo Nágera con presas y presos políticos' *Ayer, Revista de Historia Contemporánea* Volume 44, No. 4 pp 227-250

Weiss, R.P. (1991) 'Introduction: Attica: The 'Bitter Lessons' Forgotten?' *Social Justice* Volume 18, No. 3(45) pp 1-12

Extended Biography

Research

In February 2014, I defended my PhD entitled 'Deviances and the Construction of a "Healthy Nation" in South Africa: A Study of Pollsmoor Prison and Valkenberg Psychiatric Hospital c. 1964-1994' at the History Faculty of the University of Oxford. This project was born several years before, when I was organising literacy workshops in Pollsmoor Prison, in South Africa, where I was studying for a year. While speaking with young inmates, I realised that they still perpetuated the prison history, in particular relating to the last years of apartheid and to the prison revolts that occurred during the country's democratic transition. Back in France, I did my Master thesis at Sciences Po Paris on the topic, before going to England and writing up my PhD on the links between Pollsmoor Prison and Valkenberg psychiatric hospital during the second half of the apartheid regime up until the end of the democratic transition. This project led to several publications in scientific journals. The different publications focus, among other things, on gender issues in prison, psychiatric institutional violence, resistance, and collaboration inside prisons, as well as the links between police and prison forces during the South African democratic transition.

While doing research for my PhD I decided to write up an essay mixing the style of the historical novel with extracts from sociological interviews. The idea was for Pollsmoor prisoners' voices to reach a broader public than the academic one. This essay, entitled *Brûler les prisons d'apartheid* (Éditions Syllepse), was published in 2012. Parallel to this, I began translating books and articles from English to French. This work culminated in 2014 with the translation of South African freedom fighter and philosopher Steve Biko's *I write what I like* (*Conscience noire*, Éditions Amsterdam).

After finishing up my PhD I became a Research Associate for the History Workshop of Witwatersrand University (Johannesburg). I am currently working on two research projects. The first one aims to study theories and concrete cases of penal abolitionism and reconciliatory justice in different historical contexts such as South Africa, Spain and the United States. The second one focuses on a comparison between South African and Spanish prison revolts during the countries' respective democratic transitions. More broadly, my aim is to contribute to the dissemination of prisoners' requests, subjectivities and experiences as historical actors to a larger public. The idea is that the study of different historical configurations proves that it is possible to question the existence of prison institutions as a means of social control.

Activism, Organisation work, and/or Professional Membership

This academic involvement with the issue of prison, police and psychiatric hospitals was paired with a personal involvement in activist groups. While studying in South Africa, in addition to the literacy workshops in Pollsmoor Prison, I worked on the issue of networking with an association providing support for HIV-positive people. In France, I worked alongside other activists and comrades on three different things: helping out with the task of spreading information about French prisoners' requests and conditions of survival, offering support to families victim of state violence, be it regarding police violence or prison violence, and organising workshops and debates on the judicial strategies available to those suffering from state violence.

While working on the Spanish historical context, I have become involved in movements promoting the development of worker cooperatives in rural areas. I have also discovered and become closer to different groups mobilised around the theme of prison and state violence at a local level. Many existing platforms and mechanisms base themselves on the idea of a necessary bridge between academic research and activist involvement. I am referring to, for instance, the *Observatori del Sistema Penal i els Drets Humans*, the *Centre Iridia*, the group *Defender a Quien Defiende* and the SIRECOVI mechanism (International System of Recording and Communication on Cases of Institutional Violence). These platforms and mechanisms are particularly interesting in that they bring together researchers, lawyers, and groups such as unions of street vendors, prisoners' family associations and former prisoners mobilised to preserve the memory of their struggle.

Selected works

Filippi, N. (2016) 'Institutional Violence and the Law in Apartheid South Africa' *Journal of Colonialism and Colonial History* Volume 17, No. 3 DOI: 10.1353/cch.2016.0038

Filippi N. (2016) 'Women's Protests: Gender, Imprisonment and Resistance in South Africa (Pollsmoor Prison, 1970s-1990s') *Review of African Political Economy* Volume 43, No. 149 pp 436-450

Filippi, N. (2016) 'Révoltes carcérales, maintien de l'ordre et transition démocratique en Afrique du Sud (1976-1994)' *Crime, Histoire & Sociétés* Volume 20, No. 1 pp 5-25

Filippi, N. (2012) *Brûler les prisons d'apartheid* Paris: Syllepse

Filippi, N. (2011) 'Deviance, Punishment and Logics of Subjectification during Apartheid: Insane, Political and Common-Law Prisoners in a South African Goal' *Journal of Southern African Studies* Volume 37, No. 3 pp 627-643

Contact Details

Email: natacha.filippi1@gmail.com

7

'It's not a Protest, it's a Process': Protest, Resistance and the War of Position in the Advanced Capitalist State

Samantha Fletcher

Introduction

My research is concerned with exploring new social movements, protest, and resistance, utilising such phenomenon as a vehicle to continue to analyse and better understand the complex manifestations and nuanced workings of the state, state power, the state corporate-nexus, and ultimately the dominant classes' ability to maintain the status quo of capitalist accumulation of wealth by the few, at the expense of the many. To this end my doctoral research studies the Occupy movement, and mobilises this as a case study to present certain abstractions regarding the exhibition of the aforementioned conceptual concerns, that are tied up in 'state' based anxieties and political class struggle. It does so whilst simultaneously paying due deference to spatial and temporal variations in a movement that is as local as it is global, alongside seeking to avoid any problematic reification of the concepts it explores (Jessop 2008; 2015). I should perhaps add at this point that my research was not always so eloquently and overtly regarding the Occupy movement. My original PhD proposal was regarding an exploration of the cooperative movements in pubs as a form of resistance and contestation. It was however, during the initial stages of this research in 2011 when I ventured into Liverpool City Centre to speak with the newly formed Occupy Liverpool camp residing on the aptly named Communication Row that I fell deeply in adoration for this long awaited post 2008 global movement. From that moment on I decided that engaging in this new and exciting 'incubator of knowledge', to borrow an expression from Kelley (2002: 8 cited in: Choudry, 2012: 175), was where my future research trajectories lay.

Occupy, the Advanced Capitalist State and the War of Position

In September of 2011 in what Butler (2011: 193) described as an 'unprecedented display of popular will' approximately 200 people, growing in future months to up to 2000 people (Schneider, 2011 cited in: Davenport, 2011: 87) descended onto the streets of New York to undertake an occupation of a (quasi) public space in Zuccotti Park which would come to be known as Occupy Wall Street (OWS). In the subsequent two months, leading up to its violent physical dismemberment by a state-corporate collaboration (Bratich, 2014; Dellacioppa *et al.*, 2013; Pickerill and Krinsky, 2012; Wolf, 2012), this occupation style of protest spread to an estimated 950 – 1500 cities worldwide (Feigenbaum *et al*, 2013; van Gelder, 2011). To summarise briefly just some of the concerns arising from this diverse group, they included: the lie of the 'American dream', inadequate healthcare, lack of upward mobility, increasing inequality, economic injustice, the reckless action of the banking and finance industry, joblessness, multinational corporations, growing debt, rising mass incarceration, a culture of war and violence, the increasing influence of the wealthy, and corrupt politicians (Acemoglu and Robinson, 2012; Colvin, 2011; Council of Elders, 2011; Foroohar, 2011; Kroll, 2011; Scherer, 2011)[1]. The movement's message was clear, despite attempts by various factions to discredit it by attesting otherwise, unfettered capitalism and gross inequality must be challenged and changed.

Although intrigued by the role played by both historical and contemporary movements in terms of inspiration for and/or connectivity with the Occupy movement[2] both the literature (predominately narratives stemming from Occupy camps in the US) and empirical sites of investigation for this research (Occupy camps in London and Liverpool in the UK) remain very much embedded in a Western context. As a consequence the research has a particular set of concerns, or in more formalised research terms and expression, a set of theoretical 'constants' and considerations underpinning this specific work: namely the *advanced*

---

[1] For the Declaration of the Occupation of New York City see:
http://www.yesmagazine.org/people-power/declaration-of-the-occupation-of-new-york-city

[2] For historical examples of inspiration see for example: Climate Change Camps, The Zapatistas and the Anti/Alter globalisation movement (Feigenbaum, *et al*, 2011). For contemporary examples that inspired and/or ran parallel to the Occupy movement see: The Indignados, Aganaktismenoi and the 'Arab Spring' (Brown, 2011; Douzinas, 2013; Kennedy, 2011, van Gelder, 2011).

capitalist state and the *war of position,* both of which we now turn to and examine in greater depth.

The advanced capitalist state describes a state where capitalism has been distinctly and acutely integrated into a society for a lengthy period of time, arguably adapting during this period to avoid any revolutionary overturning of the system. There are many reasoned characteristics of the advanced capitalist state. Firstly, arguably there is a set of visible indicators: economic catastrophe, debt financing, and the weakening of unions alongside the accumulation of capital by even fewer members of the dominant classes. These are all often soundly encapsulated under an overarching category of *perpetual crisis* (Wolfe, 1983; Hay, 1999, Peck, 2010). The apprehension here however, is not to labour the point regarding the visible featurettes of perpetual crisis but instead it is to recognise that the advanced capitalist state denotes the presence of particular and far more complex stealth like systematics. These are perhaps best described by Green (1993: 175) who states that the distinct peculiarity of the advanced capitalist state lies in "a capitalist state [that] is premised upon a certain realm of civil society which endows all its citizens with equal legal subject hood, and obscures and mediates the reality of bourgeois political and economic domination". It is from this point that we can bring in the notion of the war of position, a termed utilised by Antonio Gramsci, as one of the key features of political class struggle in the state of advanced capitalism.

The war of position is best summarised as entrenched ideological struggle, where a war over hearts and minds must be won before seeking to commandeer state apparatus and enact change. The war of position (lengthy cultural, political and ideological class struggle) lies in contrast to a war of manoeuvre (the commandeering of the coercive state apparatus). The relationship between the advanced capitalist state and the war of position is made clear where it is argued that 'advanced capitalist societies [that] possess political and ideological resources [...] make necessary a transition from war of manoeuvre to a long war of position' (Forgacs, 1988: 223: also see: Brittain, 2008: 75). The distinct positioning of the US and UK based Occupy camps as within this war of position terrain is further demonstrated by Chomsky (2012: 69) who spoke of the argued need for Occupy to 'transition from the tents [...] into the hearts and minds of the masses'. The spatial and temporal Western specificity of the Occupy movement, in comparison to some of its parallel occurring counterparts, is perhaps best illustrated by Fischer (2011: 1) who states that "some have likened Occupy to the Arab Spring. That analogy suggests that Occupy will get the US military to turn on Washington and displace the federal government. Not too likely". Both the *advanced capitalist state* and *the war of position* are however, mindfully and purposefully referred to as 'constants' in quotation marks, to denote and acknowledge their inevitable perpetual fluidity at the hands of the ever ambiguous, elusive and ambidextrous state (Coleman *et al*, 2009; Peck, 2010).

Occupy as Ostensibly Counter-Hegemonic

In terms of conceptualising the Occupy movement it is neither desirable nor appropriate to place static conceptual parameters around this consortium either, not least out of respect for a movement that itself deliberately avoided such forms of classification (Harcourt, 2013). However, having said this there is one graspable feature of the movement that seems largely agreeable, even from the most disparate arms of the wider movement, and that is its supposed counter-hegemonic nature. This can be gleaned through a thorough reading of the emerging published narratives from those on camp who are unfailingly keen to pitch the converseness of their ways; their nonviolence against the violence of capitalism and war, their disobedience and dissent against the status quo of public order rhetoric (see: Solnit, 2011; Vitale, 2011) to name but just a few examples. As Taussig (2013: 30–31) so unmistakably attests:

> We use our magic to thwart their magic. They have pepper spray. We have burning sage. They prohibit microphones. We have the people's microphone. They prohibit tents. We improvise tents that are not tents but what nomads used before North Face [...] each day, each week, sees another deterritorialisation of their reterritorializations.

Through these discourses the Occupy movement is arguably posited as the antithesis, the David to the unencumbered Goliath, of capitalism and inequality. This is most pertinently seen in the, albeit statistically inaccurate but instead highly symbolic (Chomsky, 2012), 1 per cent vs. 99 per cent homily[3]. However, as argued by Taylor (2013: 742) whilst

---

[3] The language of the 1% Vs the 99% was used to symbolise the disproportionate amount of wealth held by the top 1% of the world's population in comparison to the rest of the world. We are the 99%' became one of the key slogans of the Occupy movement. The

'rhetorically powerful, the slogan's elegant simplicity reveals as much as it conceals'.

Hegemonic 'Catch 22s' and the Occupy Safer Spaces Policy

As multifarious Occupy camps unfolded across the globe, although tied up in variant concerns regarding the manifestation of the crisis of capital at a local level, there remained deep connections between camps (Tharoor, 2011). One noticeable commonality across most camps was the adoption of a templated Safer Spaces policy[4]. Within this policy lay a 13 point manifesto that called for a series of highly agreeable aspects that centred around "respectful awareness for language used, the unacceptable nature of various forms of prejudice and encouraging mediation and reverent challenges to any such objectionable forms of behaviour" (Fletcher, 2015: 8). To use Occupy London as an example, although the same policy was reproduced almost identically at all sites, amongst these highly agreeable points lay the more peculiar point 13: "Occupy London is an alcohol and drugs free space". Although not immediately peculiar in the sense that there is almost an immediate recognition that Occupy was a protest camp present in 'public' spaces that have clear restrictions on consumption of alcohol (see: Licensing Act 2013 actualised through Designated Public Place Orders) and the more homogenous prohibition of various narcotics under the Misuse of Drugs Act 1971, it was noticeable to some of my interviewees as a problematic conflation: that drug and/or alcohol (mis)use be placed on a list of banned behaviour next to, for example, racism and sexism. Through extended dialogue with participants both on and off camp, this almost innocuous point 13 that one might easily miss amongst the more popularised and common place Occupy interchanges, has become a cornerstone of investigation within my research leading to a much more in-depth exploration of the significance of the very existence of point 13 within the Occupy Safer Spaces policy.

There is not sufficient time here to unpack all the nuanced discourses that have emanated from exploring the Occupy Safe Spaces policy (for a full preliminary analytical account see: Fletcher, 2015). In brief, it has

---

original Tumblr blog where the slogan derives from can be accessed here: http://wearethe99percent.tumblr.com/ or read an interview with the creators of the slogan here: http://www.motherjones.com/politics/2011/10/we-are-the-99-percent-creators

[4] For the Occupy London Safer Spaces Policy see:
http://occupylondon.org.uk/about/statements/safer-space-policy/

allowed the exploration of the workings of both, in Gramscian terms, *coercion* (the metaphorical iron fist that might strike down the drug or alcohol user and Occupy) and *consent* (the ideological depoliticiation of drug and alcohol users) in tandem and in turn, its impact on and what it can help us understand about the contemporary political class struggle within the war of position terrain, with a seemingly resultant 'no win' catch 22 situation. An exploration of this peculiarity has given rise to revisiting notions from seminal works such as Piven and Cloward (1979: x) and further recognition of the analytical importance "to understand that the main features of contemporary popular struggles are both a reflection of an institutionally determined logic and a challenge to that logic", and that to delve into the heart of resistance and contestation movements to confront this, is arguably not to be critical of the counter-hegemonic efforts but instead to support them in unveiling the ever more intricate operations of its adversary.

Conclusion

Recapping the main components of my research thesis, a consideration of the conditions of the advanced capitalist state leading to acknowledging a war of position in tandem can arguably act a as crucial departure point when examining contemporary protest, resistance and dissent in the Western context. It is argued that it can also lead us to a requirement of 'fundamental diagnostic concern' (Fletcher, 2015: 13) about what it means to be ostensibly counter-hegemonic under such conditions and perhaps most importantly about how a diagnostic on such matters might lead to renewed understandings of how the dominant classes maintain their prominent position of power and gross accumulation of wealth at the expense of the vast majority. Ultimately, what my research seeks, and will continue to seek to do, is to make theoretical, conceptual and analytical contributions to critical discourse about the functionalities and peculiarities of the state, state power and the state-corporate nexus, through an intricate examination of new social movements, protest and resistance.

Acknowledgements

I wish to thank my doctoral supervisory team Dr Giles Barrett, Dr Sara Parker and Professor Joe Sim for their guidance and patience through my often turbulent and unconventional challenges on the road to completion.

I also extend a thank you to the many different members of the European Group for the Study of Deviance and Social Control who continue to support me in numerous, wonderfully diverse, and significant ways.

References

Acemoglu, D. and Robinson, J, A. (2012) 'Against political capture: occupiers, muckrakers, progressives' pp 100 – 112 in Byrne, J. (ed) *The Occupy Handbook* New York: Hachette Book Group

Bratich, J. (2014) 'Occupy all the dispositifs: memes, media ecologies, and emergent bodies politic' *Communications and Critical/Cultural Studies* Volume 11, No. 1 pp 64–73

Brittain, J, J. (2008) 'The differing revolutionary positions of Gramsci and Trotsky in relation to classical Marxism, the peasantry, and the majority world' *Socialist Studies: The Journal of the Society for Socialist Studies* Volume 3, No. 2 pp 65-92

Brown, W. (2011) 'Occupy Wall Street: return of a repressed res-publica' *Theory and Event* Volume 14, No. 4 p1

Butler J (2011) 'Bodies in Public' pp 192 – 194 in: Taylor, A., Gessen, K. and editors from n+1, Dissent, Triple Canopy and The New Inquiry (eds) *Occupy: Scenes from Occupied America*, Brooklyn: Verso

Chomsky, N. (2012) *Occupy* London: Penguin

Choudry, A. (2012) 'On Knowledge Production, Learning and Research in Struggle' pp 175 – 194 in Fanelli, C. and Lefebvre, P. (eds) *Uniting Struggles: Critical Social Research in Critical Times* Ottawa: Red Quill Books

Coleman, R. Sim, J. Tombs, S. and Whyte, D. (2005) 'Introduction: state, power, crime' pp 1 – 19 in Coleman R, Sim J, Tombs, S and Whyte D (eds) *State, Power, Crime,* London: SAGE

Colvin, G. (2011) 'Are the bankers to blame?' pp 64 – 71 in TIME Magazine (ed) *What is Occupy? Inside the Global Movement* New York: TIME Books

Council of Elders (2012) 'Occupy Wall Street statement of solidarity' pp 56 - 57 in Schrager Lang A and Lang/Levitsky D (eds) *Dreaming In Public: Building The Occupy Movement* Oxford: New Internationalist Publications

Davenport, B. (2011) 'Occupy Complexity: Using Complexity to Examine The Occupy Wall St Movement' *E:CO* Volume 13, No. 4 pp 87– 93

Dellacioppa, K. Soto, S. and Meyer, A. (2013) 'Rethinking resistance and the cultural politics of Occupy' *New Political Science* Volume 35, No. 3 pp 403 – 416

Douzinas, C. (2013) *Philosophy and the Resistance in the Crisis* Cambridge: Polity Press

Feigenbaum, A. Frenzel, F. and Mccurdy. P. (2013) *Protest Camps* London: Zed Books

Fischer, C. (2011) 'Occupy! Now what?' *Made in America: Notes on American Life From American History* Available from: https://madeinamericathebook.wordpress.com/2011/11/08/occupy-now-what/ (accessed on 24th February, 2017)

Fletcher, S. (2015) 'Negotiating the resistance: catch 22s, brokering and contention within Occupy safer spaces policy' *Contention: The Multidisciplinary Journal of Social Protest* Volume 3, No. 2 pp 10 – 20

Forgacs, D. (1988) 'Foreword' Forgacs, D. (ed) *The Antonio Gramsci Reader: Selected Writings 1916 – 1935* London: Lawrence and Wishart

Foroohar, R. (2011) 'Whatever happened to upward mobility' pp 77-85 in TIME Magazine (ed) *What is Occupy? Inside the Global Movement* New York: TIME Books

Green, C, (1993) 'Advanced capitalist hegemony and the significance of Gramsci's insights: A restatement' *Social and Economic Studies* Volume 42, No. 2/3 pp 175-207

Harcourt, B, E. (2013) 'Chapter 2: Political Disobedience' pp 45 – 92 in Mitchell W, J, T. Harcourt B, E. and Taussig, M. (2013) *Occupy: Three Inquiries in Disobedience* Chicago: The University of Chicago Press

Hay, C. (1999) 'Crisis and the structural transformation of the state: interrogating the process of change' *The British Journal of Politics & International Relations* Volume 1, No. 3 pp 317-344

Jessop, B. (2008) *State Power* Cambridge: Polity Press

Jessop, B. (2015) *States and State Power: A Strategic-Relational Approach* Available from: http://bobjessop.org/2015/02/27/states-and-state-power-a-strategic-relational-approach/ (accessed on 24th February, 2017)

Kennedy, M, D. (2011) *Global Solidarity and the Occupy Movement Possible Futures: A Project of the Social Science Research Council* Available from: http://bjsonline.org accessed: (accessed on 16th February 2014)

Kroll, A. (2011) 'How Occupy Wall Street really got started' pp 16 – 21 in van Gelder, S. and staff of YES! Magazine (eds) *This Changes Everything: Occupy Wall Street and the 99% Movement* San Francisco: Berrett-Koehler Publishers

Peck, J. (2010) 'Zombie neoliberalism and the ambidextrous state' *Theoretical Criminology* Volume 14, No. 1 pp 104 – 114

Pickerill, J. and Krinsky, J. (2012) 'Why does Occupy matter?' *Social Movement Studies* Volume 11, No. 3-4 pp 279 – 287

Pliven, F, F. and Cloward, R, A. (1979) *Poor People's Movements: Why They Succeed, How They Fail* New York: Vintage Books

Scherer, M. (2011) 'Introduction: Taking it to the Streets' pp 5 – 12 in TIME Magazine (ed) *What is Occupy? Inside the Global Movement* New York: TIME Books

Solnit, R. (2011) 'Throwing out the master's tools and building a better house' pp 146 – 156 in Taylor, A. Gessen, K. and editors from n+1, Dissent, Triple Canopy and The New Inquiry (eds) *Occupy: Scenes from Occupied America* Brooklyn: Verso

Taussig, M. (2013) 'Chapter 1: I'm so Angry I made a sign' in pp 3 – 44 Mitchell W, J, T. Harcourt, B, E. and Taussig, M. *Occupy: Three Inquiries in Disobedience* Chicago: The University of Chicago Press

Taylor, B. (2013) 'From Alterglobalization to Occupy Wall Street: neoanarchism and the new spirit of the left' *City: Analysis of Urban Trends, Culture, Theory, Policy, Action Volume* 17, No. 6 pp 729-747

Tharoor, I. (2011) 'Hands across the world' pp 25 – 33 in TIME Magazine (ed) *What is Occupy? Inside the Global Movement* New York: TIME Books

The Occupy Wall Street General Assembly (2011) 'Declaration of the occupation of New York City' pp 36 – 38 in van Gelder, S. and staff of YES! Magazine (eds) *This Changes Everything: Occupy Wall Street and the 99% Movement* San Francisco: Berrett-Koehler Publishers

Van Gelder, S. (2011) 'Introduction: How Occupy Wall Street Changes Everything' pp 77 – 82 in van Gelder S and staff of YES! Magazine (eds) *This Changes Everything: Occupy Wall Street and the 99% Movement* San Francisco: Berrett-Koehler Publishers

Vitale, A. (2011) 'NYPD and OWS: A clash of styles' pp 74–82 in Taylor, A. Gessen, K. and editors from n+1, Dissent, Triple Canopy and The New Inquiry (eds) *Occupy: Scenes from Occupied America* Brooklyn: Verso

Wolfe, D. (1983) 'The crisis in advanced capitalism: an introduction' *Studies in Political Economy* Volume 11, No. 1 pp 7–26

Wolf, N. (2012) 'Revealed: How the FBI coordinated the crackdown on Occupy' *The Guardian* [online] Available from: http://theguardian.com/commentisfree/2012/dec/29/fbicoordinated-crackdown-occupy (accessed on 12th August, 2013)

Extended Biography

Research

I began my expedition into Higher Education when I studied for a BA (Hons) in Geography at Liverpool John Moores University graduating in

2007. Although I currently, in the most part, identify as a Critical Criminologist and often Zemiologist, the discipline of Geography, and all the wonderful critical thinkers that have emerged from this sector of thought, remains incredibly close to both my work and my heart. The next 10 years hence have been marked by extraordinary opportunity and variety. In terms of further study, during this time I completed a Master of Arts in EU Politics at the University of Liverpool alongside returning to Liverpool John Moores University to complete a Postgraduate Certificate in Learning and Teaching in Higher Education. Alongside these more conventional patterns of study and qualification progression I worked at Liverpool John Moores University for many years in the capacity of both a Sessional Lecturer and Research Support Officer. These roles have afforded me opportunities to work on numerous research projects including, but not limited to, issues relating to corporate crime, Black and Minority Ethnic persons' experience of policing, and ageing populations. These research ventures have taken me physically to, as close as, only a few streets from my home in Liverpool in the UK to as far as China and Nepal. In October of 2012 I joined Staffordshire University and resided there for over 4 years as a Senior Lecturer in Criminology and Sociology facilitating learning in both undergraduate and postgraduate courses pertaining to innovation in research methods, transnational organised crime, new social movements/protest/resistance, policing, the crimes and harms of the powerful, terrorism, and surveillance and security. In March 2017 I joined The Open University as a Lecturer in Criminology producing learning material for matters regarding Crime and Global Justice.

At the time of writing I am in my fifth year of part time study for my PhD with some of the thesis rudimentary themes, summary and trajectories outlined in the preceding chapter. Although my current research thesis pertaining to my doctoral study has class struggle as its fulcrum what has unveiled itself through the research process is a whole host of other lateral, yet equally vital, issues that can be carried forward and explored within either the Occupy setting and/or within any other protest and resistance groups seeking meaningful change, be they in existence now or in the future. For example alongside the aforementioned central trajectories of the research, the study has also revealed all sorts of various intriguing tangential avenues for further research and exploration including for example investigating the possible use of Psychological Operations (PSYOPS) by both public and private policing actors against contemporary protest movements. Despite being a strictly prohibited practice under US Federal Law in the context of 'home soil', documentary evidence such as that found in the revelatory film Gasland II shows that such practices are occurring in other protest sites such as domestic anti-fracking protests in the US. In the aforementioned documentary a recording of Matt Pitzarella from Range Resources speaking at the Texas Oil and Gas Industry Conference states: "We have several former PSYOPs folk that work for us at Range because they are very comfortable in dealing with localised issues and local governments [...] Having an understanding of PSYOPS in the Army and in the Middle East has applied very helpfully here for us in Pennsylvania". Participants at the empirical sites of data collection at different Occupy camps in London have expressed concerns and suspicions that such forms of policing may be occurring. This and many other possible tangents and trajectories can be explored demonstrating once again how protest and resistance movements are so very much incredibly precious sites of knowledge generation.

What all this leads me to conclude is that essentially what ties all these strands of research together, both past, present, and future, is a commitment to active scholarly research concerned with social justice, meaningful change, and reducing inequality that simultaneously challenges and brings to account the crimes and/or harms of the powerful in their many different and complex forms.

Activism, Organisational Work and/or Professional membership
Coordinator of the Crimes of the Powerful Working Group c/o The European Group for the Study of Deviance and Social Control
The Occupy Movement (most notably Occupy Democracy and Occupy the Media Billionaires)
Activism in Sociology Forum c/o British Sociological Association

Selected Works

Fletcher, S. (2014) 'Protest' pp 41 – 44 in Atkinson, R. (ed) (2014) *Shades of Deviance: A Primer on Crime, Deviance and Social Harm* Oxon: Routledge

Fletcher, S. (2015) 'The Occupy movement vs. capitalist realism: seeking extraordinary transformations in consciousness' pp 238 – 255 in Sollund, R, A. (ed) (2015) *Green Harms and Crimes: Critical Criminology in a Changing World* Hampshire: Palgrave MacMillan

Fletcher, S. (2015) 'Negotiating the Resistance: Catch 22s, Brokering and Contention within Occupy Safer Spaces Policy' *Contention: The Multidisciplinary Journal of Social Protest* Volume 3, No. 2 pp 10–20

8

Creating and Developing Inclusive Learning Environments Beyond the Prison Gates

Helena Gosling

Introduction

> *'You want me to come to university? To be honest, I don't think I like students.'*

Once an individual has endured the complex and unforgiving web of the criminal 'justice' system, participation in society is transformed forever, as labels such as '(ex)offender' and 'lawbreaker' as well as bureaucratic processes such as those conducted by the Disclosure and Barring Service (DBS) dictate and dilute the quality and quantity of opportunities that are available to an individual. The Prisoners' Education Trust (2017) have recently utilised a series of case studies (from individuals with a criminal record who have recently applied to do a university degree) to explore how this phenomena plays out within and around the higher education sector. Rather unsurprisingly, all individuals involved in the afore-mentioned study faced numerous obstacles and barriers, with the application process seemingly proving to be the most complex and testing hurdle.

In this short discussion piece, I will provide a concise overview of a project, called Learning Together that I am currently co-leading with Dr Lol Burke at Liverpool John Moores University, which aims to create and develop inclusive learning environments within the higher education sector for those who have extensive experience of the criminal 'justice' system. To do so, the following discussion is divided into three sections. The first will outline what Learning Together is and how it came about. The second will explore the teaching and learning methods that are employed during Learning Together in an attempt to create democratic learning environments, and the third, will critically reflect upon some of the emerging findings from the project.

A Short Introduction to Learning Together: The Story so Far…

The Learning Together initiative was originally co-produced by criminologists Amy Ludlow and Ruth Armstrong from the Institute of Criminology, Cambridge University and governing staff at HMP Grendon who aimed to provide an opportunity for university students to learn alongside serving prisoners. The initiative was developed to promote learning amongst and between people who, ordinarily, would not have met or had the opportunity to learn from one another. It aims to do this through the co-creation of learning spaces within custodial environments whereby students who are imprisoned study alongside students from a local University (Armstrong and Ludlow, 2016). Through Learning Together, communities of learning develop that hold the potential to fill gaps and address deficits in current education provision in prison whilst simultaneously challenging the exclusivity that surrounds the educational experience of many university students (Armstrong and Ludlow, 2016). Although the Learning Together initiative is delivered primarily within the custodial estate, it has become a springboard for promoting and developing inclusive learning environments both within and beyond the prison gates.

Since September 2016, Lol Burke and I have designed and delivered a university-based Learning Together initiative for males and females who have personal and/or professional experience of the criminal 'justice' system to learn alongside postgraduate criminal justice students. The programme consists of 12, two-hour sessions and is designed to run twice per academic year. Learning Together is open to all Master of Arts (MA) Criminal Justice students as an additional learning opportunity, and individuals from the local community who have personal and/or professional experience of the criminal 'justice' system. Interested parties must apply via a standard application form and be willing to meet with Lol and I before being offered a place on the course. Given the varied skill set and educational attainment amongst Learning Together participants, the admission process is very much focused upon individual potential, rather than previous academic attainment/official qualifications. We have also designed a bespoke admission process, alongside a local charity who work with individuals who have experience of the criminal 'justice' system, which although rigorous and in-line with university policies and procedures, provides a more welcoming and personable introduction to higher education.

All Learning Together participants are registered as students. They are subsequently granted full access to all university buildings and libraries, a student card, e-mail address and access to the virtual learning environment. The initiative is designed to introduce students to an array of contemporary issues in criminal justice. Each session is based upon a criminological question from 'how do we explain crime and criminality' to 'why do people stop offending.' Lol and I set a series of essential readings and key questions for students to consider before each session, which helps to stimulate discussion that is informed by academically credible sources. Although we have a series of session aims and objectives, the way in which we tackle the subject within the classroom is very much influenced by the students and what aspects of the is considered, by them, to be important. This co-operative teaching and learning approach is something that Lol and I are further exploring as Learning Together continues to unfold.

Our Approach: Co-operative Teaching and Learning

Over the last decade, student-centred teaching methods have become increasingly popular throughout the higher education sector (Baeten *et al.*, 2010). One such method is co-operative learning (a philosophy and teaching style adopted by Lol and I when designing, delivering and evaluating Learning Together). Millis and Cottell (1998) claim that co-operative learning is able to enhance life-long learning, and influential scholars such as Fink (2003), Hattie (2009), and, Biggs and Tang (2011) have recommended co-operative learning as an important teaching/learning tool for university students. The distinguishing features of co-operative learning is the recognition and encouragement of both formal and informal teaching and learning methods associated with staff-peer and peer-peer interaction (face-to-face interaction, deliberate training of social skills and group evaluation of the process, to name just three components). The co-operative learning literature argues that efficient co-operation depends on two elements: positive group interdependence and individual accountability (Millis and Cottell, 1998; Johnson *et al*, 2007; Millis, 2010).

When designing the Learning Together programme, Lol and I ensured that positive group interdependence and individual accountability were at the forefront of our plans. We felt that it was important for the group to rely on each other, utilise the different skill sets that were present within the group, and take responsibility for their learning environment. Given the diverse nature of the student body involved in Learning Together, Lol and I decided to create 'learning partnerships' amongst the students. A learning partnership currently consists of two Learning Together students; one MA Criminal Justice student and one Learning Together only student. The aim of the partnership is to bring together two people, who may have different skill sets, so that they can learn from each other and enhance each other's learning, both inside and outside of the classroom. Throughout the duration of the course every student is set a series of tasks that they are expected to work on both individually and collectively (within their learning partnerships). This helps to invoke a sense of individual accountability as well as a sense of belonging to a learning environment that is both formal and informal.

More recently, Lol and I have managed to secure a small amount of money to pay two Learning Together students, one day per week for eleven weeks, to work alongside us on a project that specifically explores the role and value of co-operative learning within the higher education sector. The interns consist of one MA Criminal Justice student and one Learning Together only student. They are expected to work collaboratively with each other (supported by Lol and I), drawing upon each other's skill sets to conduct a small-piece of research that can, and will, be used to steer the future direction of Learning Together. We felt that it was important to provide an opportunity for Learning Together students to 'progress' onto something else/something different once their initial involvement in the project drew to a close.

Emerging Findings and Visions for Future Practice

Although the initiative is still in its infancy, a number of interesting findings are beginning to emerge. As our Learning Together project is based within the community (as opposed to a custodial setting) we are able to be more creative and work towards challenging, and hopefully changing the status quo which surrounds the admission and integration of individuals with criminal convictions into the higher education sector. We are currently evaluating the initiative and hope that the findings will illustrate the individual, institutional, and social benefits that can emerge from inclusive learning projects. To date, I have found that the ability of Learning Together to genuinely widen participation in higher education by 'opening up' the university space to include an atypical student population (criminal justice service users and practitioners) to be one of the challenges and rewards of the project.

Preliminary findings from our research suggest that every lecturer who has been involved in the project has 'thought differently' or 'thought more' about the session that they delivered to the Learning Together students. Although this is something that we are still exploring, I am left wondering what this means and whether these findings raise fundamental questions about how 'we' as teachers/lecturers/academics, view, define and engage with those that we teach on a day-to-day basis. The dynamic student population involved in Learning Together has allowed the initiative to organically create and develop into a 'community of praxis' whereby scholarly activity, life events, and professional experiences are recognised, applied and practiced within and beyond the classroom. To date, we have found that this 'community of praxis' provides a safe space for practitioners to discuss work-place issues and occurrences, a new place and space for criminal justice service users to practice and embrace a 'new' and/or 'different' identity (as student) to those forced upon them by society and enhance the conventional teaching and learning experience for the mainstream student population.

Acknowledgements

I would like to take this opportunity to thank Lol Burke and Eleanor Surridge for their tireless commitment and support on the Learning Together project. I would also like to thank all staff and students who have engaged with the initiative and helped to steer its design and delivery. Your participation, time and feedback has been invaluable.

References

Armstrong, R. and Ludlow, A. (2016) 'Educational Partnerships between Universities and Prisons: How Learning Together can be Individually, Socially and Institutionally Transformative' *Prison Service Journal No.* 225, pp 9 – 18

Baeten, M. Kyndt, E. Struyven, K. and Dochy, F. (2010) 'Using Student-Centred Learning Environments to Stimulate Deep Approaches to Learning: Factors Encouraging or Discouraging their Effectiveness' *Educational Research Review* Volume 5, No. 3 pp 243 – 260

Biggs, J. and Tang, C. (2011) *Teaching for Quality Learning at University: What the Student Does* Fourth Edition Buckingham: Open University Press

Fink, L. D. (2003) *Creating Significant Learning Experience: An Integrated Approach to Designing College Courses* San Fransisco: Jossey-Bass

Hattie, J. (2009) *Visible Learning: A Synthesis of Over 800 Meta-analyses Relating to Achievement* London: Routledge

Johnson, D. W. Johnson, R. T. and Smith, K. (2007) 'The State of Cooperative Learning in Postsecondary and Professional Settings' *Educational Psychology Review* Volume 19 No. 1 pp 15 – 29

Millis, B. J. (2010) *Cooperative Learning in Higher Education: Across the Disciplines, Across the Academy* Sterling, VA: Stylus Publishing

Millis, B. J. and Cottell, P. G. (1998) *Cooperative Learning for Higher Education Faculty* Westport, CT: Oryx Press

Prisoners' Education Trust (2017) Boxed in? Applying to Uni with a Criminal Conviction [online] Available from: http://www.prisonerseducation.org.uk/news/applying-to-uni-with-a-criminal-record (accessed on: 27th February 2017)

Extended Biography

Research
Before becoming a full-time Senior Lecturer in Criminal Justice, I obtained a BA (with hons) Criminology in 2009; a MA Criminal Justice in 2010; and PhD in 2015. Throughout the duration of my studies, I worked in and around the alcohol and drug treatment sector, within prison, community and residential settings, occupying both voluntary and paid positions. I have experience of conducting ethnographic research within relatively hidden spaces alongside hard-to-reach individuals and has a particular interest in Therapeutic Communities, alternative responses to law-breaking and inclusive learning environments. I hope to continue to develop the Learning Together initiative and I am currently conducting research into the sustainability of innovative learning projects such as Learning Together.

Selected Works
Scott, D. and Gosling, H. (2016) 'Before Prison, Instead of Prison, Better than Prison: Therapeutic Communities as an Abolitionist Real Utopia' *International Journal of Crime, Justice and Social Democracy* Volume 5, No.1, pp 52-66

Gosling, H. (2016) 'All This is About is Money and Making Sure that Heads are on Beds.' Perceptions of Payment by Results in a Therapeutic Community' *Probation Journal: The Journal of Community and Criminal Justice Volume* 63, No. 2, pp 144 – 152

Gosling, H. (2016) 'Payment by Results. Challenges and Conflicts for the Therapeutic Community' *Criminology and Criminal Justice* Volume 16, No. 5, pp 519 – 533

Gosling, H. (2017, forthcoming*)* 'A critical Insight into Practitioners Lived Experience of Payment by Results in the Alcohol and Drug Treatment Sector' *Critical Social Policy. A Journal of Theory and Practice in Social Welfare*

Contact Details
Email: H.J.Gosling@ljmu.ac.uk
Twitter: @helena_gosling

9

'Social Justice' in Women's Centres? Experiences and Impact of Gender-Specific Service Provision

Kirsty Greenwood

Introduction

This chapter provides an outline of my ongoing doctoral research. The working title of my thesis is 'Women's Centres, Gender Specificity and the Criminological Gaze: Implications for Female Offenders'. My PhD is concerned with evaluating Women's Centres using policy documents, statistics and the direct experiences of service providers and service users. This aims to afford new insights and possible challenges to existing limited understandings of the origin, aims and operationalisation of Women's Centres within the penal landscape, including the impact they have upon the lives of all women accessing their services. Whilst Women's Centres, as a gender-specific service are said to address the failures of the prison by being more constructive in terms of meeting women's individual and complex needs (O'Neill, 2011; PRT, 2015), very little is currently known about how different sanctions and measures are used in Women's Centres and even less is known about how they impact upon different aspects of women's lives (McIvor *et al*, 2010). It has been emphasised by many researchers including Fitzgerald (2014: 68) that in order for effective implementation of gender-specific services, "further research into, and evaluation of the particular needs and circumstances of female offenders" needs to be conducted, which this research aims to address.

Women's Centres as a Means of Achieving Social Justice?

The potential to prevent the unnecessary criminalisation of women by exploring the relationship between criminal and social justice and attempting to address women's gendered social and structural needs outside of the prison, underpinned the inception of Women's Centres following the Corston Report in 2007 (McIvor *et al*, 2009; Petrillo, 2015;

PRT, 2016). Gender-specific practice initiatives for criminalised women emerged organically following years of promotion work from charities and campaigning organisations, and academic research. This "consistently underlined the inadequacies or inappropriateness for women of most conventional criminal justice interventions" (Radcliffe and Hunter, 2016: 976-7) including the "revolving door of prison" (PRT, 2016: 7) and the Social Exclusion Unit Report in 2002. It was 2007 marked the official prompt to recognise women offenders' distinctive needs in policy and practice (Corston, 2007).

Gender-specific programming recognises women's gendered pathways into offending by understanding and addressing gendered risk factors that contribute to women's criminality (O'Neill, 2011). It considers the "distinctive features of women's lives and needs" to facilitate effectiveness, by recognising their needs as being interrelated, multiple and complex (Bloom *et al*, 2003; Gelsthorpe *et al*, 2007: 200). Gender-specificity could be theorised as being part of the "emerging gendered enterprise" which goes further than "rendering the female offender more visible" by outlining how women's social, personal, structural, and economic marginalisation impacts upon their experiences, treatment, and outcomes within the criminal justice system (Evans and Jamieson, 2008:244).

Whilst the number of female prisoners decreased from 6.0% to 4.6% between 2004 and 2014, the number of women held on remand continued to increase between 2013 and 2014 (MOJ, 2015). This points to the increasingly problematic situation of women being held on remand for trivial and low level offences, only then to be released from custody or to be sentenced to prison for less than six months (Carlton and Segrave, 2013; Malloch and McIvor, 2013). Questions regarding the capacity of gender-specific Women's Centres to respond to the complex and diverse experiences of women as a non-homogenous group need to be raised (Bloom, 1999), due to both the continued increase in the number of women held on remand and no evidence of a significant decrease in the female prison population despite the operation of Women's Centres since 2007.

Because of the continued growth of women on remand within the prison system, evaluations of Women's Centres have become consumed by recidivism rates and rates to re-arrest, alongside a desire to locate evidence to justify the operation of their gender-responsive schemes as feasible *alternatives* to imprisonment (PRT, 2016; see: Brennan *et al*, 2016). This ultimately results in a 'what works' rhetoric in the task of legitimisation which directly informs the growth of gender-responsive policies, practice and initiatives which claim to rehabilitate women (PRT, 2016).

Sharpe (2015: 2), whilst referring to the youth justice system, draws upon previous research by Goodkind (2005), debating that gender-specificity assumes an essentialised notion of the female subject with her problems needing "individual therapeutic recovery and transformation" through empowerment and self-esteem enhancement programmes. However, the ability of such programmes to empower, whilst being part of a criminal justice system aimed at "punishment and social control", requires exploration (Malloch and McIvor, 2013: 206).

Women's Centre services are enacted within a risk reduction and offending prevention framework to assist female offenders and those 'at risk' of offending. Moore and Scraton (2014) contend that individuals are encouraged to think and behave differently, which resonates more with neo-classical perspectives that place an emphasis on personal responsibility. The focus on delivering an "individual, therapeutic, criminal justice response" displaces the social, structural and economic conditions that shape the lives of marginalised women and therefore contradicts the very nature of gender-responsive justice (Radcliffe and Hunter, 2016: 977; Moore and Scraton, 2014). The target for intervention is the individual female rather than society, and oppressive social experiences are translated into individual risks and needs, rather than wider marginalisation (Radcliffe and Hunter, 2016). Whilst there are currently other research projects taking place in Women's Centres, exploring their role for specific client groups and for those with experience of imprisonment (see: Barr, 2017; Elfleet, 2017; Harding, 2017), this is arguably one of the only studies exploring the role of Women's Centres, for *all* client groups – offenders, non-offenders, and staff – both qualitatively and quantitatively.

By critically examining existing literature and policy initiatives relating to the origin, aims and operation of Women's Centres as arenas of gender-specific provision for women, it has become apparent that several issues dominate this area. Key issues include the continued escalation of the female remand population and no significant reduction in the general female prison population, despite the operation of Women's Centres which brings into focus concerns around human rights and social justice (Barton and Cooper, 2013). The potential decontextualisation of women's social marginalisation when addressing offending behaviour and an over-reliance upon women's personal responsibility (Shaw and Hannah-Moffat,

2011; Carlton and Segrave, 2013) directly contradicts Corston's premise of "society" being responsible for "supporting women" and is also an area of contention (Corston Report, 2007: 7). Finally, the legitimacy of Women's Centres as key arenas in the rehabilitation of women, with most in receipt of no government funding and with an increasing number of women accessing their services each year (Malloch and McIvor, 2013; Howard League, 2016), highlights the potential issues concerning their sustainability and future operationalisation in a time of austerity (Gelsthorpe and Hedderman, 2012).

In November 2016, the Howard League published a report *Ten years after the Corston Report, is this the end of successful Women's Centres?*, claiming that Women's Centres are at risk of becoming a "thing of the past" due to funding struggles under the new Community Rehabilitation Company structure (Howard League, 2016: 1). The Asha Women's Centre; pioneered as a gender-specific and specialist needs-led support service for female offenders and women at risk of offending in 2006, and which Corston (2007) referred to as a model of good practice, was forced to close in January 2017 due to a lack of funding. This is therefore an extremely appropriate point in time to be critically examining this topic.

Methods

The methods utilised in this research include a policy analysis, quantitative analysis and qualitative analysis via semi-structured interviews. By undertaking a policy analysis, Women's Centres are being theoretically conceptualised within their historical, political, social and economic context. This is being achieved by exploring the language used within setting the objectives of policy and legislation, the choice and design of policy and legislation, and the mechanisms of implementation in practice.

As there are currently no datasets indicating the number of women accessing Women's Centre services in England and Wales, a quantitative analysis is being undertaken to chart their territory. Firstly, by tracing their total numbers, geographical location and secondly the date of inception using the publicly available Charity Commission database. Charity Commission data is also being used to explore the number of women with whom Women's Centres are working and on what basis they are accessing the services in terms of age, offence, ethnicity, and offending history. In addition, being conducted is a numerical analysis of operational data for Women's Centres including what interventions are provided and quantifying any possible outcomes or impacts as a direct result of these interventions.

Qualitative semi-structured interviews are currently being undertaken with stakeholders and service-users at one research site – a case study Women's Centre in the North West of England. The Women's Centre provides a series of targeted interventions which are tailored to individual women via a multi-agency, problem solving approach; acknowledging her pathway into the criminal justice system as well as providing support to women who are not involved in the criminal justice system. Interviews with service-providers are enabling an analysis of the origins of the Women's Centre and its day-to-day operation. They also enable perspectives on the effectiveness and impact of Women's Centre provisions on service-users to be analysed, as well as eliciting views and opinions on any gaps in policy and service provision and how they could be overcome.

Furthermore, service user interviews enable an analysis of the legitimacy and effectiveness of the Women's Centre in meeting their gender-specific needs. Both offending and non-offending women are being interviewed as those attending Women's Centres voluntarily are often marginalised within academic research. Interviews are exploring service-users' involvement with the Women's Centre, highlighting areas of good practice, documenting areas for improvement and noting any barriers faced when accessing services. The impact of Women's Centre service provision on service-users' lives is also being examined. All interview responses are women's own personal experiences, opinions and viewpoints which recognises that they are not a homogenous group; their experiences of punishment and gender-specific services vary alongside other structural dimensions such as age and ethnicity (Malloch and McIvor, 2013; Malloch *et al*, 2008; McIvor *et al*, 2010).

Social Justice Theoretical Approach

Gender-specificity in the form of gender-specific programming in Women's Centres has been designed to address the significant disadvantage and social problems that both women at risk of offending and those who have made formal contact with criminal justice services possess. Gender-specific punishment was designed to tackle the structural characteristics of women's lawbreaking (Carlton and Segrave, 2013) by referring to the gendered needs of criminalised women (Medlicott, 2007). In practice, gender-specific models of punishment contradict the medical model whereby individual "deficits" are defined as the root cause of offending requiring clinical treatment, in favour of the "holistic needs-based services" provided under gender-sensitive operationalisation (Rumgay, 2004: 108). Women attending community interventions tend to be the most socially and structurally marginalised in society. They are "disproportionately poor, formally undereducated, of colour, and have experienced high levels of physical, emotional and sexual violence" (Lawston, 2013: 115). One of the main factors contributing to gender-responsive programming is "instilling a sense of empowerment" into female service users by enabling women to "gain more knowledge about their own skills and experiences" and demonstrating "how they can apply them to their lives outside of punishment" (DeCou, 2002: 105).

A social justice theoretical approach is thus being utilised to examine how the rhetoric of penal reform and penal policy (Hudson, 1993) translates into effectiveness, legitimacy and impact for women's treatment in Women's Centres in England and Wales. In this research, the term social justice is understood within the framework set out by the Commission on Social Justice (1993 cited in: Cook, 2006: 21) which states that the principles of social justice include: equal worth of all citizens; all citizens having the ability to meet their basic needs for food, income, shelter, education and health; a reduction or elimination in inequalities; and equal worth via the widest spread of opportunities and life chances. Whilst Hudson (1993: 149) stated that "in spite of so much activity in both penal practice and penal discourse, criminal justice continues to be a disaster", this research explores the possibility that Women's Centres, established as a direct result of the Corston (2007) report, may offer a new way of achieving social justice for criminalised women. Hudson (1993) believes that to achieve social justice, the oppressive power of the State must be lessened, citizens must have increasing dominion over their own lives and social cohesion and harmony must be promoted. Women's Centres as sites of "possibility" and "advocacy" to pursue and achieve justice for marginalised women and to enable them to overcome social, economic and political exclusion is explored throughout the PhD (Keddie, 2012: 263; Cook, 1997; Fraser, 2008).

Although it is argued by Carlton and Segrave (2013: 6) that the operation of gender-specific justice serves to emphasise women's individual failures which in turn overrides the possibility to focus upon and address broader contextual factors of "subordination, control" and "multiple levels of disadvantage" beyond gendered stereotypes, this research allows for a consideration of the political landscape in which

Women's Centres in England and Wales operate (Malloch and McIvor, 2013). A social justice approach is a "productive lens", which permits for an analysis of the key ways in which different dimensions of injustice are either being addressed or are hindering women's participation, experiences, and outcomes of accessing gender-specific services in Women's Centres (Keddie, 2012: 276). It explores how Women's Centres may or may not address matters of discrete injustices such as inequalities in the provision of education, housing, and health care; unemployment; poor physical and mental health; social isolation and victimisation, with participation being a key element of this approach (Fraser, 2008).

Whilst Women's Centres may operate to address the multiple and complex needs of vulnerable women, the voices of those subject to gender-specific justice need to be heard. Proponents of gender-specific justice services "too often speak for, rather than listen to, the political positions and expressed needs" of those subject to services and interventions (Shaylor, 2009: 151). Producing new knowledge from the voices of the excluded will expose "the political context" in which criminological knowledge surrounding the operation of Women's Centres is produced and re-produced within a neoliberal society (Hudson, 2000: 177), giving a voice to the powerless and providing a platform for their voices to finally be heard. This research project is currently at the data collection stage and therefore no analysis has been conducted as of yet.

Acknowledgements

The PhD would not be possible without the Graduate Teaching Assistant (GTA) studentship I am in receipt of from Liverpool John Moores University under the guidance of Dr Janet Jamieson.

References

Barr, U. M. (2016) 'Ontological theory and women's desistance: Is it simply a case of 'growing up'?' *Early Career Academics Network Bulletin, The Howard League for Penal Reform Justice and Penal Reform Conference*, Volume 30 pp 3-13

Barton, A. and Cooper, V. (2013) 'Hostels and Community justice for women: The "semi-penal" paradox' pp 136 – 151 in Malloch, M., and McIvor, G. (eds) *Women, Punishment and Social Justice*, London: Routledge

Bloom, B. (1999) 'Gender-responsive programming for women offenders: Guiding principles and practices', *Let's Talk/Entre Nous Newsletter, Correctional Services for Canada*, [online] Available from: http://www.csc-scc.gc.ca/research/forum/e113/113f_e.pdf (accessed 11th January 2017)

Bloom, B. Owen, B. and Covington, S. (2003) *Gender-responsive strategies: Research, practice and guiding principles on women offenders,* Washington, DC: National Institute of Corrections

Brennan, I.R. Green, S. and Sturgeon-Adams, L. (2016) 'Early Diversion and Empowerment Policing: Evaluating an Adult Female Offender Triage Project', *Policing and Society*, Volume 26, No.4 pp 1-18

Carlton, B. and Segrave, M. (2013) (eds) 'A radical vision for system social change' *Women Exiting Prison: Critical Essays on gender, post-release support and survival*, London: Routledge

Cook, D. (1997) *Poverty, Crime and Punishment*, London: CPAG Ltd

Cook, D. (2006) *Criminal and Social Justice*, London: Sage

Corston, J. (2007) *The Corston Report: A Review of women with particular vulnerabilities in the criminal justice system*, London: Home Office

DeCou, K. (2002) 'A gender-wise prison, opportunities for, and limits to, reform' in Carlen, P. (Ed.) *Women and Punishment*, Cullompton: Willan Publishing

Elfleet, H. (2017) 'Empowered to be resilient: Neo-liberal Penal Rhetoric and The Corston Report (2007)', *Prison Service Journal*, 230, pp 33-8

Evans, K. and Jamieson, J. (2008) 'Conclusion: gender and crime – the legacy?' pp243 - 251 in Evans, K., and Jamieson, J. (eds) (2008) *Gender and Crime: A Reader*, Maidenhead: Open University Press

Fitzgerald, F. (2014) *Strategic Review of Penal Policy: Final Report*, Dublin: Government of Ireland

Fraser, N. (2008) 'Reframing justice in a globalising world' in Olson, K. (ed) *Adding Insult to Injury: Nancy Fraser debates her critics*, London: Verso

Gelsthorpe, L. Sharpe, G. and Roberts, J. (2007) *Provision for Women Offenders in the Community*, London: Fawcett Society

Gelsthorpe, L. and Hedderman, C. (2012) 'Providing for women offenders: the risks of adapting a payment by results approach', *Probation Journal*, Volume 59, No.4 pp 374-390

Goodkind, S. (2005) 'Gender-specific services in the juvenile justice system: A critical examination', *Affilia*, Volume 20, No. 1, pp 52-70

Haney, L. (2010) *Offending Women: Power, Punishment and the Regulation of Desire,* London: University of California Press.

Harding, N. (2017) 'Picturing Subjugated Knowledge' in K. Atkinson, A. R. Huber, and K. Tucker (eds.) *Voices of Resistance: Subjugated knowledge and the challenge to the criminal justice system*, London: EG Press

'Social Justice' in Women's Centres?

Howard League (2016) *Ten Years after the Corston Report, is this the end of successful Women's Centres?*, [online] 6th November Available from: http://howardleague.org/wp-content/uploads/2016/11/Is-it-the-end-of-womens-centres.pdf {accessed 8th January 2017)

Hudson, B. (1993) *Penal Policy and Social Justice*, Basingstoke: Macmillan

Hudson, B. (2000) 'Critical Reflection as Research Methodology' pp 328 – 344 in Jupp, V. Davies, P. and Francis, P. (eds) *Doing Criminological Research*, London: Sage

Keddie, A. (2012) 'Schooling and social justice through the lenses of Nancy Fraser' *Critical Studies in Education*, Volume 53, No.3 pp 263-79

Lawston, J. (2013) 'Prison, gender responsive strategies and community sanctions' pp 109 – 120 in Malloch, M., and McIvor, G. (eds) *Women, Punishment and Social Justice*, London: Routledge

Malloch, M. McIvor, G. and Loucks, N. (2008) '"Time Out" for women: Innovation in Scotland in a context of change', *Howard Journal of Criminal Justice*, Volume 47, No.4 pp 383-399

Malloch, M. and McIvor, G. (eds) (2013) *Women, Punishment and Social Justice*, London: Routledge

McIvor, G. Trotter, C. and Sheehan, C. (2009) 'Women, resettlement and desistance' *Probation Journal*, Volume 56, No.4 pp 347–361

McIvor, G. Malloch, M. Gelsthorpe, L. Loucks, G. Moore, L. Pollack, S. and Larrauri, E. (2010) Women, Punishment and Community Sanctions: Human Rights and Social Justice, Glasgow: Scottish Universities Insight Institute

Medlicott, D. (2007) 'Women in Prison' in pp 245 – 267 Jewkes, Y. (ed) *Handbook on Prisons*, Cullompton: Willan Publishing

MOJ (2015) *Justice Data Lab: Reoffending Analysis - Women's Centres throughout England*, London: MOJ

Moore, L. and Scraton, P. (2014) *The Incarceration of Women: Punishing Bodies, Breaking Spirits*, London: Palgrave Macmillan

O'Neill, J. (2011) 'The Inspire Women's Project: Managing Women Offenders within the Community', *Irish Probation Journal*, Volume 8, pp 93-108

Petrillo, M. (2015) 'You get plenty of punishment', [online] *Centre for Crime and Justice Studies*, Available from: https://www.crimeandjustice.org.uk/resources/you-get-plenty-punishment (accessed 22nd January 2017)

PRT (2015) *Why Focus on Reducing Women's Imprisonment?*, London: Prison Reform Trust

Prison Reform Trust (2016) *Is this the end of Women's Centres?*, [online] , 8th November, Available from http://howardleague.org/wp-content/uploads/2016/11/Is-it-the-end-of-womens-centres.pdf (accessed 29th March, 2017)

Radcliffe, H. and Hunter, G. (2016) '"It was a Safe Place for Me to be": Accounts of Attending Women's Community Services and Moving beyond the Offender Identity', *British Journal of Criminology*, Volume 56, No.5 pp 976-994

Rumgay, J. (2004) 'Scripts for Safer Survival: Pathways out of Female Crime, *The Howard Journal*, Volume 43, No.4 pp 405-419

Sharpe, G. (2015) 'Re-Imagining Justice for Girls: A New Agenda for Research', *Youth Justice*, Volume 16, No.1 pp 1-15

Shaw, M. and Hannah-Moffat, K. (2011) 'How cognitive skills forgot about gender and diversity' pp 90 – 121 in Mair, G. (ed) *What Matters in Probation*, London: Routledge

Shaylor, C. (2009) 'Neither Kind Nor Gentle: The Perils of "Gender-Responsive Justice"' pp 145 - 163 in Scraton, P. And McCulloch, J. (eds) *The Violence of Incarceration*, Abingdon: Routledge

Extended Biography

Research

I am a second year doctoral student in Criminology at Liverpool John Moores University, in receipt of a Graduate Teaching Assistant (GTA) studentship. The working title of my thesis is 'Women's Centres, Gender Specificity and the Criminological Gaze: Implications for Female Offenders'. Prior to commencing the PhD, in 2014 I completed a Master of Research (MRes) degree in Critical Social Science and in 2013 I attained a BA Honours degree in Criminology. Both were undertaken at Liverpool John Moores University.

I won the Merseyside Woman of the Year £1,000 bursary for academic excellence in June 2013 and received the David McEvoy prize for outstanding performance at Honours degree level study in July 2013. My undergraduate dissertation, supervised by Professor Joe Sim, was entitled 'Punishing Deviant Women: A Feminist Analysis of Liverpool Female Penitentiary 1850-1900'. My Master's thesis, written under the direction of Dr David Scott, was entitled 'Regulating Deviant Women: The Production of Feminine Docile Bodies in Liverpool Female Penitentiary 1809 – 1921'. In this I investigated the disciplinary regimes utilised in controlling, regulating and producing feminine docile bodies within the semi-penal institution of Liverpool Female Penitentiary between 1809 and 1921. The thesis was shortlisted for the Howard League of Penal Reform

'Social Justice' in Women's Centres?

John Sunley Prize and I was also awarded the LJMU MRes in Arts, Professional and Social Studies (APSS) Achievement Award for the highest degree mark across the Faculty in December 2014.

As a GTA in Criminology at LJMU, I teach on several undergraduate modules including Contemporary Issues in Criminology, Introduction to Criminological Theory and Inside the Criminal Justice System. I have also delivered several sessions on the MRes degree programme for the Critical Social Science Project Development module. I have been a Visiting Lecturer for the department of Social and Political Science at Chester University since 2015 where I have delivered lectures for the level six undergraduate module Advanced Social Theory and have contributed to the level four module Crime, Continuities and Change. I have also undertaken sessional lecturing at Keele University.

My undergraduate dissertation formed the foundation of my Master's thesis and recent publications. My dissertation provided a critical feminist account of the social control of women resident in the semi penal institution of Liverpool Female Penitentiary (LFP). For my Master's thesis I then adopted a Foucauldian feminist theoretical approach to analyse specific regimes of feminisation, infantilisation and religious instruction imposed upon 'deviant' women housed in LFP between 1809 and 1921. In this work I explored how these regimes co-existed and intersected to render female inmates docile and subservient. I also analysed the tension between the overarching Christianisation of the institution and the imposing nineteenth century discourse of positivism with its corresponding medical treatments.

I adapted these research findings and bridged Foucauldian theorisations with theories of carcerality to produce an interdisciplinary book chapter for the edited book 'Carceral Mobilities'. My chapter contributes to criminological, human geographical and historical research by providing the first analysis of an historical semi-penal institution within a carceral mobilities theoretical framework. I drew together Foucault's concepts of discipline and governmentality and concepts of social and physical mobility from mobility theory to explore methods of social, bio-political and physical control utilised to punish deviant women in nineteenth and early twentieth century Liverpool.

The working title of my PhD thesis is 'Women's Centres, Gender Specificity and the Criminological Gaze: Implications for Female Offenders'. My research is one of the the first criminological studies to examine the shape and space of Women's Centres within the penal landscape in England and Wales via statistical analysis. It is also currently understood to be the first study to explore the operation and impact of Women's Centres using qualitative semi-structured interviews with a specific focus on the experiences and opinions of *all* service-users and staff.

The motivation for my PhD research project in the very early stages, stemmed from an academic curiosity of possible continuities between historical semi-penal institutions and contemporary Women's Centres. After undertaking an extensive review of the literature it became clear that while little knowledge exists exploring this possible connection, even less is known within Criminology about the current operation of Women's Centres, with significant gaps in knowledge related to their origin, aims and operation as a form of gender-specific community intervention. In addition, it also became apparent that they had also been subject to minimal theoretical scrutiny. This inspired me to construct a research proposal to explore these areas of unfamiliarity whilst simultaneously aiming to provide a platform for the voices and experiences of socially and structurally marginalised women.

Activism, Organisational Work and/or Professional Membership
I am a student member of the Howard League for Penal Reform, a member of the European Group for the Study of Social Control and Deviance and a member of Our Criminal Past: Caring for the Future.

Future Aspirations
My immediate future research plans include commencing data analysis for my PhD, beginning the writing up period in January 2018 and submitting in November 2018. I then plan to apply for University Lecturer positions in the UK and continue to teach Criminology. Post-doctorally, I aim to disseminate my PhD findings widely and to bridge my historical research on the semi-penal institutionalisation of women in England with my contemporary exploration of gender-specific punishment in Women's Centres.

Selected works
Greenwood, K. (In press June 2017) 'Deviant Women' in Turner, J., Taylor, P., Corteen, K., and Morley, S. (Eds.) *A Companion to Crime and Criminal Justice History*, Bristol: Policy Press.

Greenwood, K. (2017) 'Semi-penal institutions' in Taylor, P. (Ed.) *A Companion to State Power, Rights and Liberties,* Bristol: Policy Press.

Greenwood, K. (2017) 'The Mobilisation of "deviant" female bodies: Carceral regimes of discipline in Liverpool Female Penitentiary, 1809-1921' in Peters, K., and Turner, J. (Eds.) *Carceral Mobilities: Interrogating Movement in Incarceration*, Oxford: Routledge.

Greenwood, K. (2015) 'Applying the philosophical methodological approach of Collingwood to the Foucauldian feminist analysis of State responses to "deviant" women via the use of semi-penal institutions in Liverpool (1809-1983)', *Under Construction Postgraduate Journal*, Keele: Keele University Press.

Greenwood, K. (2014) 'The Oppression, Regulation and Infantilisation of 'Deviant' Women: Liverpool Female Penitentiary (1809-1921), *European Group for the Study of Deviance and Social Control: Summer Newsletter 2,* available at http://www.europeangroup.org/media/256#overlay-context=media/255

Contact Details
Twitter: @KGreenwood91

10

Why Feminist Criminology Must Pose a Methodological Challenge to Male-centred Criminological Theory

Nicola Harding

Introduction

The purpose of this chapter is to consider the contribution that feminist criminology can offer to understandings of women's lived experience of community punishment. In particular it considers how the use of Participatory Action Research (PAR) can pose a methodological challenge to theories that have been conceived and developed within the context of a male-centred Criminology. Specifically, this piece will examine the role of relationships within current desistance theory, arguing that the complex nature of the role of victimisation and resistance to victimisation has not been fully explored in relation to female desistance. Drawing upon evidence collected during a PAR cycle[1] with women subject to community punishments in North West England, an argument will be made that whilst some characteristics of desistance theory are shared across gender lines, many aspects are male focused and inadequately explain the processes of women desisting from crime.

This research is framed within a social constructionist ontology, underpinned by critical feminist perspectives. As such the research recognises that terms such as 'deviant' and 'offender' hold values and meanings that are used to oppress certain groups within society. Using these terms can pose the risk of colluding with those who use them to label and 'other' the individuals to whom they are applied. When used within this text they are done so in a reflection and critique of the way society, practitioners and some criminologists label women with

---

[1] A PAR cycle refers to a series of workshops within which the women co-produced the research. The participants were involved at each step of the research including design, implementation, action, reflection and finally dissemination. Each group of participants attended a five-week cycle.

convictions. However, the contested nature of such terms is acknowledged here, specifically the role labelling plays within processes of social control and oppression of marginalised groups. The concept of measuring desistance perpetuates this further by extending the period by which an 'offender' is labelled indefinitely and collaborating with criminal justice interventions that are reliant upon the measurement of outcomes. It is argued here that by formulating a female theory of desistance, we may be able to re-frame desistance away from a descriptor of the absence of crime, towards the emotional experience of life after punishment.

Male-centred Criminology

Almost half a century has passed since Heidensohn (1968) challenged the lack of attention paid to women with convictions within the social sciences. Periodically since, other scholars have acknowledged that while more studies have focused upon female participants, there are still areas of the study of deviance that neglect gender differences and the experiences of criminalised women (Estrada and Nilsson, 2012; Smith and Paternoster, 1987). This central base of male focused criminological study has produced theoretical models that remain at the heart of criminological enquiry today; strain theory (Cloward and Ohlin, 1960), subcultural theory (Cohen, 1955; Miller, 1958), differential association (Sutherland and Cressey, 1978), and control theory (Reckless *et al*, 1957; Reckless *et al*, 1956, Hirschi, 1969) are just some examples (Smith and Paternoster, 1987). Heidensohn (1968) explains that it is the appearance of low participation in 'deviant' activities that accounts for the neglect of the criminalised female experience from the criminological imagination; due to this perceived low participation, criminalised women are not constructed as of pressing concern for legislators.

The close relationship between criminological research and the criminal justice system means that criminologists carefully navigate the interests of organisations of social control, accepting funding for research that originates from within both public and private spheres of the criminal justice system. Research agendas are then set by such agencies or legislators, who even when not directly funding the research, can influence research through their gatekeeper roles. With such emphasis upon the accumulation of funding grants within the neoliberal university, those who are marginal within the criminal justice system can become invisible in research. This leads to a distinct lack of attention paid to the experiences of women, with theories of deviance formulated by male researchers, traditionally based upon the experiences of men (Henne and Shah, 2016; Leonard, 1982).

This is evident in England and Wales when comparing legislative inquiry in recent years. In 2007 Baroness Corston compiled a report that examined women in the criminal justice system, making forty-three recommendations to the government regarding changes that need to be made relating to women in custody (Coyle, 2011; Corston, 2007). After 9 months silence, the recommendation of replacing female prisons with "suitable, geographically dispersed, small, multi-functional custodial centres within 10 years" (Coyle, 2011: 21) was dismissed as too costly as it would reduce resources in other (male-focused) areas. In contrast, 3 reports produced by Lord Carter (2001; 2003; 2007), focusing upon the predominantly male criminal justice system and recommending the costly creation of a National Offender Management Service, were actioned the very same day (Coyle, 2011).

Understanding Male Desistance

The concept of desistance is problematic, with Laub and Sampson (2001: 1) highlighting that desistance studies have been "hampered by definitional, measurement, and theoretical incoherence". Desistance, put most simply, is ceasing from committing crime (Laub and Sampson, 2001). However, law is constructed and changes – what is considered a crime is not static and can affect future categorisation as criminal without a change in behaviour. A person can commit further crimes without detection, does that impact the measurement of desistance? However, most crucially, once a person is convicted and punished, having 'served their time' their status should not be that of 'ex-offender' but reinstated as just 'person'. The whole notion of desistance is that those who have committed a crime before must always be labelled as criminal or desisting. This serves to continue oppression long after the label of 'offender' can no longer be legally applied.

Studies that attempted to understand the process of desisting from crime do so by predominantly focusing upon the accounts of males. Rumgay (2004: 406) highlights how the trend for male centred theory in deviance studies is mirrored in desistance theory by asserting that "studies of desistance from crime, like so many other fields of criminological enquiry, have largely ignored the experiences of women" (Giordano *et al*, 20002; Laub and Sampson, 2001; Uggen and Krutschnitt, 1998). The few studies that do compare gender in relation to desistance generally suggest "that there are more similarities than differences in desistance processes of men and women" (Rumgay, 2004: 406; Graham and Bowling, 1995; Uggen and Krutschnitt, 1998), with the differences not significant enough to warrant further enquiry (Rumgay, 2004). However, studies that do assess gender difference in desistance theory do so within existing frameworks and theories that have been conceived within general male-centred criminological theory (Uggen & Krutschnitt, 1998; Rumgay, 2004). It appears that efforts being made by a small number of scholars to formulate an understanding of female desistance from crime, do so through reliance upon the aspects of male centred theory that 'fit', disregarding the elements of female experience that challenge or refuse categorisation by existing theories of desistance. It is time for researchers to address the lack of female focused Criminology, in the hope of formulating a comprehensive theory of female desistance that focuses upon the lived experience of desistance rather than the ability to measure it. By applying feminist perspectives that situate the subjugated knowledge of the female deviant within the wider context of women's subordination and the promotion of feminist methodologies, a challenge to male-centred Criminology can be posed.

Feminist Methodology and Participatory Action Research

With the acceptance that established theories of deviance and desistance have been conceived with a focus upon male populations, often by male scholars, we must also recognise that the methods by which data is collected and knowledge is produced are also devised within male-dominant schema. Many studies that do include women do not include a significant enough number to draw theoretical conclusions from (Heidensohn, 1968). Therefore, more studies need to be completed that focus solely on the experiences and behaviour of women. Ultimately, to focus fully upon the experiences of women, and pose a challenge to male centred theory, feminist research methods that prioritise the voices and experience of those whose knowledge is subjugated need to be deployed. Participatory Action Research (PAR) offers such opportunity.

Positioning research within a PAR framework disrupts and destabilises "the characterisation of traditional knowledge-production and social science research as objective, apolitical, and democratic" (Brydon-Miller *et al*, 2003; Houh and Kalsem, 2015: 263). PAR places deviant women at the centre of each stage of the research cycle, from developing the research agenda, to selecting data collection methods (including deciding what can be considered data), collecting data, and performing analysis; the research is positioned and remains led by the participants. This is important; it is no longer enough to simply theoretically 'look to the bottom', by examining the lives or concerns of the most marginalised and unheard in society, instead we must treat those "at the bottom" 'as equal research partners who are presumptively best situated to identify, analyse, and solve problems that directly affect them' (Houh and Kalsem, 2015: 263). It is by conducting research in this way that meaningful challenges to male centred theory can begin to be developed.

This chapter now draws upon an exchange that occurred between two women during a PAR workshop with women subject to punishment in North West England. Within the study, women who are currently subject to community supervision and/or sanctions, and women with convictions who are 'actively desisting'[2] by performing the role of a peer mentor, became co-producers of knowledge about their experiences of punishment. Some of the data collection methods chosen by the women were creative writing (letters), map making, photovoice, and photo-elicitation. After data collection, the women completed thematic analysis of the maps, letters, and photographs within group and individual settings which were mostly audio-recorded. The women pose significant challenges to male centred Criminology within this body of participatory research, with this chapter relating a specific example regarding their experiences of relationships and how this can pose a challenge to male centred desistance theories.

Relationships, Victim Status, and Desistance

Laub and Sampson (1993) present a desistance theory that builds on the popular 'ageing out' of crime curve, and they demonstrate how informal social controls rooted in quality family and work ties act as 'turning points' in criminal careers, promoting desistance. In later work, Laub *et al* (1998) build upon this idea to demonstrate how 'good' marriages will promote desistance over time. Maruna (2001) summarised this neatly with employment and "the love of a good woman" forming the key equation

---

[2] 'Actively desisting' is a term discussed with the women as a way of describing their feelings about their risk of committing crime. They felt that to be actively desisting they must be taking part in activities that reinforce their belief that they will not commit another crime. This was in recognition of the passive nature of some of their convictions and the energy that they were expending in order to craft crime free futures through education, employment and volunteering.

that produces male desistance. In response to this Katz (2000) asserted that female deviance, and therefore desistance, can be predicted though women's experiences of victimisation through their life course. This relates to earlier assumptions about the origin of female deviance; that it is a result of victimisation, or some individual mental insufficiency (Heidensohn, 1968).

These three short excerpts taken from a group elicitation session offer some explanation of how relationships affect offending and desistance. Whilst sorting photographs taken during an earlier photovoice workshop, Sarah and Jess[3], are prompted into discussion by pictures they had taken themselves. This led to a short exchange about domestic violence. All the 32 women involved in the study recalled instances of domestic violence at some point in their lives. Sarah and Jess discuss the impact of the quality of their relationships (past and present) and how this related to their offending.

> If it was physical at least I knew where I stood, mentally it landed me up in that court (Sarah).

Here Sarah is attributing a controlling relationship as a contributor to her offending behaviour. When Jess experienced physical abuse, she knew that she could walk away and be supported in this decision by friends, family and support services.

> [He] never touched me all the way through the pregnancy though so I was in quite a good place at the time that he was born and it was only after we left the bedsit and had gone to our first proper house together that it started again and I said to him "the first time you touch me I am gone, you're not doing that, not while I have got a baby to think of now" and he put his hands around my neck and I don't know whether he was messing or whether he was being serious but the next day I packed my stuff and went (Jess).

Both Sarah and Jess agree that mental and emotional abuse is much harder to recognise, reject and recover from.

> Long lasted damage as well, longer lasting, you can get over a smack (Sarah).

---

[3] Names have been changed to ensure confidentiality.

This short exchange highlights issues with assigning victim status and explaining deviant behaviour or desistance as a response. When physically abused, Jess was able to leave. Health interventions experienced in her pregnancy enabled her to do so and rather than feeling victimised, she felt empowered. Sarah had also experienced and removed herself from violent domestic abuse. However, she went on to experience a controlling relationship that she feels led to her obtaining a conviction. Both agree that when faced with violence they could 'save' themselves. But when facing controlling behaviour, the boundaries of what is acceptable behaviour in a relationship within wider society were not clear; they could not easily differentiate between control and care or love. Both women recognised that domestic violence that involved physical violence was a legitimate reason to leave their partners, support (amongst peers, family and agencies) was easy to find and the signs of a violent relationship easier to identify. Within a controlling relationship this was not the case; controlling behaviour was viewed as 'normal' with less support from friends, family and support services to leave.

Both women's experiences occurred prior to the implementation of section 76 of the Serious Crime Act 2015 'Controlling or Coercive Behaviour in an Intimate or Family Relationship' (CPS, 2015). With no legal protection, there was very little support for them when they tried to seek help, unlike when they experienced violent domestic abuse. This is reflective of the way in which violence against women has become less acceptable in recent years, but raising awareness of domestic violence has not necessarily impacted other forms of abuse. While reflecting upon this exchange later Sarah and Jess felt that their experiences were not unique to a woman with convictions, but the wider experiences of all women. The ability to become their own saviour when experiencing domestic abuse was heavily dependent upon what was considered unacceptable behaviour within a relationship by those around them. The lack of understanding of controlling abuse within society further compounds the experiences of the women subject to emotional or mental abuse. Katz (2000) identified this as women's unique socialisation, in that females are socialised to be subordinate to men. However, these women could resist this in some aspects when given permission and the tools to resist by wider society. While an argument may be made for a relationship between the victimisation of women and the promotion of 'deviant' behaviour, this study shows that the complex nature of the role of victimisation and resistance to victimisation has not been fully explored in relation to female desistance.

This study directly contradicts the view that good marriages promote desistence (Laub and Sampson, 1993; Laub *et al*, 1998). The level of domestic abuse found in the study suggested that even if relationships began as 'good marriages' they did not remain this way, with some of the women stressing how relationships had contributed to their offending behaviour. The women who were actively desisting[4] chose to keep relationships that had self-imposed distance, with statements such as *"I won't have another man in my house now, he has his house and I have mine"* and *"I will never give another man the power of having his child"*. During analysis, the women discussed the constraints of relationships with men. They felt that a relationship made them responsible for the man, describing male partners *"like having another child"*. If men need employment and the "love of a good woman" to desist from crime, women become responsible for the behaviour of their man. Radcliffe and Hunter (2015:3) support this assertion, finding that for women "relationships frequently do not have a protective effect on supporting desistance, in fact quite the reverse since all too often male partners have not played a supportive, prosocial role".

Conclusion

Theories of desistance are almost exclusively developed whilst examining the experiences of men and boys. Where women are included in the study, the aspects of their experiences that are not shared by men are discarded or dislocated from the wider social restraints experienced by all women within a patriarchal society. The impact of this upon criminal justice interventions in England and Wales is clear to see; the last major enquiry focusing on women with convictions occurred ten years ago, yet many of the recommendations are still to be fully addressed.

Feminist Criminology has an opportunity to redress this by developing a feminist research methodology that elevate the experiences of women with convictions to challenge male dominated hierarchies of knowledge. Rather than continue to clumsily overlay male centred criminological theory and the experiences of men onto those of women, PAR offers the potential for new female focused theories of desistance to emerge, led directly by the women themselves. By doing so, contested theories such as desistance may be rethought as a way of understanding the emotional

---

[4] See note 2 above.

and psychological experience of life after punishment, rather than individuals experience reduced to measurable criminal justice outcomes.

> When notions of right and wrong, justice and injustice, are examined not from an abstract position but from the position of groups who have suffered through history, moral relativism recedes and identifiable normative priorities emerge (Matsuda, 1987: 325).

It was not intended that this chapter propose a new theory of female desistance, nor is it meant to underplay the contributions of criminologists who are focusing upon women's relationship to desistance theory. Rather this is a call for feminist researchers to go further and continue to develop feminist research methodologies such as PAR in order to disrupt and destabilise the notion that male centred criminological theory can be used to adequately provide understandings for female deviance or desistance.

Acknowledgements

I am grateful to Manchester Metropolitan University for funding this research. Many thanks to Dr Paul Gray, Professor Hannah Smithson, and Dr Steven Millington for their continued supervision and support. I would also like to show gratitude to the support and encouragement given by Dr Mary Corcoran and Professor Anne Worrall. To my partner Peter Harding, and the Harding five, I am truly grateful.

References

Brydon-Miller, M. Greenwood, D. and Maguire, P. (2003). 'Why Action Research?' *Action Research*, Volume 1, No. 1 pp 9-28

Carter, P. (2001). *A Review of PFI and Market Testing in the Prison Service*. London: HMSO

Carter, P. (2003) *Managing Offenders, Reducing Crime* London: Stratedgy Unit

Carter, P. (2007) *Securing the future - Proposals for the efficient and sustainable use of custody in England and Wales* London: Ministry of Justice.

Cloward, R. A. & Ohlin, L. E. (1960) *Delinquency and Opportunity* New York: Free Press

Cohen, A. K. (1955) *Delinquent Boys* New York: Free Press

Corston, J. (2007) *Corston Report* London: The Home Office

Coyle, A. (2011) 'Taking Gods' name in vain: Carter mark 3', *Criminal Justice Matters* Volume 71, No.1 pp 20-21

CPS. (2015) 'DPP: Controlling and coercive behaviour can "limit victims' basic human rights" as new domestic abuse law introduced'. The Crown Prosecution Service: http://www.cps.gov.uk/news/latest_news/new_domestic_abuse_law_introd uced/

Estrada, F. and Nilsson, A. (2012). 'Does it cost more to be a female offender? A life-course study of childhood circumstances, crime, drug abuse, and living condition', *Feminist Criminology* Volume 7, No.3 pp 196-219

Giordano, P. C. Cernkovich, S. A. and Rudolph, J. L. (2002) 'Gender crime and desistance: toward a cognitive theory of transformation' *American Journal of Sociology* Volume 107, No.4 pp 990-1064

Graham, J. & Bowling, B. (1995) *Young People and Crime*. Home Office Research Study No.145 London: Home Office.

Heidensohn, F. (1968) 'The Deviance of Women: A critique and an enquiry' *The British Journal of Sociology* Volume 19, No.2 pp 160-175

Henne, K. & Shah, R. (2016) 'Feminist Criminology and the Visual', *Crime Media and Popular Culture* pp 1-28 DOI: 10.1093/acrefore/9780190264079.013.56

Hirschi, T. (1969) *Causes of Delinquency* Berkley: University of California Press.

Houh, E. & Kalsem, K. (2015) 'Therorizing Legal Participatory Action Research: Critical Race/ Feminism and Participatory Action Research' *Qualitative Inquiry* Volume 21, No.2 pp 262-276

Katz, R. S. (2000) 'Explaining Girls' and Women's Crime and Desistance in the Context of their Victimization Experiences' *Violence Against Women* Volume 6, No.6 pp 633 - 660

Laub, J. H. and Sampson, R. J. (1993) 'Turning Points in the Life Course: Why Change Matters to the Study of Crime' *Criminology* Volume 31, No.3 pp 301-325

Laub, J. H. and Sampson, R. J. (2001) 'Understanding Desistance from Crime' *Crime and Justice* Volume 28, pp 1 - 69

Laub, J. H. Nagin, D. S. and Sampson, R. J. (1998) 'Trajectories of Change in Criminal Offending: Good Marriages and the Desistance Process' *American Sociological Review* Volume 63 pp 225-238

Leonard, E. B. (1982) *Women, Crime and Society* New York: Longman.

Maruna, S. (2001) *Making Good: How ex-convicts reform and rebuild their lives* London: American Psychological Association.

Matsuda, M.J. (1987) 'Looking to the Bottom: Critical Legal Studies and Reparations' *Harvard Civil Rights-Civil Liberties Law Review* Volume 22, pp 232-400

Miller, W. B. (1958) 'Lower class culture as generating milieu of gang delinquency' *Journal of social issues* Volume 14, No.3 pp 5-19

Radcliffe, P. & Hunter, G. (2015) ''It was a safe place for me to be' Accounts of attending womens community services and moving beyond the offender identity' *British Journal of Criminology* Volume 56, No.5 pp 976 - 994

Reckless, W. G. Dinitz, S. & Kay, B. (1957) 'The Self Component in Potential Non-Delinquency' *American Sociological Review* Volume 22, No.5 pp 566-570

Reckless, W. G. Dinitz, S. & Murray, E. (1956). 'Self-concept as an Insulator Against Delinquency' *American Sociological Review* Volume 21, No.6 pp 744-746

Rumgay, J. (2004) 'Scripts for Safer Survival: Pathways out of female crime' *The Howard Journal of Crime and Justice* Volume 43, No.4 pp 405-419

Smith, D. A. & Paternoster, R. (1987). 'The Gender Gap in Theories of Deviance: Issues and Evidence' *Journal of Research in Crime and Delinquency* Volume 24, No.2 pp 140-172

Sutherland, E. H. & Cressey, D. R. (1978) *Criminology (10th ed.)* Philadelphia: Lippincott

Uggen, C. & Krutschnitt, C. (1998) 'Crime in the breaking: gender differences in desistence' *Law and Society Review* Volume 32, No.2, pp 339-366

Extended Biography

I returned to education in my late 20s, completing an Access to Higher Education qualification in Social Sciences at St Helens College, Merseyside. I went on to study for a BA in Criminology and Sociology at Keele University, where I achieved first-class honours and won Keele University's Student of the Year 2014. With the assistance of Dr Andy Zieleniec I secured a student fellowship scholarship of £5,000 from Santander. This was awarded for travel to Chile during August 2014, where I completed photo-ethnographic research of Latin American graffiti and street art. Upon returning from Chile, I resumed postgraduate study at Keele University, completing an MA in Criminology and Criminal Justice which I passed with distinction in 2015. I am now a PhD candidate in Sociology at Manchester Metropolitan University.

Prior to my studies I volunteered as a peer mentor at Apex Trust, a charitable trust that assists women with convictions to engage with education, training or to secure employment. During my undergraduate degree, I volunteered with Staffordshire and West Midlands Probation Trust as a literacy mentor; teaching the Toe-by-Toe literacy system to individuals with very low levels of literacy who were subject to probation supervision. Throughout this time, I also worked as a Life Skills Tutor in a unit for women with convictions, and went to night school to earn a Preparing to Teach in the Lifelong Learning Sector (PTLLS) teaching qualification to enhance my ability to teach basic literacy, numeracy, and the skills needed for prisoner resettlement and everyday life. Whilst a postgraduate taught student, I served as Secretary of Keele Postgraduate Association, and worked within the university Advice and Guidance Office. I have recently worked as an Associate Lecturer at Staffordshire University and currently at Manchester Metropolitan University, alongside marking sociology GCSE papers for Cambridge Assessment.

Research

My studies have produced a variety of research projects on a range of topics, including sex work, probation and policing, and graffiti[5]. In addition to my academic research I have also recently completed an independent research project with the Whitworth gallery in Manchester and REALab (University of Manchester). Here I co-designed, pitched, and implemented a participatory action research evaluation with children and young people from the local area. This research consisted of a creative evaluation using community mapping, photovoice and photo elicitation to provide an evaluative report of a new installation by Anya Gallaccio situated within Whitworth Park, Manchester. The research methodology was based upon the design on my current PhD research, which advocates a participatory approach to researching and engaging with individuals and groups traditionally assumed 'hard to reach'.

My current research forms a response to the part privatisation of probation triggered by the report 'Transforming rehabilitation: a strategy for reform' in 2015. The report discusses penal intervention as occurring within either *custody* or *community*, with Chris Grayling stating that 'not enough is being done to connect custody to community' (Grayling, 2013:

---

[5] My graffiti research was presented at the British Sociological Association annual conference on 5th April 2017, in a paper titled 'Instagraff: How the rich kids of Instagram killed the graffiti writer'. This was reported in local and national media; including an interview BBC Radio 4 today show (5/4/2017), and The Times
https://www.thetimes.co.uk/article/instagram-kills-off-the-graffiti-rebel-qbg30lcb0 (5/4/2017) among others.

7). However, notions of community are vague, placing imagined responsibility on the individual to 'payback' to some imagined community, and responsibility on this imagined community to rehabilitate the individual. With all who are supervised beyond the prison gates now being imagined as part of a community, my research incorporates elements of Human Geography to critically examine how community is communicated to women with convictions as aspiration for belonging, which when achieved is expected to result in desistance from crime.

Building upon this, I then seek to understand how community interventions and sanctions placed upon women with convictions can intersect, contradict or ignore their understanding of place, community and belonging. Looking to feminist criminology, this research, partly discussed in this chapter, seeks to uncover the subjugated knowledge possessed by women subject to community punishments. By facilitating a Participatory Action Research (PAR) project with women with convictions, this research champions the formation of a more democratic form of knowledge production; situating participants as the experts in their own lives.

Activism, Organisational Work and/or Professional Membership

I am the editor of the British Society of Criminology postgraduate blog, where I publish blogs written by postgraduate students about their research, opinion pieces, and responses to current events by postgraduate students in Criminology. I am a co-director of @Creative_Crim, an online network for creative criminology, which is open to all criminologists who are already using or are interested in using creative research methods. I am also a member of the British Sociological Association and the European Group for the Study of Deviance and Social Control.

Selected Works

Crossley, C. and Harding, N. (2016) *'The Problem with Participatory Action Research'* (Blog post) Manchester Centre for Youth Studies (MCYS) Blog [online] Available at http://www.mcys-mmu.org.uk/the-problem-with-participatory-action-research/

Harding, N. and Smith, R. (2016) *RESEARCH in the Park: A participatory community evaluation of the Anya Gallaccio installation, Whitworth Park, Manchester* [Online] Available at https://www.academia.edu/31059569/RESEARCH_in_the_Park_A_participato

ry_community_evaluation_of_the_Anya_Gallaccio_installation_Whitworth_P
ark_Manchester

Harding, N. & Crossley, C. (2017) ''Are we lost?' Participatory Action Research, creative methods and map making with individuals experiencing disadvantage'. British Sociological Association Annual Conference 2017, University of Manchester, April 2017.

Harding, N. (2017) 'Instagraff – How the rich kids of Instagram killed the graffiti writer' British Sociological Association Annual Conference 2017, University of Manchester, April 2017.

Harding, N. (2017) 'Insta-graff. How the rich kids of Instagram killed the graffiti writer' (Blog Post) Manchester Centre for Youth Studies (MCYS) Blog [online] Available at http://www.mcys-mmu.org.uk/insta-graff-how-the-rich-kids-of-instagram-killed-the-graffiti-writer-by-nicola-harding/

Contact Details
Email: nicola.ann.harding@gmail.com
Twitter: @NicolaAHarding and @Creative_Crim
Academia: https://mmu.academia.edu/NicolaHarding

11

Criminal Records and Conditional Citizenship: Towards a Critical Sociology of Post-Sentence Discrimination

Andrew Henley

Introduction

The critical sociology of punishment has a long-established tradition of exploring issues such as: the differential application of penal sanctions across class, race and gender divisions; the harms associated with confinement in penal and semi-penal institutions; and the expansion of the carceral continuum into community settings. More recently, North American scholarship has explored the extent to which criminalisation may generate a number of 'collateral consequences' for those previously subjected to punishment. However, this term arguably fails to convey what is at stake when those who have served their sentences are denied access to the full range of rights and entitlements associated with meaningful citizenship. Indeed, for many people with convictions, the discrimination that they face in their *post*-sentence lives may be experienced as equally or even more painful than the original sanctions for lawbreaking. Moreover, given the often precarious status of those targeted for punishment in many advanced capitalist economies, this discrimination against convicted populations is likely to intensify and exacerbate pre-existing marginality. This requires that post-sentence disadvantage should be considered as *central* to the social process of punishment and not merely 'collateral' to it.

In this short chapter, I provide a brief exploration of some the issues arising from criminal records within England and Wales. In doing so, I hope to demonstrate the potential for a broader sociological agenda concerned with discrimination against people with convictions during their post-sentence lives. That is, a field of enquiry which does not merely 'chart' different forms of discrimination against people with convictions, but which also: (1) explores the rationalities which underpin it; (2) examines the lived experience of those subjected to it; and therefore (3) opens up various forms of discrimination to critical scrutiny and contestation.

Criminal Records, 'Less Eligibility' and 'Non-Superiority'

Over 10.5 million people in Britain have a previous criminal conviction (Unlock, 2014). The 'criminal records' pertaining to these convictions can cause multiple disadvantages for people in their post-sentence life (Henley, 2014). These disadvantages can stem from both *de jure* exclusions where the law prohibits or disqualifies people with certain convictions from, for example, undertaking specified jobs (Thomas, 2007), serving on juries (HM Courts Service, 2015), or running for various public offices (Electoral Commission, 2013a; 2013b; 2013c). However, the less favourable treatment of people with convictions is more often the result of *de facto* discrimination stemming from the policies and practices of both state and private-sector actors. For instance, some employers may not be willing to consider people with convictions when recruiting, even if there is no specific law requiring them to consider criminal records as part of the process (Working Links, 2010; Larrauri, 2014). Moreover, many providers of insurance policies, mortgages and other financial products might treat a criminal conviction as evidence of an enhanced 'risk' and either refuse to offer their services or charge an enhanced premium for doing so (Unlock, 2013). Similarly, private landlords may be reluctant to let a property to a person who declares a previous conviction (Shelter, 2012). This amorphous range of *de jure* exclusions and *de facto* forms of discrimination has obvious potential to restrict the life chances of former lawbreakers in a number of spheres.

Historically, the Benthamite principle of 'less eligibility' associated with both systems of poor relief and, subsequently, with penal confinement, dictated that those either in workhouses or prisons were required to be held in conditions not more favourable than those available to the lowest ranks of the (non-offending) working population (Sieh, 1989). This persistent ideology has continued into contemporary political discourses, with strong objections raised to improvements in the treatment of prisoners or other lawbreakers on the grounds that they would cause offence to the purportedly 'law-abiding majority' or to victims of crime (Drake and Henley, 2014). However, Mannheim (1939) described how the less-eligibility principle also applied to the treatment of convicted people *post-sentence* by suggesting that they were often subject to a standard of 'non-superiority'. This he defined as "the requirement that the condition of the criminal *when he has paid the penalty for his crime* should be at least not superior to that of the lowest classes of the non-criminal population" (57, emphasis added).

In the present-day, the effects of this 'non-superiority' are seen most obviously within the labour market where those with convictions are placed at a distinct disadvantage (in 2011 of the 1.21 million people claiming Job Seekers Allowance, 33 per cent appeared on the Police National Computer, MOJ/DWP 2011). When 'structural unemployment' and 'labour market flexibility' are central tenets of neoliberal globalised economies (Standing, 2009) it is easy to see how these disadvantages are readily sustained. As outlined above, non-superiority also applies to access to positions of responsibility within civil society. For example, the opportunity to perform jury service or to run for public office is, in many circumstances, denied to people with convictions. However, the non-superiority principle has also been applied to the distribution of scant welfare goods. Indeed, in some US states various forms of social security (e.g. food stamps) are denied to those with specified drug felony convictions (see *inter alia* Wacquant, 2009; American Bar Association, 2013; The Sentencing Project, 2015). In the UK these restrictions have, to date, been less dramatic. However, Garland (1985) amongst others has identified a close historical nexus between domestic penal and welfare strategies and, in recent years, attempts have been made to exert quasi-punitive effects through the 'welfare state'. For instance, Harlow Council in Essex has attempted to introduce measures that would deny social housing to people with specified convictions (BBC News, 2013). Also, in many cases, previous convictions have the effect of either reducing or withholding completely the possibility of receiving state-funded compensation from those who sustain injuries as victims of crime (Criminal Injuries Compensation Authority, 2012).

Partial Rehabilitation and Discriminatory Biopolitics

My doctoral research (Henley, 2016) explored the emergence and erosion of the Rehabilitation of Offenders Act 1974 (ROA) as a legal mechanism designed to mitigate various forms of exclusion and discrimination which can potentially affect people with old criminal records. The ROA allows convictions resulting in sentences of less than four years' imprisonment to become 'spent' after a specified period of time. Once a conviction becomes spent it need not be declared for *most* purposes. However, those who have received sentences of more than four years' imprisonment or an indeterminate term are permanently excluded from the provisions of the ROA. Therefore, these individuals remain vulnerable to possible discrimination based on their criminal records for life. In 2014 alone, some 7,010 people received a conviction which can *never* become spent (Ministry of Justice, 2015). Furthermore, a significant (and growing) number of occupations are now subject to 'enhanced' criminal background checks which reveal *all* convictions and cautions (even those which are 'spent') thus rendering the ROA ineffective in many cases. Over four million background checks of this nature are conducted for employment purposes each year (Larrauri, 2014). This issue of 'unspent' convictions, the ubiquity of criminal background checks and the resultant potential for discrimination and exclusion of convicted individuals *post-sentence* raises serious questions about whether the effects of state punishment ever truly end and if 'rehabilitation' is currently given effective articulation in law.

My research theorises these issues by drawing on the work of Michel Foucault on governmentality and biopolitics (Foucault, 2007; 2008). It considers whether the emergence of criminal records databases since the 19th Century and systems of disclosure in the 20th Century (Thomas, 2007) has (partly by contingency and partly by design) facilitated the development of a *moral technology for the regulation of life chances*. I suggest that discriminatory 'ways of acting' (such as criminal background checks and statutory exclusions) are underpinned by neoliberal political rationalities which regard members of society who have contravened the law as having made a rational choice to do so. They thus render the convicted population vulnerable to the exercise of a regulatory power which 'disallows life' (Foucault, 1978: 138) by exposing former lawbreakers to less favourable treatment and potentially condemning them to permanent membership of an emerging global 'precariat' (Standing, 2011). By contrast, this exclusionary biopolitics has the effect of improving the relative life chances of 'good citizens' by ensuring that they have a strategic advantage over people with convictions in the competition for employment and in other opportunities for self-improvement. Thus, previous convictions operate not just as markers of potential 'risk' or danger as many scholars have noted (see: Castel, 1991; Hudson, 2003; O'Malley, 2010; Mythen, 2014), but also as *indices of relative desert*, through which government can, through various legal and policy instruments, guide the conduct of non-state actors towards the convicted members of the population and their associates. This may be achieved by adjusting the period of time it takes for a conviction to become 'spent' under rehabilitation legislation or, for instance, by expanding or restricting the circumstances under which certain convictions can be considered. This administration of the boundaries of redemptive possibility can occur in response to either shifting penal sensibilities or due to conditions of economic 'necessity' (i.e. by restricting access to employment to those regarded as 'good citizens').

Citizenship: from Universality to Conditionality

In Marshall's (1950) classic essay, citizenship was conceived of as a status bestowed on those who are *full members* of a community. For Marshall, citizenship involved an evolution of rights: from *civil* rights in the eighteenth century (e.g. the right to life and liberty, due process and equality before the law); *political* rights in the nineteenth century (e.g. the right to vote, stand in elections, participate in political life and civil society); and *social* rights in the twentieth century (e.g. the right to an adequate standard of living and social protection). After the Second World War, frameworks for rights emerged such as the Universal Declaration of Human Rights in 1948 and the International Covenants on Civil and Political Rights and on Economic, Social and Cultural Rights in 1966. Whilst these frameworks and theoretical approaches sought to assert the principle of *universal* rights, the actual enjoyment of rights has tended to be experienced as a facet of *national* citizenship. Indeed, Bobbio (1990) has described how national identity has involved a 'melting' of the notion of rights with modern citizenship. That is, of citizenship entailing one's belonging to an entity such as a sovereign nation and one's entitlement to rights being a function of that belonging. The conditionality of one's enjoyment of rights upon national citizenship has clear implications for migrants and refugees. In his work on the emerging 'precariat' class, Standing (2011: 14) deploys the notion of the *denizen* to convey the idea of a person who "for one reason or another, has a more limited range of rights than citizens do". He also notes how, in Roman times, the idea of the denizen "applied to foreigners given residency rights and rights to ply their trade, but not full citizenship rights" (ibid). However, Standing also suggests that, whilst *most* modern denizens are still migrants, "one other category stands out – the large layer of people who have been criminalised, the convicted" (ibid).

My future research agenda takes up the challenge of charting the status of 'criminalised denizens' in modern society. As already alluded to, their partial enjoyment of rights occurs within the context not only of an elevated concern with 'risk' but also an increasingly politicised law and order discourse which implicitly constructs 'offenders' as having actively forfeited their rights by virtue of their lawbreaking (Drake and Henley, 2014). This ideological shift advances the view that somehow granting rights too liberally will be to the detriment of 'victims' or the 'law-abiding', further polarising our understanding of what it means to be a citizen (ibid). Kivisto and Faist (2007: 49; emphasis added) have suggested that citizenship *"confers an identity* on individuals by binding them to and defining them as members of a political community". However, processes of criminalisation have the effect of weakening this bind and the convicted individual's membership of the community because a restriction of liberty and suspension of 'full' citizenship has traditionally been justified on the basis that lawbreaking 'breaches the social contract'. Consequently, lawbreakers are placed within the ambit of what Foucault (1977: 11) once termed "an economy of suspended rights" involving, for instance, a restriction of normal engagement with civil society. What remains ambiguous, however, is precisely when and how this 'suspension' of rights comes to an end and when 'normal' citizenship, if indeed it was ever present in the first place, can be resumed and on what terms.

In *A Theory of Justice*, Rawls (2009 [1971]) reworked traditional social contract philosophy to resolve the problem of distributive justice (that is, of how to achieve a socially just distribution of goods in a society). Within his theory, Rawls derived two principles of justice: the liberty principle and the difference principle. The liberty principle supported an "equal right to the most extensive basic liberty compatible with a similar liberty for others" (53) such as, for instance, the right to run for public office. The difference principle, on the other hand, proposed that social and economic inequalities could only be justifiable to the extent that they are to the benefit of the least advantaged. Within this framework, the achievement of a Rawlsian conception of 'Justice as Fairness' for the sizeable convicted population is problematic when it so clearly conflicts with the utilitarian principles of 'less eligibility' and 'non-superiority' described earlier. That is, the possession of a criminal record in modern society poses difficult questions about the extent to which meaningful citizenship can be enjoyed precisely because the denial of full citizenship is no longer given effect merely for the duration of an individual's sentence, but through the as yet uncharted and expanding array of exclusions and forms of discrimination which continue into *post-sentence* life.

References

American Bar Association (2013) 'National Inventory of the Collateral Consequences of Conviction' [online] Available from: http://www.abacollateralconsequences.org/map/ (accessed 13 October 2015)

BBC News (2013) 'Harlow Council Plans Social Housing Ban for Criminals' [online] 11th February Available from: http://www.bbc.co.uk/news/uk-england-essex-21408021 (accessed 13 October 2015)

Bobbio, N. (1990) L'etá dei diritti [The Age of Rights]. Rome: Einaudi

Castel, R. (1991) 'From Dangerousness to Risk' pp 281-298 in G. Burchell, C. Gordon and P. Miller (eds) *The Foucault Effect: Studies in Governmentality* London: Harvester Wheatsheaf

Collateral Consequences Resource Center (2015) 'Collateral Consequences of Criminal Conviction and Restoration of Rights: News, Commentary, and Tools' [online] Available from: http://ccresourcecenter.org/ (accessed 23 October 2015)

Criminal Injuries Compensation Authority (2012) The Criminal Injuries Compensation Scheme 2012 [online] Available from: https://www.gov.uk/government/uploads/system/uploads/attachment_data /file/243480/9780108512117.pdf London: Ministry of Justice (accessed 13 October 2015)

Drake, D. H. and Henley, A. J. (2014) ''Victims' Versus 'Offenders' in British Political Discourse: The Construction of a False Dichotomy' *The Howard Journal of Criminal Justice* Volume 53, No. 2 pp 141-157

Electoral Commission (2013a) *Guidance for Candidates and Agents: UK Parliamentary By-Elections in Great Britain* [online] Available from: http://www.electoralcommission.org.uk/__data/assets/pdf_file/0008/154439 /UKPE-CA-by-election-guide.pdf (accessed 27 August 2013)

Electoral Commission (2013b) *Local elections in England and Wales: Guidance for Candidates and Agents Part 1 of 6 – Can You Stand for Election?* [online] Available from: http://www.electoralcommission.org.uk/__data/assets/pdf_file/0007/141784 /Part-1-Can-you-stand-for-election-LGEW.pdf (accessed 27 August 2013)

Electoral Commission (2013c) *Police and Crime Commissioner Elections in England and Wales Guidance for Candidates and Agents. Part 1 of 6 – Can You Stand for Election?* [online] Available from: http://www.electoralcommission.org.uk/__data/assets/pdf_file/0009/148743 /PCC-Part-1-Can-you-stand-for-election.pdf (accessed 27 August 2013)

Foucault, M. (1977) *Discipline and Punish: The Birth of the Prison* London: Penguin

Foucault, M. (1978) *The History of Sexuality – Volume 1: An Introduction* New York: Pantheon Books

Foucault, M. (1990) 'Critical Theory/Intellectual History' pp 17-46 in Kritzman, L. (ed) *Michel Foucault: Politics, Philosophy, Culture. Interviews and Other Writings 1977-1984* London: Routledge

Foucault, M. (2007) *Security, Territory, Population: Lectures at the Collège de France, 1977-1978* Basingstoke: Palgrave Macmillan

Foucault, M. (2008) *The Birth of Biopolitics: Lectures at the Collège de France, 1978-1979* Basingstoke: Palgrave Macmillan

Garland, D. (1985) *Punishment and Welfare: A History of Penal Strategies* Aldershot: Gower

Henley, A. J. (2014) 'Abolishing the Stigma of Punishments Served' *Criminal Justice Matters*, Volume 97, No. 1 pp 22-23

Henley, A. J. (2016) *Criminal Records and the Regulation of Redemption: a Critical History of Legal Rehabilitation in England and Wales* Unpublished PhD Thesis Keele: Keele University

HM Courts Service (2015) *Guide to Jury Summons* London: Ministry of Justice

Hudson, B. (2003) *Justice in the Risk Society* London: SAGE

Justice (1972) *Living It Down: The Problem of Old Convictions* London: Stevens and Sons

Kivisto, P. and Faist, T. (2007) *Citizenship: Discourse, Theory, and Transnational prospects* Oxford: Blackwell

Larrauri, E. (2014) 'Legal Protections Against Background Checks in Europe', *Punishment and Society* Volume 16, No. 1 pp 50-73

Mannheim, H. (1939) *The Dilemma of Penal Reform* London: George Allen and Unwin

Marshall, T H. (1950) *Citizenship and Social Class: And Other Essays.* Cambridge: Cambridge University Press

Ministry of Justice (2015) *Criminal Justice System Statistics publication: Sentencing: Pivot Table Analytical Tool for England and Wales* [online] Available from: https://www.gov.uk/government/uploads/system/uploads/attachment_data/file/428941/sentencing-data-tool.xls (accessed 13 October 2015)

Mythen, G. (2014) *The Risk Society: Crime, Security and Justice* Basingstoke: Palgrave Macmillan

O'Malley, P. (2010) *Crime and Risk* London: SAGE

Rawls, J. (2009 [1971]) *A Theory of Justice* Harvard: Harvard University Press

Shelter (2012) *Policy Briefing: Unlocking Stable Homes – Housing Advice for Ex-offenders.* London: Shelter Available from:

Criminal Records and Conditional Citizenship

http://england.shelter.org.uk/__data/assets/pdf_file/0004/596794/Unlocking _Stable_Homes_final_2.pdf (accessed 27 August 2013)

Sieh E.W. (1989) 'Less Eligibility: The Upper Limits of Penal Policy' *Criminal Justice Policy Review* Volume 3, No. 2 pp 159-183

Standing, G. (2009) *Work after Globalization: Building Occupational Citizenship.* Cheltenham: Edward Elgar Publishing

Standing, G. (2011) *The Precariat: The New Dangerous Class*. London: Bloomsbury

The Sentencing Project (2015) *A Lifetime of Punishment: The Impact of the Felony Drug Ban on Welfare Benefits* [online] Available from: http://sentencingproject.org/wp-content/uploads/2015/12/A-Lifetime-of-Punishment.pdf (accessed 24 February 2017)

Thomas, T. (2007) *Criminal Records: A Database for the Criminal Justice System and Beyond* Basingstoke: Palgrave Macmillan.

Unlock (2013) 'Insurance and Convictions – A Simple Guide' [online] Available from: http://hub.unlock.org.uk/knowledgebase/insurance-convictions-simple-guide/ (accessed 13 October 2013)

Unlock (2014) *Number of People with Convictions - Home Office Freedom of Information release CR33517* Maidstone: Unlock

Wacquant, L. (2009) *Punishing the Poor: The Neoliberal Government of Social Insecurity* London: Duke University Press

Working Links (2010) *Prejudiced: Tagged for life - A Research Report into Employer Attitudes Towards Ex-offenders* London: Working Links

Extended Biography

Research

I am currently employed as a Lecturer in Criminology in the School of Social Science and Public Policy at Keele University in Staffordshire, UK. Prior to this I worked at Keele as a Graduate Teaching Assistant whilst conducting my doctoral studies under the supervision of Dr Mary Corcoran and Professor Ronnie Lippens. My PhD, entitled 'Criminal Records and the Regulation of Redemption: A Critical History of Legal Rehabilitation in England and Wales', was submitted in September 2016. Before joining Keele, I undertook an MA in Social Sciences at the Open University.

My research interests are primarily in the areas of punishment and social control. In particular, I am interested in the impact of criminal records and post-sentence control measures on the life chances and human rights of people with convictions. Whilst I have previously used quantitative analysis in some of my published work on Multi-Agency Public Protection Arrangements, my doctoral thesis and other research is predominantly qualitative and archival, drawing theoretical inspiration from the works of Michel Foucault on discourse, power and governmentality.

Activism, Organisational Work and/or Professional Membership
My research agenda is also inspired by my involvement with the award-winning charity Unlock, which supports people with convictions with information, advice, and advocacy to help them overcome the disadvantage which can arise from the stigma associated with criminal records. My first involvement with Unlock was as a volunteer researcher for its online Information Hub whilst I was studying for my Master's degree. I later became a member of the Board of Trustees in July 2013 and assumed the role of Chair in October 2016. Further information about Unlock and its work can be found online at www.unlock.org.uk.

Selected Works
Henley, A. J. (forthcoming, 2017) 'Civil and Social Death: Criminal Background and the Loss of the Self', in Read S. Santatzoglou, S. and Wrigley, A. (eds.) *Loss, Dying and Bereavement in the Criminal Justice System* London: Routledge

Hudson, K.J. and Henley, A.J (2015) 'Disparities in Public Protection Measures Against Sexual Offending in England and Wales: an Example of Preventative Injustice?' *Criminology and Criminal Justice* Volume 15, No. 5 pp 561–577

Hudson, K., J. Taylor, C. and Henley A. J. (2015) 'Trends in the Management of Registered Sexual Offenders across England and Wales: a Geographical Approach to the Study of Sexual Offending' *Journal of Sexual Aggression* Volume 21, No. 1 pp 56-70

Henley, A. J. (2014) 'Abolishing the Stigma of Punishments Served' *Criminal Justice Matters* Volume 97, No. 1 pp 22-23

Drake, D .H. and Henley, A. J. (2014) ''Victims' Versus 'Offenders' in British Political Discourse: The construction of a False Dichotomy' *The Howard Journal of Criminal Justice* Volume 53, No. 2, pp 141-157

Contact Details
Twitter: @AndyHenley1

12

Life in Prison through the Lens of Deafness: The Experiences of Deaf Prisoners in England and Wales

Laura Kelly

Introduction

The majority of existing prison research has been focused on the type of prisoner that prison was initially designed for and continues primarily to contain: the young able-bodied lower class male (Cheney, 2005). However, increasing attention is now being given to individuals who do not fit this mould, including female, older and foreign national prisoners (see: Scott and Codd, 2010; Phillips, 2012; Moore and Scraton, 2013; Mann, 2016). As a result of this, it has become apparent that these prisoners experience prison differently and often feel the pains of imprisonment (Sykes, 1958) more intensely than their peers. This is despite being theoretically protected by the Equality Act 2010, a legislative framework which places a legal duty on public bodies in the United Kingdom (such as the Prison Service) to exercise their functions in a way that is designed to reduce inequality. This chapter explores the experiences of another minority group in prison, one that is rarely given meaningful attention: Deaf prisoners. In order to do this, it presents findings from my recently completed doctoral research entitled 'Silent Punishment: The experiences of d/Deaf prisoners', showing that these prisoners undoubtedly experience disproportionate pain in prison for a multitude of reasons. As part of this, details about the aims of the research and the methodology that was used are also provided.

Many hearing people view those who are d/Deaf as simply having the misfortune to live in a world without sound (Lane *et al*, 1996; Ladd, 2003), d/Deafness is in fact much more complex than this. The extent to which a person is d/Deaf varies significantly from those whose hearing is only slightly impaired, to individuals who are severely deaf, and finally to those who are Deaf. Although there are different ways of categorising these levels of d/Deafness, for the purposes of the research severely deaf referred to those with little or no functional hearing, who usually need to rely on lip reading even with hearing aids, and Deaf to individuals who identify as being culturally and linguistically Deaf, and commonly use British Sign Language (BSL) to communicate. The lives of those who are d/Deaf have been studied at length within the academic discipline of Deaf Studies, where individuals who identify as being *deaf* (but not Deaf) are commonly shown to view their deafness negatively (Higgins, 1980), and where *Deaf* people are seen as being part of a distinct group known as the Deaf Community which is comprised of people who are proud to be Deaf and share the same language, values and life experiences (Baker and Padden, 1978; Higgins, 2002). The distinction between *deafness* and *Deafness* was vital to my thesis, where it was shown that the way an individual identifies with their d/Deafness has a profound impact on the way they experience prison.

The Existing Literature

Prior to the completion of this study, available literature relating to the experiences of d/Deaf people in prison was limited. Of the literature that was available, most was anecdotal and very small scale, and was often based on either American prisons or accounts of ex-prisoners (O'Rourke and Reed, 2007). Furthermore, even the most recent and comprehensive sources (McCulloch, 2010, 2012) failed to acknowledge the complexity of d/Deafness or to differentiate meaningfully between the experiences of *deaf* and *Deaf* prisoners. Despite these limitations, there was consensus in such literature that d/Deaf prisoners suffer disproportionately as a direct result of their d/Deafness, with communication barriers, resource issues and a lack of d/Deaf awareness being cited as key causes of this (Fisken, 1994; Royal National Institute for the Deaf, 1995; Ackerman, 1998; Gerrard, 2001; Izycky and Gahir, 2007; McCulloch, 2010, 2012). Research carried out in England and Wales suggested that the Prison Service is ill-equipped to meet the needs of d/Deaf prisoners, with McCulloch (2010, 2012) arguing that their treatment equates to a violation of the Equality Act 2010, which stipulates that reasonable adjustments must be made to ensure that those with a protected characteristic such as d/Deafness are not discriminated against.

Research Aims and Methodology

The primary aim of my doctoral research was to provide a more detailed and rigorous study of the lives of d/Deaf people in prison in England and Wales than what was already available, and to further explore existing claims that they suffer disproportionately during their time in custody. Another aim was to meaningfully consider the role of imported identity in prison and to examine the experiences of *deaf* and *Deaf* prisoners separately, thus fusing together the fields of prison studies and Deaf studies in a way that had not been done before. The final main aim of the research was to explore whether the Prison Service is currently adhering to the legal duty imposed by the Equality Act 2010.

In order to address these aims, a qualitative approach was taken. As part of this, 28 semi-structured interviews were carried out at seven adult male prisons in England with a sample of hard of hearing/d/Deaf prisoners, and staff members who had worked with them. In addition to this, observations were made at each establishment, and later recorded in a fieldwork journal. Where necessary, a BSL interpreter was used during interviews with Deaf prisoners.

Key Findings

While the research included a sample of prisoners with varying levels of d/Deafness, for the purposes of this chapter focus is given to the culturally and linguistically Deaf prisoners, as it is they who were shown to experience the pains of imprisonment most severely[1].

There were seven culturally and linguistically Deaf prisoners interviewed as part of the research, five of whom were situated in one establishment (HMP Bowdon[2]), and the remaining two being the only Deaf prisoners at their respective prisons (HMP Sale and HMP Wilmslow). All of these individuals communicated using BSL and used common Deaf behaviours such as touching and prolonged eye contact. They saw themselves as being intrinsically different to hearing people, preferring to be with other Deaf people, and viewing the hearing world with hostility and resentment as a consequence of their experiences in wider society, as highlighted here by one participant:

---

[1] I plan to publish a paper discussing the different experiences of deaf and Deaf prisoners.
[2] The names of all the establishments included in the study have been changed for the purposes of confidentiality and anonymity.

> Hearing seem to look down at me [...] They think I am simple because I can't interact on their level. They think that I'm no good to them, they don't want to know. I get that all the time, that's why I walk away from them. Don't get me wrong, there are good hearing who have got time and patience to listen to me. There are good, but there are also bad.

These perceptions and behaviours had a profound impact on the way these individuals experienced prison, with all seven prisoners attempting to maintain their cultural and linguistic Deaf identities throughout their time in custody. Evidence of this was provided in the fact that they continued to communicate in BSL, to use culturally distinct Deaf behaviours, to gravitate towards other Deaf prisoners (where possible), and to view hearing people (be it prisoners or staff members) negatively.

Despite attempting to remain culturally and linguistically Deaf, it became clear that there was little room for such profound difference in prison. There are a number of reasons for this, the first relating to the role sound plays in prison. A key argument posited in the thesis was that prison as an institution relies on sound in order to operate, with tannoys, voices, bells, and alarms all being central to the prison regime. While sound is also key in wider society (Higgins, 1980) it is even more important in prison where it is used to regulate the "batch" (Goffman, 1961: 17) of prisoners and to guide them through their daily routine. With this in mind, it was argued that an ability to hear is a necessity if a prisoner is to fulfil the requirements of the prisoner role, and therefore for individuals to whom sound is not available, prison automatically becomes more difficult.

In addition to sound, verbal communication also plays a key part in the penal regime. Therefore, in order to adjust to their designated prisoner role, Deaf prisoners also require regular provision of qualified BSL interpreters, as well as access to other prisoners/staff members who can communicate fluently in BSL. However, establishments were shown to be largely ill-equipped to adapt their regimes to accommodate Deafness, and mapping on to findings from existing literature (see: Gerrard, 2001, McCulloch, 2010, 2012), were not providing the prisoners with access to BSL interpreters or specialist equipment in any consistent way. While this was slightly less isolating for the prisoners at HMP Bowdon because they had other Deaf people to communicate with (at times), for the remaining participants who had no one else with whom to communicate in BSL, this lack of provision led to almost total communication isolation, as shown here:

> In the gym they all go round together; the Russians, the Romanians, the Latvians, the Africans, the Blacks. Everybody's in their own little groups, and I'm just on my own in there. If there was a Deaf group I know I would be part of it, but there isn't one so I'm on my own [...] Everybody else talks to each other but I don't know what they are talking about, and it's really difficult depending on the situation. Nobody signs, so I just keep myself to myself really. I have brief chats with people with paper and pen but it's very brief. To get anything out, and to communicate, that would be great. It would help me sleep better.

Issues relating to Deaf awareness on the part of staff members were found to be key to this lack of provision, as without a certain level of understanding about the complexity of d/Deafness and the needs of Deaf people, prison officials failed to understand how to appropriately respond to these prisoners[3]. It was demonstrated that in the absence of such awareness, staff members either left Deaf prisoners to their own devices, or attempted to communicate with them in a variety of largely ineffective, and at times inappropriate, ways. Strategies for communication ranged from speaking louder and writing things down (many Deaf people cannot read), to attempting to use staff members with low levels of BSL comprehension as interpreters, to finally using a Deaf prisoner who could sign and speak as an interpreter. This final strategy was perhaps the most concerning, as it gave this prisoner an unprecedented level of power without any means of monitoring the accuracy of his interpretations.

As HMP Bowdon was the only prison included in the research that was holding multiple Deaf prisoners, it had been anticipated that the interviewees there would have had less difficulty behaving as culturally and linguistically Deaf. However, it became apparent that a lack of Deaf awareness on the part of many staff members inhibited the maintenance of such difference. Officials commonly had little understanding about why it could have been beneficial to keep them on the same wing, and often

---

[3] It is important to acknowledge that findings were presented which indicated that a small number of staff members do have some level of Deaf awareness, thus meaning that the general trends discussed throughout the remainder of this paragraph do not necessarily apply to them.

viewed Deaf behaviour such as signing and touching as being suspicious or inappropriate, as shown here by one staff member:

> But then there are negative attitudes about how the Deaf prisoners interact with each other, which I don't necessary think is about rules, but rather staff not being aware of Deaf culture [...] They fear that they don't know what's going on because they can't understand what they are saying [when the Deaf prisoners are communicating in BSL], or what's happening, [and they worry] that they might be able to group together and make plans and plot.

Without appropriate resource allocation or Deaf awareness, it was shown that Deaf prisoners often become almost completely isolated from prison life. In line with other literature (see: McCulloch, 2010) the Deaf interviewees were often unable to partake in education, training or rehabilitative programmes, to access medical assistance or legal aid with an interpreter, or to gain a meaningful understanding of the penal regime or the expectations of their prisoner role. This, combined with a lack of access to other Deaf people meant that the pains of imprisonment (Sykes, 1958) were being experienced differently and much more intensely by the Deaf interviewees, to the point that they were often living in a continual form of solitary confinement through no fault of their own. Findings were presented which showed that Deaf people are certainly punished disproportionately in prison to the extent that it could have a negative impact on their mental health, with all of the Deaf prisoners appearing anxious, lonely, fearful, frustrated, and stressed. This is highlighted here in a quote from a Deaf participant (this individual was the only Deaf person at HMP Wilmslow):

> My son emailed me and said 'Don't worry'. He is a doctor and he said that I must be strong, I must be patient, I must be strong. And I must read the Quran and pray every day. So I am trying to be patient and do that. But it is very difficult because there is no communication. Who do I talk to? With my colleagues there is a barrier between us and I can't communicate with them, they just leave me alone [...] Inside and mentally I feel that I want to communicate, I want to get stuff out, but I can't. And even with jokes, humour, there's nothing. I get very emotional [...] Very stressed. I want to get it out, and I don't want to get mentally ill, but I have to keep it all inside and be patient. That's all I can do.

This interview was very difficult to conduct because the individual became extremely distressed on a number of occasions, and while transcription does not fully convey the extent to which he was affected by being the only Deaf person at HMP Wilmslow, it does provide an indication of the way he was feeling. A further example of this is provided in the following extract from the interview:

> Participant: It's a real problem for me inside. I keep it in. We are communicating now at this appointment, and I was EXCITED to come here. I was excited to see you because I knew I would be communicating with people. But out there I have to hold it all in, and I really do struggle.
> Interviewer: So is it nice to have somebody that you can sign with then?
> Participant: Yeah. It is.
> Interviewer: Okay. Just a couple of questions, I know I've kept you for ages so thank you.
> Participant: *Starts crying*
> Staff: I'll go and get a tissue.
> Interviewer: Oh no, are you okay? Are you alright?
> Participant: Yeah, I just get upset because I need to communicate. If I was in a Deaf prison, I would be able to communicate so it is really emotional for me.

Conclusion

This short chapter has provided a brief insight into the findings from my doctoral research, which has highlighted the presence of a group of prisoners in establishments throughout England and Wales who are often forced to exist in almost complete isolation, with little option for rehabilitation or inclusion in prison life. By drawing attention to the significant issues currently being faced by Deaf people in prison, my research has shown that the Prison Service is currently failing to meet the needs of these prisoners, or to adhere to the Equality Act 2010 in any consistent way.

Acknowledgements

I would like to thank my PhD supervisors Martin O'Brien, David Scott and Frank Harrington for all of their help throughout the duration of my PhD. Martin, you are amazing – you transformed my PhD with our brainstorming sessions, your dedication and your belief in me. David, your knowledge, support and humour, particularly over the last few months, has been so brilliant, and I am so incredibly grateful for that. Finally, Frank, thank you for helping me to learn about the lives of a group of people for whom I previously knew nothing about, and for your patience with me (the highest maintenance PhD student ever!).

When I started my PhD I had no idea what it would actually entail, or the level to which it would take over my life. I am so lucky that I have the support network around me that I do – my mum, my dad, my grandparents, my Uncle Mike – to you all, you have helped me so much – thank you. Most of all, I have to thank Tom Corless; without you I could not have done it. I truly couldn't. You are my rock, and I am so incredibly, incredibly grateful that I have you, and my life with you.

Finally, as always, to the prisoners and staff members who were involved in my research – I hope my research has done your views justice, and I hope that it goes at least some way to improving the experiences of d/Deaf people in prison going forwards.

References

Ackerman, N. (1998) *Deafness and Prisons - A Study of Services for Deaf Prisoners and the Experience of being Deaf within a Prison Environment* [An unpublished dissertation] Oxford: Oxford Brookes University

Baker, C. and Padden, C. (1978) *American Sign Language: A Look at its Story Structure and Community* Silver Spring, MD: T.J. Publishers Inc

Cheney, D. (2005) 'Prisoners' pp 547-566 in Hale, C. Hayward, K. Wahidin, A. Wincup, E. (eds) *Criminology* Oxford: Oxford University Press

Fisken, R. (1994) *The Deaf in Prison* (unpublished dissertation) Cambridge: University of Cambridge

Gerrard, H. (2001) *Double Sentence* Birmingham: BID

Goffman, E. (1961) *Asylums* New York: Anchor

Higgins, P. (1980) *Outsiders in a Hearing World: A Sociology of Deafness* London: SAGE

Higgins, P. (2002) 'Outsiders in a Hearing World' pp 23-31 in Gregory, S. and Hartley, G. (eds) *Constructing Deafness* London: Pinter

Izycky, A. and Gahir, M. (2007) *The Adverse Effects of Imprisonment on Deaf Prisoners' Mental Health: A Human Rights Perspective.* [Online] Available from: www.britsoc.co.uk/NR/rdonlyres/8EA09898-A67A-4B68-91D6-BFC589345D9D/0/AdverseEffectsofImprisonment.ppt (accessed 3rd April 2013)

Ladd, P. (2003) *Understanding Deaf Culture: In Search of Deafhood* Clevedon: Multilingual Matters

Lane, H. Hoffmeister, R. Bahan, B. (1996) *A Journey into the Deaf World* San Diego: Dawn Sign Press

Mann, N. (2016) 'Older Age, Harder Time: Ageing and Imprisonment' pp 514-529 in Jewkes, Y. Crewe, B. And Bennett, J. (eds) *Handbook on Prisons* Second Edition London: Routledge

McCulloch, D. (2010) *Not Hearing us? A Critical Exploration of the Current Experiences of Profoundly Deaf Prisoners in Anglo Welsh Prisons* (unpublished dissertation) Birmingham: Birmingham City University

McCulloch, D. (2012) *Not Hearing Us: An Exploration of the Experience of Deaf Prisoners in English and Welsh prisons. A Report for the Howard League for Penal Reform* London: The Howard League for Penal Reform

Moore, L. and Scraton, P. (2013) *The Incarceration of Women: Punishing Bodies, Breaking Spirits* London: Palgrave

O'Rourke, S. and Reed, R. (2007) 'Deaf People and the Criminal Justice System' pp 257-274 in Austen, S. and Jeffery, D (eds) *Deafness and Challenging Behaviour: The 360 Perspective* Chichester: John Wiley & Sons

Phillips, C. (2012) *The Multicultural Prison: Ethnicity, Masculinity, and Social Relations among Prisoners* Oxford: Oxford University Press

Reuss, A. (2000) 'The Researcher's Tale' pp 24-48 in Wilson, D. and Reuss, A. (eds) *Prison(er) Education: Stories of Change and Transformation* Hook: Waterside Press

Royal National Institute for the Deaf (1995) *Disabled Prisoners' Needs: The Urgency of a Policy Response* London: RNID

Scott, D. and Codd, H. (2010) *Controversial Issues in Prisons* Maidenhead: Open University Press

Sykes, G. (1958) *The Society of Captives: A Study of a Maximum Security prison* Princeton, N.J: Princeton University Press

Extended Biography

Research

I studied Criminal Justice and Criminology at the University of Leeds from 2007-2010. I then went on to complete an MA in Criminal Justice studies at the University of Leeds, receiving a distinction. As part of my MA I carried out qualitative prison research at HMP Leeds looking at the role of arts based programmes in the desistance process, which then inspired me to do a PhD. However, while I knew that I wanted to do a PhD in the field of prison studies, I did not know the exact direction I wanted to take. At this point I began to look at advertised PhDs, and saw that the University of Central Lancashire was advertising a bursary for an interdisciplinary doctorate, combining the fields of Deaf studies and prison studies, and looking at the experiences of Deaf people in prison. I was immediately fascinated by this, having never given meaningful consideration to the experiences of such a group in prison, and knowing very little about d/Deafness more broadly. After deciding to apply for the PhD and being successful in my application, I began my doctorate in January 2013 and submitted in 2016.

My PhD thesis examined the experiences of hard of hearing and d/Deaf people across the prison estate in England and Wales, providing a rigorous and more detailed understanding about their lives than was previously known. In doing this, a picture was painted of a group of individuals whose lives often become characterised by isolation, frustration, anxiety and subordination, and for whom the pains of imprisonment are undoubtedly intensified. As part of this research a qualitative methodology was adopted, with semi-structured interviews being carried out with hard of hearing, severely deaf, and profoundly Deaf prisoners, and staff members across seven prisons in England, and observations being made at each establishment.

While promoting policy change was not a core aim of the thesis, the findings presented throughout had obvious implications for Prison Service policy. In order to ensure that establishments are able to comply with the legal stipulations of the Equality Act 2010 going forwards, a set of recommendations for change for the Prison Service were outlined in the concluding chapter of the thesis. I am aiming to disseminate this information across a number of places, with the hope of attaining some positive change.

Currently, I am preparing a number of articles for publication based on the findings of my PhD research. As part of my role as a Criminology lecturer at the University of Central Lancashire I am also running a pilot scheme at a local prison, facilitating debates on contemporary topics with students and prisoners. The aim of this is to break down boundaries and to create a positive environment where all participants can learn together as equals.

Activism, Organisational Work and/or Professional Membership
I am a member of the Howard League for Penal Reform, the Prison Research Network, and the European Group for the Study of Deviance and Social Control.

Future Aspirations
Going forwards I would like to raise awareness about the issues faced by d/Deaf people in prison. I hope to publish my findings widely with the aim of contributing to some improvement in the provisions for these prisoners. While I was mindful to ensure that I did not become "contaminated by sympathy" (Reuss, 2000: 40) during the research process, I found it extremely difficult to hear about the extent of the problems that these individuals face in the prison environment, and I very much hope that my research can change that, even if it is just in the smallest way. Another aspiration of mine is to secure a book contract to publish my thesis as a single authored book, something which I will begin working towards in the near future.

As the subject of d/Deaf people in prison (and the criminal justice system more broadly) is so under-researched, there is also significant scope for me to do further research on this topic, and to build on what I have already found. Furthermore, as part of the research process I kept fieldwork journals detailing my thoughts and feelings about my time in prison, and I would also like to publish these in some form, as these experiences had a profound impact on me both during and after the fieldwork was over.

Selected Works

Kelly, L. M. (2014) 'Imprisoned by Deafness: The Experiences of Deaf Prisoners' European Group for the Study of Deviance and Social Control, July 2014 Newsletter

Kelly, L. (2017) 'HMP Kirkham: Student/Prisoner Debate' *UCLan Law Blog* [online] Available From: https://uclanlaw.co.uk/2017/02/09/hmp-kirkham-studentprisoner-debate/

Kelly, L. (forthcoming) 'Sounding out d/Deafness: The Experiences of d/Deaf Prisoners', *The Journal of Criminal Psychology* [Prison Research Network Special Edition entitled: PRisoN Research: Expanding our Network]

Contact Details
Email: lauramargaretkelly@gmail.com
Twitter: @lauramargaret3

13

An Alternative to Zero-Tolerance Policies? The Project Implemented in the Multi-Ethnic 'Piave' Neighbourhood in Mestre, Venice

Claudia Mantovan

Introduction

This chapter reflects upon achievable policies within the neighbourhoods where there has been an increase in the presence and visibility of immigrants and socially excluded people, which gives rise to the phenomena of social conflict, through the case study of the *quartiere Piave* in Mestre (Venice)[1]. Adopting a critical criminological approach, this research[2] deconstructs the dominant narratives describing petty crime as the biggest problem in these types of neighbourhoods. The problems experienced by residents and shop-owners are much more complex and are rather the result of environmental and social incivility, low levels of interpersonal and institutional trust, and the poor quality of the urban

---

[1] Mestre forms part of the municipality of Venice but, unlike the islands of the city's historical centre, it is on the mainland.

[2] The chapter describes some of the results of a research project entitled *La partecipazione di autoctoni e migranti alla vita della città come fattore di sicurezza urbana: due casi studio nei Comuni di Padova e Venezia* [Participation of the autochthonous and immigrant populations in city life as a factor of urban security: two case studies in the municipalities of Padua and Venice], designed by Claudia Mantovan and funded by the *Fondazione Cassa di Risparmio di Padova e Rovigo*. The research was conducted from January 2011 to January 2014, based on a composite method: review of background data on the districts under analysis; press review of the daily newspapers *Il Mattino di Padova* and *La Nuova Venezia* (two daily newspapers from Padua and Venice, respectively); ethnographic observation in the public spaces and retail shops in the districts; 50 semi-structured interviews with politicians, spokespeople from the citizens' committees, exponents of the autochthonous associations and cooperatives, and of the associations of immigrants; analysis of the documentation produced by the local administrations, district councils and other organisations. The full results of the research were published in Mantovan and Ostanel, 2015.

spaces. Beginning in 2006, Venice City Council implemented a project that aims to be an alternative to the quite popular 'zero tolerance' policies that emerged in the 1990s in many Western cities. The project's aim is to recognise, and therefore manage, the complex and multifaceted nature of the problems that affect a neighbourhood that is undergoing rapid social changes, where an autochthonous community that is also, to a large degree, elderly, is increasingly exposed to daily interactions with people of different ethnicities, cultures and social mores. This chapter analyses the Venice City Council project, highlighting its strengths and pointing out its limitations, in an effort to distil those elements that may be useful in understanding and implementing policies to manage an increasing super-diversity (Vertovec, 2007) within the neighbourhoods of many Western cities.

Rising Protests in the Piave Neighbourhood: the Problems Experienced by Residents and Shopkeepers

In May 2006, some residents of the Piave district called a meeting to complain about their area's problems. The tone of the meeting was 'inflamed': the citizens protested loudly, calling for a stronger police presence in the district. What triggered their concern was the fact that the pedestrian zone in San Francesco square had become a meeting place for people with drug problems, but the issues they discussed were broader, including the rapid demographic and commercial transformation underway in the district as a result of the rising numbers of immigrants among residents and shopkeepers. A review of the citizenship status of residents and shopkeepers of the neighbourhood, compared with the figures from the entire Council area, does indeed reveal that this neighbourhood hosts many foreigners. Whereas immigrant residents make up 10.8% (29,281 persons) of the total population in the Venice Council (270,884 persons), they constitute 24% (5,079 persons) of the total population of the Piave neighbourhood (21,082 persons). Regarding the neighbourhood businesses: of the 124 located on via Piave street, the neighbourhood's main artery which connects the railway station to the city centre, 32 (25.8%) are managed by foreigners as opposed to the 92 (74.2%) operated by Italians.

Certain trends underway in Western cities today are indeed particularly evident in areas near railway stations (such as the *quartiere Piave*, fronting the Mestre's railway station), and include: an increasing social complexity, ethnic and cultural diversity; social fragmentation;

growing social exclusion; and the construction of material and symbolic boundaries between different social groups. Despite the dominant representation of this district as highly insecure, the interviews with residents and shopkeepers show that only a minority state that they have been victims of a crime. Most of the problems reported by them have to do with episodes of turf wars among drug dealers, fighting among immigrants who may have had too much to drink, relief of bodily functions on the streets, leaving rubbish such as empty bottles, rude or intimidating behaviour (such as cat calls to female pedestrians from drug dealers, or mendicancy). Several people complained about immigrants simply being in public areas (the word choice reveals an *us/them* rift, and the feeling of having been invaded) as well as the high concentration of 'ethnic' businesses in the neighbourhood. The locals complained about the progressive disappearance of locally owned and operated businesses, on the one hand because they represented a social landmark, especially for the elderly, but also because the merchandise sold at the immigrants' stores are not as appealing to them. Other issues highlighted by those who were interviewed relate to chaotic and excessive traffic, insufficient green space as well as a lack of meeting spaces and common areas.

The Entrance of *Equipe Territoriale Aggregazione Minorile* (ETAM) and of the *Gruppo di lavoro Piave*: a 'Kaleidoscope' of Schemes Co-ordinated by the Local Authority

In response to the aforementioned angry meeting in the Piave district, the local authority tried to enlist these individuals and involve them directly in organising action to deal more constructively with the problems they reported. Rather than simply heeding the protests of some by strengthening policing and repression of the 'problematic' segments of the population, the Venice Council's coordinated effort in the Piave neighbourhood attempts to operate directly on the diverse and complex causes of residents' and shopkeepers' dissatisfaction. It does so by promoting a process of communication and familiarity among the various ethnic, social and generational groups within the neighbourhood, as well as improving the quality of public areas. In particular, the then alderman for social policies appointed the local authority's *Equipe Territoriale Aggregazione Minorile* (ETAM) unit, specialising in Community and Territorial Animation, to take action in the Piave district. Two ETAM educators were assigned to a project for the Piave district. Consistently with the community animation approach, these educators promoted activities that were to be organised by small groups of residents. This gave birth to the *Gruppo di lavoro Piave* [Piave working group]. This working group has chosen to remain informal, and is loosely composed of about 15 people, almost all of them autochthonous district residents with a medium-to-high formal education. The majority of them are pensioners. Since this category of person has more free time; anyway, a number of more heterogeneous people in terms of age and national origin collaborate with the group, even though it is in a less systematic way.

In cooperation with ETAM, the working group began to organise a number of micro-activities and micro-projects that all served the general purpose of promoting mutual understanding, social harmony and cohesion in the Piave area. At the 'heart' of the measures implemented by the Piave working group and ETAM there are, above all, actions that focus on socio-cultural animation and the promotion of intercultural encounters. One of the flagship undertakings is undeniably the multi-ethnic choir *Voci dal Mondo* [Voices from the world]. Other activities have become well established too, like the 'barter markets' for children and adolescents up to 13 years old, or the *cena di quartiere* [street party].

Another aspect of the complex and multifaceted kaleidoscope of measures for the Piave district, concerns the work done on the topic of communication, perceptions and representations, undertaken mainly through the medium of the figurative arts. A periodical entitled *Le voci di via Piave* [Voices of the Piave road] aims to challenge the distorted and alarmist pictures of the district painted by the local press. Various public meetings have been organised about local residents' security issues too, and on the changes underway in the district. Several photography exhibitions have been held too, showing old and new citizens of Mestre and the Piave area, also with a view to providing food for thought on the social phenomena underway in the district.

The fact that so many coordinated, and coherent schemes have been implemented in the Piave district, is largely thanks to the local authority's role as 'director' and coordinator, through its ETAM unit. On several occasions during our interviews, the founders of the Piave working group mentioned how important the ETAM unit's support had been to the success of their undertakings.

Another effect of the project has been to pinpoint those immigrants with a stronger desire to commit themselves to the territory, to join forces and develop a network, and to emerge on the public stage. Also several exponents of a committee called *Un impegno per la città* [A commitment to the city] (established by a number of Piave district residents living nearest to the railway station to protest against the area's urban decay) have quite often been involved in activities promoted by the Piave working group. The work done by the ETAM educators thus also involves listening to the citizens (and especially to those taking a more confrontational stance), making them feel that the institutions take an interest in their needs, and helping them put their problems in the right perspective.

The Episode of *via Monte San Michele* and *via Trento*, and the Interrupted Mediation

However, there is an area within the neighbourhood where ETAM's attempt to involve the residents in a process of mediation with those accused of being the source of urban decay did not have a positive outcome: the part of *via Monte San Michele* that intersects with *via Trento*, which also happens to be closest to the railway station. In the span of just a few years, several businesses have sprung up that are managed by Sub-Saharian immigrants, mainly Nigerian. These shops have attracted a population of African customers, most of whom reside in other neighbouring councils, and have become a social gathering point as well as a place where customers find merchandise from their home countries. African customers would buy beer from their fellow countryperson's shop, and then drink and socialise while sitting on the narrow footpaths in front of the business; the groups could sometimes swell up to around fifty people. Those who tended to converge in this manner seemed, for the most part, to belong to lower-middle social strata (unemployed, day labourers), and appeared to be somewhat isolated from the other immigrant' communities of the neighbourhood, who were instead able to coalesce into more visible forms of associations. The African shops are located on the ground floor of residential high rise buildings, whose residents started to complain about: loitering patrons who obstructed access; loud noise and yelling; some patrons repeatedly urinating in the rubbish bins; the habit of leaving glass beer bottles lying around on the floor; supposed drug dealing and drug use on the premises; and the occasional fight or brawl amongst immigrants. In this area, after some attempts at social mediation carried out by an ETAM operator which have not been successful among residents, the local government's choice was to counter the presence of African regulars by forcing some African shops to close at 2.30 pm. Between the conflicting interests of the

African immigrants (for the shopkeepers, to be able to operate their businesses in the most profitable hours; for the customers, to have a social point of reference), and those of the local residents, the decision was made to drastically favour the latter.

Concluding Remarks

A positive aspect of the Venice Council's action in the Piave neighbourhood is the positive and proactive role of the local government in guiding and promoting a form of *governance* that networks and values several social actors operating in the area (*Gruppo di lavoro Piave*, immigrants' associations, citizens' groups). Several scholars have highlighted the importance of a local government that is able to guide and shape the evolution of its geographic area, by promoting and coordinating a network of public and private stakeholders in the various sectors of policy making (see: Germain, 2012; Bassoli, 2011; Pitch, 2001).

A major critical aspect among many is, surely, the difficulty of having to tackle issues that in part have a global nature, such as rise in immigration, social exclusion, and the shift from a social state to a penal state (Wacquant, 1999) with local remedies. The recent birth of more 'citizens' committees' in Mestre, and some of the measures undertaken by the local government (such as removing park benches, or forcing the early closure of some businesses run by immigrants) remind us that the issues are far from being resolved. The objective of some politicians in the Council of Venice to deconstruct the dominant 'safety' paradigm, and to interpret security as much as possible as social security and, as the security of the rights of everyone (Baratta, 2001), is constantly being undermined by protests from some of the residents, on the one hand, and on the other by the politicians' and the police's irresistible urge to pander to them; a phenomenon that is in part happening in Mestre like in other places. This is especially true for those situations that are more complicated and difficult to manage, such as the one in *Monte San Michele* street at the corner with *Trento* street, where a repressive approach is seemingly easier and quicker to implement, and is a lot more useful in how it plays out politically, insofar as it appeals to the constituents' point of view, as opposed to social assistance projects of a medium and long term nature, where results cannot be predicted with confidence.

The story of Mestre's 'African corner' also highlights a further issue: measures aimed at 'developing a community', ironically, are the hardest to implement in areas that need them most, where the high turnover of residents makes stable and long lasting relations hard to develop. In order for these initiatives to 'stick' and be successful, there needs to be a core 'community' that is stable and pre-existing. Moreover, the process requires people with economic, cultural and social resources who are willing to take an active role and participate (as is the case of the *Gruppo di lavoro Piave*). These community-based initiatives typically see the participation of white-caucasian citizens who are for the most part of upper-middle class extraction (Herbert, 2006; Davis, 1998): at a local level it appears that the deliberative process favours citizen organisations composed by these particular types (Melo and Baiocchi, 2006). This is the reason why a governance approach occasionally runs the risk of 'empowering the powerful' (Bassoli, 2011): in governance instances, the presence of less organised and structured associations are scarce, as they often do not have the staff resources to participate actively in functions of a participant nature. Therefore, those members of civil society who should theoretically be the main contributors (and, in part, the beneficiaries) of processes of *governance*, in reality often end up abandoning them. The fact that the project carried out in the Piave district failed to involve the less integrated and the most vulnerable immigrant groups demonstrates, as argued by critical approaches to the concept of 'social cohesion', that to promote social cohesion and intercultural dialogue we must not only act at the cultural level, but also at the material level, promoting social integration and work for all the people living in a city. There is no social cohesion without economic and social inclusion.

Acknowledgements

I would like to thank Samantha Fletcher and Holly White for having done such a great work of coordination to produce this edited book collection, and also for reading my chapter with care and attention, making meaningful suggestions and comments, and supervising the English translation.

References

Baratta, A. (2001) 'Diritto alla sicurezza o sicurezza dei diritti?' pp 22-36 in Anastasia, S. and Palma, M. (eds) (2001) *La bilancia e la misura. Giustizia, sicurezza, riforme* Milano: Franco Angeli

Bassoli, M. (2011) 'La governance locale: alcuni aspetti teorici' pp 15-37 in Bassoli, M. and Polizzi, E. (eds) (2011) *La governance del territorio. Partecipazione e rappresentanza della società civile nelle politiche locali* Milano: FrancoAngeli

Davis, M. (1998) *Ecology of fear: Los Angeles and imagination of disaster* New York: Metropolitan Books

Germain, S. (2012) 'Le retour des villes dans la gestion de la sécurité en France et en Italie' *Déviance et Société* Volume 36, No. 1 pp 61-84

Herbert, S. (2006) *Citizens, cops and power. Recognizing the limits of community* Chicago: The University of Chicago Press

Mantovan, C. and Ostanel, E. (2015) *Quartieri contesi. Convivenza, conflitti e governance nelle zone Stazione di Padova e Mestre* Milano: FrancoAngeli

Melo, M. and Baiocchi, G. (2006) 'Deliberative democracy and local governance: towards a new agenda' *International Journal of Urban and Regional Research* Volume 30, No. 3 pp 587-600

Pitch, T. (2001) 'Sono possibili politiche democratiche per la sicurezza?' *Rassegna Italiana di Sociologia*, Volume 42, No. 1 pp 137-156

Vertovec, S. (2007) 'Super-diversity and its implications' *Ethnic and Racial Studies*, Volume 30, pp 1024-1054

Wacquant, L. (1999) *Les prisons de la misère* Paris: Éditions Raisons d'Agir

Extended Biography

Research
My doctoral research, completed in 2005, addressed the theme 'citizenship and immigration' through the analysis of the forms of mobilisation and participation of migrants at the urban level in the Veneto Region (Italy). Thereafter, my focus shifted even more to the study of urban issues, and in particular, the urban effects (with particular reference to the processes of urban segregation) of general forms of stratification and inequality related to ethnicity, immigrants' legal status, social class; and the effects that spatial configurations have on social relations. In more detail, I have dealt with the effects in terms of the

social stigma of living in segregated urban areas inhabited almost exclusively by lower class immigrants. I also analysed some 'sensitive' neighbourhoods, studying their perception by residents, workers and city users; their representation in public and media discourse; the policies and projects caused by these representations and by the mobilisation of the inhabitants ('comitati di cittadini').

Entering into further detail of the research projects, the first project researched a desegregation programme carried forth by the city of Padua, in Anelli street, where there is a residential development made up of 6 buildings that saw a very high degree of ethnic segregation and social deviance (mainly drug dealing), beginning in the 1990s. The analysis of this case study was preceded by a review of the available academic literature pertaining to segregation processes and desegregation programs in the United States and in Europe (France in particular). Being familiar with the experience of other countries was a fundamental step in being able to analyse the case of Padua. Specifically, some of the exceptions taken by certain scholars to the programs that attempted to achieve urban renewal through a process of *mixité sociale*, were also proven to be relevant in Padua.

A second research project analysed an initiative of the Venice city council, aimed at facilitating Roma and Sinti's housing insertion. Where, at the national level, the traditional strategies usually resulted in either confinement into camps or into expulsion, this local policy took an alternative approach by actively tackling these groups' housing issues and needs. My research took stock of the advantages, as well as the flaws of the Venice project. A third research project on urban issues was titled: 'The participation of autochthonous and immigrant residents in city life as a factor of urban security: two case studies in the cities of Padua and Venice' and focused on two districts near the railway stations of Padua and Mestre (North-Eastern Italy). The comparison between these two areas is interesting because, generally speaking, in Italian cities of a certain size, the areas immediately surrounding the train station share similar characteristics: a high concentration of immigrant populations; a significant presence of foreign-owned businesses and retail; a more or less important presence of trade in illegal substances and prostitution; a visible presence of socially excluded people (such as the homeless); a local media characterisation of these areas as generally unsafe and degraded; and a high degree of urban conflict, often linked to the presence of social groups with conflicting needs (e.g. regarding the use of public spaces). In some ways these areas provide an extreme example of a series of processes that are increasingly prevalent in most major urban centres today, such as a higher degree of social complexity and diversity, fragmentation, social exclusion, the creation of material and symbolic walls separating different social groups from each other. The research project is divided into two parts: an analysis of the urban textures and contexts of the neighbourhoods, and of the issues affecting their population (residents, retailers, city users). The second thread is an in depth study of the policies enacted by local governments, to address the particular issues and needs that characterise these neighbourhoods. Interestingly, the two city councils approached similar problems with radically different solutions: whereas in Venice the local government addressed social integration and perception of safety with targeted measures and policies, Padua did nothing of the sort, neglecting to develop anything approaching an organic or pro-active stance on these matters. Beyond analysing local public policies, my research project also analyses private initiatives, stemming from neighbourhood programs and associations, in an effort to show the structure and activity of local policy networks, within the framework of urban governance.

Finally, in these last month's I'm engaged in a research project that deals with a very different topic: the project is titled "One jail, two sexes and three genders: the struggle concerning the gender binarism in Italian prisons" and the situation of transgender prisoners in Italy.

Selected Works

Mantovan, C. (2017) 'Contested areas. Coexistence, conflict and governance in the districts near the railway stations of Padua and Mestre (North-eastern Italy)' in *Justice, Power and Resistance* Volume 1, No. 1 (forthcoming)

Mantovan, C. (2013) 'Cohesion without Participation: Immigration and Migrants' Associations in Italy' in *Patterns of Prejudice* Volume 47, No. 3 pp. 253-268

Mantovan, C., (2012) 'Citoyens ou étrangers? Dynamiques d'inclusion et d'exclusion dans le conflit du village Sinti de Venise' in *Déviance et Société* Volume 36, No. 1 pp. 37-60

Mantovan, C. (2010) *Muslim self-organisation and State interaction with Muslim organisations in Italy* pp. 93-110 in Bodenstein, M. and Kreienbrink, A. (eds.) (2010) *Muslim Organisations and the State-European perspectives,* Nurnberg: Bundesamt für Migration und Flüchtlinge. Available from: http://eprints.whiterose.ac.uk/43692/2/Muslim%20Organisations%20and%2 0the%20State%20-European%20Perspectives.pdf (accessed 2nd April, 2017)

Mantovan C. (2006), 'Immigration and Citizenship: Participation and Self-organisation of Immigrants in the Veneto (North Italy)', in *Forum Qualitative*

Sozialforschung/Forum: Qualitative Social Research, Volume 7, No.3. Available from: www.qualitative-research.net/fqs-texte/3-06/06-3-4-e.htm (accessed 2nd April, 2017)

Contact Details
Academia Profile: https://transumanisti.academia.edu/ClaudiaMantovan

14

"...They Didn't Ask Us to Come Here, Did They?" The Pain of the Threat of Expulsion in a Contemporary Prison

Agnieszka Martynowicz

Introduction

On the 8th February 2016, the then British Prime Minister (PM) David Cameron delivered what was the first speech by a PM in over 20 years solely focusing on prison policy. While stating his belief that "prison reform should be a great progressive cause in British politics", unsurprisingly perhaps there was little new in Cameron's framing of how those 'reforms' should take place and the speech repeated many of the earlier proposals of the so-called 'rehabilitation revolution' (Bell, 2013). His starting point, he said, was that "we need prisons" and that "punishment" is not "a dirty word". In his view however, prisoners should not be seen "as simply liabilities to be managed" but as "potential assets to be harnessed" and in a "compassionate country" they should be offered "hope" and "chances to change" to find their "way back onto the right path". To aid the process of finding that "way", his 'vision' was that prisoners will be supported in gaining education, addressing mental health needs and substance misuse issues, and in finding employment on release. In a true neoliberal fashion (Bell, 2013), all of that was to be done hand-in-hand with a large-scale investment in building new, 'better' prisons.

Whatever the merits, or indeed a lack thereof, of the proposed reforms, there were a few sentences in Cameron's speech that, as a researcher focusing on the experiences of prisoners who are not British but are incarcerated in the UK, caught my particular attention. Cameron managed to further divide the already excluded and marginalised (all prisoners) into those 'deserving' of support (British prisoners) and those 'undeserving' ('foreign' prisoners). In the case of the latter, the PM's ideas for 'reform' revolved around earlier identification by the police and the courts to enable quicker and more efficient removal beyond the national borders. Rather than supported in any way, 'foreign' prisoners were to be *managed* and *expelled*; as the PM said: "[...] there is one group I do want out of prison more quickly, instead of British taxpayers forking out for their bed and breakfast: and that is foreign national offenders."

This divisive and differential approach is, of course, not new and dates back to the 2006 'foreign national prisoner scandal' when it transpired that just over 1,000 non-British prisoners were released between 1999 and 2006 without consideration for deportation. The political 'storm' that followed forced the resignation of the then Home Secretary Charles Clarke and resulted in consecutive British governments focusing their efforts on creating the legal and policy framework for the 'management' of this group in and beyond custody. A separate system of 'foreign national'-only and "hubs and spokes" prisons with embedded immigration enforcement personnel was created, and bureaucratic mechanisms for "finding foreigners" (Kaufman, 2015: 114) were introduced across the prison system. The government's powers to expel were strengthened through the introduction of an automatic consideration for deportation in the *UK Borders Act 2007* while opportunities for prisoners to resist removal were curbed through the imposition of strict limits on access to legal aid and the introduction of the "deport first, appeal later" principle in the *Immigration Act 2014.* The government also invests large amounts of money to support this system, with the spend estimated in 2014 at £850m per year (National Audit Office, 2014). The UK's central focus in respect of 'foreign' prisoners is to effect as many expulsions as possible in the shortest possible time and the government deports over 5,000 people a year (National Audit Office, 2014).

At the same time, the daily lives of 'foreign' prisoners remain "one of the most routinely overlooked aspects of imprisonment" (Kaufman, 2012: 701). Although their vulnerability has long been acknowledged and their differential experience of prison 'regimes' increasingly documented (see, for example, Bhui, 2007; 2009; Cheney, 1993; HM Inspectorate of Prisons, 2006; 2007), there is still limited knowledge of how prisoners of different nationalities cope with their lives in prisons and what their relationships are with other prisoners and staff. My doctoral research, on which this chapter is based, was designed to explore those experiences with a group of Polish male prisoners incarcerated in Northern Ireland. The study also considered how their 'foreignness' impacts on how they experience pains of imprisonment (Sykes, 2007) and how they adapt to what is a harsh reality of prison life. Eighteen prisoners were interviewed, either individually or in small groups; views were also sought of a small number of prison staff and representatives of prison monitoring bodies. Observations of aspects of the prison 'regime' also formed part of the fieldwork. The research found that many Polish prisoners experience the pains of confinement in ways that are different and distinct to 'British' or 'Irish' prisoners.[1] This chapter, however, focuses on one of the new pains identified during the study and specifically experienced by this group: the pain of the threat of expulsion. It is to a discussion of that experience that this chapter now turns.

Living With Uncertainty and Under the Threat of Expulsion

Although the research did not set out to explore the prisoners' experiences of deportability, it quickly became evident that the threat of expulsion loomed large over Polish prisoners' time in custody. Eight out of the eighteen interviewees were potentially facing deportation, while a further six faced extradition under the European Arrest Warrant. While deportation and extradition differ in legal terms, much of the experience of the actual process is the same. Uncertainty, concern about the complexity of the legal processes related to expulsion, and most of all concern about their future lives and those of their families, were shared regardless of whether the person was to be removed to face criminal proceedings in Poland, or to be removed after serving a sentence in Northern Ireland. Where those experiences did diverge was in the area of legal advice, access to interpretation and access to the courts, with those facing deportation often left to negotiate the process on their own or with the help of other prisoners due to limited access to other resources.

Partly because of that, the majority of prisoners potentially faced with deportation did not resist it, and two specifically mentioned that they wished to return to Poland as soon as possible. Nevertheless, the prospect of removal understandably caused a lot of anxiety, and its process led to many frustrations. This usually began with the prisoners being asked by the immigration authorities to fill in lenghty questionnaires in English about many aspects of their lives, and without access to interpretation. The Home Office does not provide any translated documents and some prisoners felt pressurised into signing

---

[1] While the official definition of a 'foreign national prisoner' in England, Wales and Scotland includes anyone who does not have a British citizenship, in Northern Ireland the exclusion of 'Irish' prisoners from such categorisation reflects the right to either citizenship conferred on anyone born in Northern Ireland.

documentation without proper understanding while others understood that they agreed to be removed, but were not clear what the conditions of their deportation were; for example what would be their chances of ever returning to the UK if they were to be expelled. No advice was provided to most of the men as to how to deal with matters such as accessing their bank accounts in Northern Ireland to transfer money before or after their removal, how to access and pack their belongings left outside of the prison walls, or about any other practical aspect of deportation. Having been told that he will be deported, Artur[2] had many questions in a research group interview: "And how do they do that? How does it look like, do you know? Will they take me from here to the airport? How?" Some prisoners felt angry about the prospect of being held in immigration detention after their sentence while awaiting removal. As Jerzy stated,

> [When being deported] you have to go to England and spend two, three days in England, and only then to Poland. This is some kind of a joke! Because once I've agreed to being deported, then maybe I would like to be deported directly to Poland? I don't need to see a deportation centre in England!

Jerzy was not sure if he ever would in fact be held in immigration detention, and that uncertainty was frustrating for him. While some prisoners thought that they would only be detained if they were contesting the deportation order, others were aware that detention was possible for other reasons (such as lack of transport to Poland). It was the often lenghty wait for any information about the process of deportation or the decision from the immigration authorities that was the most painful. Kuba was asked to fill in the Home Office questionnaire at the beginning of his sentence, and while he asked to see his solicitor about it, three months later he was still waiting for someone to contact him. Paweł, who was serving two years in prison, completed his initial documentation in the first month following committal but seven months before his conditional release date, he did not know whether he would be deported or not. Bartosz, whose solicitor helped him to fill in the Home Office paperwork, was then told by the lawyer: "Maybe you will be deported, maybe not." In the information and decision-making vacuum, prisoners were trying to get some advice from other prisoners and stories

---

[2] All names are pseudonyms.

were often exchanged between them reflecting on previous experience of people they knew to have been deported. This often meant that information was contradictory and partial, increasing the feelings of anxiety and adding to apprehension about what their futures would look like. In the meantime, their release plans were put on hold as they were unable to prepare for their life after prison while not knowing where that life would be.

Discussion and Conclusions

In much of the popular discourse, migrants "continue to be portrayed as inherently dangerous, posing an existential threat to the body politic, to our way of life [...] to our standard of living, our public services, our safety and security" (Webber, 2012: 5). The "myth of immigrant crime and of immigrants as a dangerous class" (De Giorgi, 2010: 154) is used to generate societal consensus to exclusion and fear is utilised to justify the casting of "the carceral net around [...] those excluded because of their ethnicity or nationality" (Phillips, 2012: 4). When inside that net, the "bureaucratic classification" as a 'foreigner' legitimises their discriminatory treatment, "by eroding the sense of moral responsibility towards them and making the differential, more intensive application of coercive powers against this group acceptable and compatible with the standards of decency upheld in [liberal] societies" (Aliverti, 2016: 127).

That abrogation of moral responsibility is clearly articulated in Cameron's statement quoted in the introduction to this chapter that "British taxpayers" should not be obliged to "fork out" the costs of keeping 'foreigners' in prisons. Instead, deportation is seen "as a ritualized method of reasserting state authority, reinforcing a collective resentment against the groups assumed to disrupt the national order, and obscuring state responsibility for immigrant integration" (Phillips, 2012: 16). 'Foreign' prisoners are therefore doubly-punished, "not simply [just] for the crime committed, but for doing so as outsiders" (Bosworth and Guild, 2008: 712). As Aas (2013) points out by drawing on Stumpf's (2006) concept of "crimmigration", it can even be argued that contemporary "crimmigration systems" – epitomised in the UK by the network of "hubs and spokes" and 'foreign national'-only prisons - are less concerned with punishment and more with the physical removal of the person beyond national borders as a symbol of final moral rejection (Sykes, 2007).

Defining certain prisoners as 'foreigners' from the moment of entry into the prison has serious consequences for their experiences of detention and there is a growing recognition that pains of imprisonment are exacerbated by a person's status as a 'foreign national prisoner' (see, for example, Bosworth, *et al*, 2016; Warr, 2016). Over the last thirty or so years, their treatment has become stagnant in its exclusionary character and it appears that a culture of permissiveness has been instilled in relation to non-provision of support. Many, as I observed elsewhere (Martynowicz, 2016), serve their time at a considerable distance from other prisoners (outside of their immediate national group) and staff, and are often forced by their circumstances into self-reliance. Their vulnerabililty is increased due to lingustic exclusion and their "welfare and rehabilitation needs are becoming invisible" as they are "doubly disadvantaged through being at the mercy of the immigration and prison systems" (Cooney, 2013: 51).

That ever-present threat of expulsion needs to be defined as a distinct pain of imprisonment. Whether connected to extradition or deportation proceedings, this threat instilled in the Polish prisoners interviewed for this research a deep sense of uncertainty and of what I call a *temporariness of belonging* to both the 'prisoner society' and the society outside of the prison walls. While awaiting final decisions about their futures, some tried to salvage at least parts of their lives in Northern Ireland, attempting to make arrangements for their money and belongings to be ready for when they eventually have to leave. Mostly, however, they wanted to be treated with respect and to be afforded an opportunity to understand their own situation and the consequences of their decisions, taken while facing the deportation system. Even that opportunity was not always afforded to them and while some actively challenged differential treatment, others seemed resigned to their situation. As Artur put it, with certain sadness, "...they didn't ask us to come here, did they?".

An extended version of this chapter has been published as Martynowicz, A. (2017) 'Uncertainty, Complexity, Anxiety – Deportation and the Prison in the Case of Polish Prisoners in Northern Ireland' in Archiwum Kryminologii Vol.XXXVIII/2016 pp 425-439.

Acknowledgments

I would like to thank all the men who took part in my research and who so generously shared their experiences with me. Already during the fieldwork, and as my PhD thesis was being written, many of them were facing deportation or extradition, leaving behind their adopted homes in the North of Ireland and with them often their hopes for a better future. I do not know where many of them are today but this research would not have existed without them. For that, I will always owe them a debt of gratitude. This research was supported by the Department for Employment and Learning Postgraduate Research Scholarship.

References

Aas, K. F. (2013) 'The Ordered and the Bordered Society: Migration Control, Citizenship and the Northern Penal State" pp 21-39 in Aas, K. F. and Bosworth, M. (eds) *The Borders of Punishment. Migration, Citizenship, and Social Exclusion* Oxford: Oxford University Press

Aliverti, A. (2016) 'Doing Away With Decency?: Foreigners, Punishment and the Liberal State' pp 124-144 in Eriksson, A. (ed) *Punishing the Other: The Social Production of Immorality Revisited* Oxon: Routledge

Bell, E. (2013) 'The Prison paradox in Neoliberal Britain' pp 44-64 in Scott, D. (ed) *Why Prison?* Cambridge: Cambridge University Press

Bhui, H.S. (2007) 'Alien Experience: Foreign National Prisoners After the Deportation Crisis' in *Probation Journal* Volume 54, No. 4, pp 368-382

Bhui, H. S. (2009) 'Foreign National Prisoners: Issues and Debates' pp 154-169 in Bhui, H. S. (ed) *Race and Criminal Justice* London: SAGE

Bosworth, M. and Guild, M. (2008) 'Governing Through Migration Control' in *British Journal of Criminology* Volume 48, No.6 pp 703-719

Bosworth, M., Hasselberg, I. and Turnbull, S. (2016) 'Imprisonment in a Global World: Rethinking Penal Power' pp 698-711 in Jewkes, Y., Crewe, B. and Bennett, J. (eds) *Handbook on Prisons* Second Edition Oxon: Routledge

Cameron, D. (2016) *Prison Reform: Prime Minister's Speech, 8 February 2016* [online] Available from: https://www.gov.uk/government/speeches/prison-reform-prime-ministers-speech (accessed 06th March 2017)

Cheney, D. (1993) *Into the Dark Tunnel: Foreign Prisoners in the British Prison System* London: Prison Reform Trust

Cooney, F. (2013) 'Double Punishment: The Treatment of Foreign National Prisoners' in *Prison Service Journal* No. 205 January 2013 pp 45-51

De Giorgi, A. (2010) 'Immigration Control, post-Fordism, and Less Eligibility. A Materialist Critique of the Criminalization of Immigration in Europe' in *Punishment and Society* Volume 12, No.2 pp 147-167

HM Inspectorate of Prisons (HMIP)(2006) *Foreign National Prisoners: A Thematic Review* London: HMIP

HM Inspectorate of Prisons (HMIP)(2007) *Foreign National Prisoners: A Follow-up Report* London: HMIP

Kaufman, E. (2012) 'Finding Foreigners: Race and the Politics of Memory in British Prisons' in *Population, Space and Place* Volume,18, No. 6 pp 701-714

Kaufman, E. (2015) *Punish and Expel: Border Control, Nationalism, and the New Purpose of the Prison* Oxford: Oxford University Press

Martynowicz, A. (2016) 'Not So Multicultural Prison: Polish Prisoners in a Transitional prison system' in *Criminology and Criminal Justice* Volume 16, No.3 pp 337-349

National Audit Office (2014) *Managing and Removing Foreign National Offenders* London: House of Commons

Phillips, C. (2012) *The Multicultural Prison: Ethnicity, Masculinity, and Social Relations Among Prisoners* Oxford: Oxford University Press

Stumpf, J.P. (2006) 'The Crimmigration Crisis: Immigrants, Crime, and Sovereign Power' in *bepress* Legal Series Working Paper 1635 (online) Available from http://law.bepress.com/expresso/eps/1635 (accessed 6th March 2017)

Sykes, G.M. (2007) *The Society of Captives: A Study of a Maximum Security Prison* Second Edition Princeton: Princeton University Press

Warr, J. (2016) 'The deprivation of certitude, legitimacy and hope: Foreign national prisoners and the pains of imprisonment' in *Criminology and Criminal Justice* Volume 16, No.3 pp 301-318

Webber, F. (2012) *Borderline justice: The Fight for Refugee and Migrant Rights* London: Pluto

Extended Biography

Research

Much of both my formal education and research interests sit across Law and Criminology. I graduated with an MA in Law and Legal Sciences from University of Warsaw in 1998 where my dissertation examined the role of non-governmental organisations in supporting prisoners. I later gained an LLM in Human Rights Law (Distinction) from Queen's University Belfast in 2004, having researched the rights of victims appearing before international criminal tribunals. In September 2016, I successfully defended my doctoral thesis which explored the experiences of prison custody in Northern Ireland by Polish, male prisoners. I was subsequently awarded a PhD by the School of Criminology, Politics and Social Policy, Ulster University. Also in September 2016, I took up a lecturer post in the Department of Law and Criminology at Edge Hill University.

My PhD research came out of a long-standing concern about, and an interest, in the experiences of people held in detention. I first crossed the gate of a prison in 1996 when I was a *Street Law* tutor in the Rakowiecka Prison in Warsaw. I still remember the moment of realisation that any of the 16 men who took part in our classes could be our family members – our Dads, Granddads or uncles, brothers or partners … – I also remember the feeling of relief each time we left the prison behind, and its horrible smell of strong disinfectants, and the feeling of sadness that the men with whom we were learning could not easily do the same. I knew then that what started as an educational experience, will stay with me as a life-long interest. Co-incidentally, I also attended my first ever conference of the European Group in 1996 in Bangor, Wales, which with its critical focus and inclusive ethos immediately felt like an academic home.

Although I visited different prisons in Poland, Lithuania, and England and Wales after 1996, the first opportunity to work on prison issues arose when I joined the Northern Ireland Human Rights Commission (NIHRC) in 2005 as a Research Worker. There, I was privileged to work with Linda Moore and later also Ann Jemphrey, organising regular monitoring visits to places of detention; responding to policy proposals, and using national and international human rights mechanisms to highlight what was then, and still is, a desperate situation in the North's three prisons. Linked to the Commission's work on detention in all its forms was the investigation into the use of the then UK Border Agency's powers of detention which Nazia Latif and I undertook in 2007 (Latif and Martynowicz, 2009). With detainees stopped, searched, arrested, held and questioned at police stations and later often sent to prisons while awaiting removal, the inter-connection between the criminal justice and immigration systems (or what Stumpf in 2006 aptly named 'crimmigration') could not be clearer. It is that connection that I also explored as part of my PhD research with reference to the prisoners' experiences of deportability.

My interest in prisons, detention, and migrants' rights has continued in the last 10 years. While working in the Institute for Conflict Research in Belfast, I led the organisation's work on migration and, among other projects, was involved with a number of colleagues in the conduct of a first large scale study of the experiences of migrant workers in Northern Ireland in 2009. More recently, I also worked with the Irish Congress of Trade Unions on highlighting migrant workers' experiences of discrimination in the workplace (Martynowicz, 2014). While working in the Irish Penal Reform Trust (2009 - 2010), I continued to research prison conditions and the treatment of prisoners in Ireland. Together with colleagues, we were also involved in a number of Trust's campaigns, including a campaign for the introduction of spent convictions legislation, which was eventually enacted in Ireland in 2016.

I am currently involved (with Linda Moore) in a study of the use of solitary confinement in Ireland (a research project commissioned by the Irish Penal Reform Trust/IPRT) and its impact on prisoners. The findings of the research will provide evidence for IPRT's campaign on abolishing the use of solitary. I am also working to develop a research project with colleagues in Poland on post-deportation experiences of Polish prisoners formerly incarcerated in the UK.

Activism, Organisational Work and/or Professional Membership

I have been active as a volunteer in a number of organisations. Amongst those are the Women's Aid Federation for Northern Ireland (where I was a Helpline volunteer in 2009, later to become a Board member between 2012-2015) and Belfast and Lisburn Women's Aid (where I was a member of the Board between 2009 and 2015, and its Chair between 2014 and 2015). Between 2012 and 2016, I was a volunteer with the Fire Emergency Support Service (British Red Cross), supporting individuals and families in crisis. Until my move to England in November 2016, I was also a member of the West Against Racism Network (WARN) – a grassroots collective in Belfast working to challenge racism in the local communities and in political discourse.

In 2013, I was involved in the "Drop the Charges against Barbara Muldoon" campaign – a collective action of trade union and anti-racism activists in support of Barbara. An immigration solicitor and anti-racism activist, she was accused of taking part in an 'unlawful procession' following a protest against Nick Griffin (BNP) being invited to take part in BBC's "Question Time". Following the campaign, and two court hearings, Barbara was cleared of all charges in July 2013.

Selected Works

Martynowicz, A. (2017) 'Uncertainty, Complexity, Anxiety – Deportation and the Prison in the Case of Polish Prisoners in Northern Ireland' in *Archiwum Kryminologii* Vol. XXXVIII/2016, pp 425-439

Martynowicz, A. (2016) 'Not So Multi-Cultural Prison: Polish Prisoners in a Transitional Prison System' *Criminology and Criminal Justice,* Volume 16, No.3, pp 337-349

Martynowicz, A. (2014) *'It's Not How They Should Treat People'. Migrants and the Workplace in Northern Ireland* Belfast: Irish Congress of Trade Unions Northern Ireland Committee

Latif, N. and Martynowicz, A. (2009) *Our Hidden Borders: The UK Border Agency's Powers of Detention* Belfast: NIHRC

Contact Details
Twitter: @AgsMM

15

Critical Feminist Methodology: A Reflexive Account of Prison Research

Gillian McNaull

Introduction

This chapter is based on the author's PhD research which explores the experience of women's remand imprisonment in Northern Ireland. The project is framed by a critical feminist methodology, one which carries the ontological assumption that structural oppression perpetrated by patriarchal society impacts all those who vary from its subjectivity, either singularly or through various intersections (hooks, 1984; Scraton, 1990; Gelsthorpe and Morris, 1990; Hudson 2006; Renzetti 2014). Using a feminist methodology to explore the experiences of women remand prisoners gives primacy to distinct epistemic understandings of the data sought and produced. Gelsthorpe (1990: 90–104) suggests that feminist methodologies in criminology entail four dominant themes; a women centred topic, use of feminist methods, a consideration of the position of power and control in the conduct of research, and an encouragement of researcher reflexivity. The topic of the author's research, 'women's remand imprisonment', is in line with the assertion by Gelsthorpe (1990) that feminist researchers should focus on the concerns of women, with the intention of challenging their oppression. In line with critical feminist methodology, this research aims to reach an understanding of women prisoners which comes not from 'studying down', 'pathologising' the individual and their actions, but instead highlighting how "oppressive gender arrangements lead to victimisation and harsh punishment" (Chesney-Lind and Morash, 2013: 295). Epistemically responsible practice requires deviation from the subject/object relationship and instead the creation of "situations where speakers and hearers make, deliberate, take up or contest attempts to know" (Code, 2014: 19). This entails moving away from research models that privilege hierarchical "top-down models of knowing", shifting instead to a "horizontal model of knowledge–making

165

as a communal activity", which allows the "lived experience of marginalisation" to make visible that which would be unseen (Code, 2014: 19-21). This project was constructed with this aim, to give primacy to the voices and experiences of women on remand, allowing their stories to illuminate the processes that lead to their imprisonment, their position within the criminal justice system, and the impact of remand upon their life quality. An element of feminist methodology is that the researcher "locate themselves within their work", displaying a reflexivity regarding their research and their experiences whilst collecting data, rather than considering these aspects as irrelevant to the process (Gelsthorpe, 1990: 94). This chapter subsequently centres around reflection on the prison research process and researcher's positionality within the data collection and interpretative process, whilst considering the ethics of prison research in action.

Methods and Ethics: Justifying Prison Research

The research at the centre of this work used ethnographic methods to investigate prisons "as they actually exist and operate, rather than from afar and above" (Wacquant, 2002: 387). The focus of analysis is twenty-five qualitative interviews with women held on custodial remand in Ash House, Hydebank Wood Secure College and Women's Prison[1] in Northern Ireland, supplemented by twenty-three interviews with prison staff and third sector workers across grades. Participant led semi-structured interviews were carried out, with an ethnographic diary kept of both observations of processes and interactions within the prison, and reflexive experience of the prison environment. From the outset, the design of this study acknowledged the triad of relationships that exists in all prison research; the interrelationship not just of the researcher and participant, but of the monolithic prison that surrounds them both. As Malloch (2000: 14) outlines, the methods of a critical feminist framework, whilst enriched with a "feminist consciousness [...] informing the nature of the relationship between the researcher and the women being researched", are just one element of the "dual power structure" which exists in prison

---

[1] Ash House is the Women's Unit in the Northern Ireland Prison Service Hydebank Wood campus in Belfast. Hydebank Wood had until 2015 housed a Young Offenders Centre and Women's Prison, but from April 2015 had been reinvented as Hydebank Wood Secure College and Women's Prison. For the remainder of this chapter Hydebank Wood Women's Prison will be referred to as Ash House.

research, the other being the relationship "between the researcher and the context of the total institution" (ibid: 18). This is operationalised through the aim of the design; as McCorkel (2013: 9) notes, ethical justification of the use of women prisoners' voices must have its foundation in the research intention, not to "legitimate new forms of control" but instead "to interrogate these forms of control". Malloch (2000: 16) outlines the impact of the researcher's relationship with the prison on the design process; first through the hurdle of prison access, which is intensified through "'gatekeepers' expectations of what they might gain through co-operation", and second through the potential for "official definitions and controls" to effect the employment of the research. The first hurdle encountered by this project was the application for prison access with the Northern Ireland Prison Service (NIPS) research committee. The NIPS research application form prioritised the benefits any proposed research project could provide for the prison service. This did not pose a considerable problem as the remand population presents 'operational issues' for the prison service which were acknowledged. However, the application also attended to Schlosser's caution that justifications for carrying out prison research should reflect the researcher's and not the institution's position, which was achieved by cementing the application's operationalisation of research questions and concepts within the researcher's epistemology (Schlosser 2008: 1505). Moreover, the approval of the application could only be established via the authorisation of the 'NIPS Research Ethics Committee', an assembly of near mythical proportions with no established pattern for meeting. This served to create a bureaucratic barrier of Kafkaesque (1957) dimensions; access was dependant on the approval of a committee with no set form, timetable or design for gathering data, and the application received no attention for six months which impacted the progression of research data collection.

Insider, Outsider? Researcher Positionality

After access was eventually granted, a central consideration of conducting prison ethnography was the researcher's negotiation of the boundary between 'insider' and 'outsider' status (Jewkes, 2014). As Jewkes asserts, there is a necessity in prison research to recognise the tension of being positioned on one side or another, staff or prisoner; can we reconcile the ethics of 'keeping on side' the prison staff, whilst at the time of collection "doing little [...] to challenge the institution of the prison itself?" (Jewkes,

2014: 389). My role as a researcher in the prison setting was complex. Over the past decade, I have been visiting Ash House and Hydebank Wood Secure College, providing emotional support to prisoners in distress as a member of Samaritans Prison Support Team. As a researcher, there were many benefits to this experience: I was familiar with the prison setting; I had experience of talking to the women imprisoned about trauma and emotional issues; I understood and was familiar with the workings of the environment and its inhabitants; and I had a broad knowledge of NIPS policies and implementations as they have developed in Northern Ireland. In the event, there were times I found differentiating between my Samaritan and researcher roles a challenge. Whilst I had stopped Samaritan prison visits nine months prior to the data collection, to reduce overlapping perceptions of my role on the part of participants, the transition from volunteer listener with a purpose of 'being there' for women, to researcher with professional outcomes from the interactions, was unsettling. On several occasions, I found myself setting the researcher role to the side, to instead respond to women's emotional need in the moment. In a sense, this was the only way I could 'be' a researcher in prison; relating to the women as human to human and discarding the researcher role when necessary.

Once in the researcher position in Ash House, I enacted the 'observer as participant' role as outlined by Gold's typology of four participant observer roles: the complete participant, the participant as observer, the observer as participant and the complete observer (Gold, 1958). However, whilst observing and experiencing the prison setting for periods of time, this cannot be comparable to the experience of prisoners who have no power to walk away from the environment, or to shrug off the efforts to enforce total control. Nor should feminist researchers wish to be assimilated as insiders on the side of the management, positioning ourselves as experts distanced from those who we observe, participating in "prison tourism" (Jewkes, 2014: 390). On several occasions I stepped outside the researcher role to actively advocate or make referrals for the women. A number of women were caught in a bureaucratic web created by deficits in staff knowledge regarding the processes that would lead to their release, and I found myself engaging with probation officers, health workers, sentence managers and women's solicitors to try and attain and transmit the knowledge that could aid that release. I accompanied one woman as she tried to question unjust implementation of adjudication processes, advocated women's problems to staff and made referrals for others to third sector organisations within the setting that could help them with issues they were facing. The counter side of this stance was the moral dilemma that accompanied not acting, and the feelings of regret and remorse that I had not found a way to intervene in certain outcomes. For example, sitting in the pod and witnessing the arbitrary implementation of control and restraint upon a woman on the landing above, who was standing fast against being locked up for the day; waiting on a landing to make an appointment with a participant and witnessing the class officer locking the women away early because they were making too much noise chatting and enjoying each other's company.

As a researcher carrying out interviews first with the imprisoned women, and second prison landing staff, I experienced the tension between maintaining accepted distance from both groups and challenging perceived over-identification with either. I was a daily visitor to the staff 'bubble', checking in to let them know I was in the house and finding out whether any new committals had been received. The staff accepted my presence easily and at times I felt uncomfortable with the lack of boundaries they had in my company; hearing intimate information about the women that was not for my ears, witnessing a third sector counsellor returning to the bubble after seeing a prisoner and joking about the woman's unreliability regarding the issues she had relayed, arriving into the bubble late at night and the staff admitting they smuggled in a television to relieve the boredom of their night-time shifts. In a sense, my status as a researcher bridging insider/outsider status with multiple groups across the prison mirrored the title and focus of the thesis, 'the Space In-between'. I had access to all areas and to all those who resided and worked in the prison in one form or another, but while acceptance was offered, belonging could never (and should never) be provided and I occupied a particular 'in-between' space.

Safeguarding Participants: 'Do No Harm'

Recent research highlights the traumatic histories of many women prisoners (Pollack, 2004; Baldry, 2010; Carlton and Seagrave, 2011), and that the possibility of re-traumatisation through the research process exists. In response to the emotion evoked in many of her participants, Bosworth (1999: 72 - 73) made efforts to ensure the women were not left feeling worse after the process than they were before, and if women interviewed appeared uncomfortable she terminated the process. At the heart of this emotion elicitation from women prisoners are issues of both ethics and exploitation. These must be at the heart of project design and this ethical responsibility was inserted into the design from the outset. The main criterion for recruitment selection was remand status only, with no other variables included. This was an inclusive process with involvement open to all eligible candidates (Scott and Haydon, 2005), enabling the women's choice to participate (Bosworth *et al*, 2005). The women presented a diverse group; women facing long sentences if found guilty, women who were foreign nationals, women facing imprisonment for the first time, women who were recurring short term prisoners. Taking into consideration the high level of vulnerability within the prison, only participants considered able to engage actively with the process of giving voluntary, competent consent (Liamputtong, 2007) were interviewed. Other women presented as too emotionally vulnerable to engage in the process of the interview and those unable to participate at a certain point in time had the option for involvement at a later date. This was the case for a number of the women remanded in Ash House; one woman lacking capacity to participate was held on remand whilst the judge requested awaited psychiatric referral, but was trapped by the prison conundrum of her inability to participate in psychiatric assessment, with the note sent back to the judge, 'will not engage'. This systemic failure meant her bail was unattainable and weeks later she still resided in the prison. A bureaucratic web caught more than one women; one participant was remanded and the charges against her dropped, but too late as her 'unwillingness' to re-engage with the prison mental health team led to her recall and prevented release until she acquiesced to work upon her psyche. This participant relayed 'her head was too melted' to participate at the early stages of the interview process, but approached me several months later to take part.

In conducting prison interviews, ethical issues arise regarding the traumatic histories of the participants and the toll that imparting their stories and experiences can take. The processes utilised in conducting a 'women-centred' project are integral and, as advocated by Gelsthorpe (1990: 91), a positivistic, quantitative methodology was rejected and with it the masculinist paradigm framing conventional interviewing. This entailed an abandonment of one-way processes which objectify the subject, instead producing a subjective social interaction between the researcher and the researched. The interrelationship within this process aimed not to produce an exploitation of interviewees 'as sources of data' (Gelsthorpe, 1990: 93), but through honesty and transparency concerning the project's goals and objectives to instead produce an authentic and open interaction. In-depth semi-structured interviews allow a participatory approach (Wadsworth, 2005) which gives primacy to the voice and meaning-making of the participants, enabling them to tell their story in their own subjective terms, rather than through the representation the researcher projects when using alternative methods of structured interviews and psychometric testing (Richards, 2002). This was a key aspect of the interview design, to be led by the women regarding the issues and experiences that had primacy for them, rather than fulfilling a brief of my making. This had the outcome of guiding the research direction with the majority of the women placing increased emphasis on their lives outside the prison, and the daily injustices and structural oppressions they experienced. When carrying out the interviews, I was mindful of opening up issues which might play on the participant's mind when locked behind the door. Whilst it was not my intention to elicit women's narratives of trauma and harm experienced over the course of their lives, I realised these issues might be part of the stories women wanted to tell me. As a Samaritan listening volunteer I had gained experience of the issues surrounding the impact of sensitive disclosures, and used the knowledge of that context to guide the support mechanisms I inserted into the research design. I scheduled morning interviews so that the women had access to support from staff and other prisoners during the day, provided a sign-posting sheet of support services within the prison and put in place referral mechanisms to those services. I emphasised that participants had the option to stop the interview at any time and as discussed above, set aside the researcher role to provide support when needed. I also provided stamped addressed envelopes to the participants and my mobile phone number, to facilitate participants contacting me further down the line with any delayed concerns. In practice, carrying out feminist prison ethnography meant decreasing the distance between the researcher and the researched, participating in self-disclosure, offering comfort and having an "empathetic stance" (Renzetti, 2014: 11), whilst maintaining honesty about the goals of the research and the possible effects of the project (Bosworth *et al.*, 2005).

Conclusion

The prison research process poses a number of distinct ethical questions which cut to the very heart of what sociological examination should be. 'Being there', giving voice to hidden populations and challenging official discourses, raises issues of "intervention, interpretation, responsibility, complicity and identification" (Scraton, 2007: 5). Conceiving prison research, ensuring access, and collecting data in a space of total control and oppression carries ethical risks with the potential to create and reproduce numerous harms: reinforcing discourses and frameworks of the criminal justice paradigm; doing the work of prisons to make punishment 'better'; incorporation into the mechanics of imprisonment; pathologising and retraumatising vulnerable populations. Whilst a critical feminist methodology can mitigate some of the harms that prison research carries, for both the researched and the researcher some of the impacts are indelible. In efforts to balance these practices, participant wellbeing should always be central and attended to throughout conception, design, implementation and interpretation of research processes. As Moore and Scraton (2014: 67) consider: "there is an ethical responsibility in social research equivalent to the Hippocratic Oath in medicine – to guard against harm and injustice whilst maintaining confidentiality".

References

Baldry, E. (2010) 'Women in Transition: From Prison to...' in *Current Issues in Criminal Justice* Volume 22, No.2 pp 253-267

Bosworth, M. (1999) *Engendering resistance: Agency and power in women's prisons.* Aldershot: Dartmouth Publishing Company

Bosworth, M. Campbell, D. Demby, B. Ferranti, S.M. and Santos, M. (2005) 'Doing prison research: Views from inside' *Qualitative Inquiry*, Volume 11, No.2 pp 249-264

Carlton, B. and Segrave, M. (2011) 'Women's survival post-imprisonment: Connecting imprisonment with pains past and present' *Punishment & Society*, Volume 13, No. 5 pp 551-570

Chesney-Lind, M. and Morash, M. (2013) 'Transformative feminist criminology: A critical re-thinking of a discipline' *Critical Criminology*, Volume 21, No.3 pp 287-304

Code, L. (2014) 'Feminist epistemology and the politics of knowledge: questions of marginality' pp 9-25 in Evans. M, Hemmings. C and Henry. M (eds) *The Sage Handbook of Feminist Theory* London: SAGE Publications Ltd

Gelsthorpe, L. (1990) 'Feminist Methodology in Criminology: A New Approach or Old Wine in New Bottles' pp 89-106 in Gelsthorpe, L. and Morris, A (eds) *Feminist Perspectives in Criminology* Buckingham: Open University Press

Critical Feminist Methodology

Gelsthorpe, L. and Morris, A (eds) *Feminist Perspectives in Criminology* Buckingham: Open University Press

Gold, R.L. (1958) Roles in sociological field observations *Social forces* Volume 36, No.3 pp 217-223

hooks, B. (1984) *Feminist Theory: From Margin to Center* Boston: South End Press

Hudson, B. (2006) Beyond white man's justice: Race, gender and justice in late modernity *Theoretical Criminology* Volume 10, No.1 pp 29-47

Jewkes, Y. (2014) An Introduction to "Doing Prison Research Differently" *Qualitative Inquiry* Volume 20, No. 4 pp 387-391

Kafka, F. (1957) *The Castle* Middlesex: Penguin Modern Classics

Liamputtong, P. (2006) *Researching the vulnerable: A guide to sensitive research methods* London: Sage

Malloch, M.S. (2000) *Women, drugs and custody: The experiences of women drug users in prison* Winchester: Waterside Press

McCorkel, J.A. (2013) *Breaking women: Gender, race, and the new politics of imprisonment* NY: NYU Press

Moore, L. and Scraton, P. (2014) *The Incarceration of Women* London: Palgrave Macmillan UK

Pollack, S. (2004) Anti-oppressive social work practice with women in prison: Discursive reconstructions and alternative practices *British Journal of Social Work*, Volume 34, Number 5 pp 693-707

Renzetti, C.M. (2014) *Feminist Criminology* London: Routledge

Richards, G. (2002) *Putting Psychology in its Place: A Critical Historical Overview* Sussex: Psychology Press

Schlosser, J.A. (2008) 'Issues in interviewing inmates: Navigating the methodological landmines of prison research' *Qualitative Inquiry*, Volume 14, No.8 pp. 1500-1525

Scott, S. and Haydon, D. (2005) 'Barnardos Statement of Ethical Research Practice' [online] Available from: http://www.barnardos.org.uk/barnardo_s_statement_of_ethical_research_pr actice_-_dec_2005.pdf (accessed 18th April 2017)

Scraton, P. (1990) 'Scientific knowledge or masculine discourses? Challenging patriarchy in criminology' pp 10-25 in Gelsthorpe, L. and Morris, A (eds) *Feminist Perspectives in Criminology* Buckingham: Open University Press

Scraton, P. (2007) *Power, Conflict and Criminalisation* Abingdon: Routledge

Wacquant, L. (2002) 'The curious eclipse of prison ethnography in the age of mass incarceration' *Ethnography*, Volume 3, No. 4 pp 371-397

Wadsworth, Y. (2005) 'Gouldner's child? Some reflections on sociology and participatory action research' *Journal of Sociology*, Volume 41, No. 3 pp 267-284

Extended Biography

Research

I am currently undertaking a Department for Employment and Learning (DEL) funded PhD in the School of Law, Queen's University Belfast (QUB), entitled 'The Space In-between: An examination of Women's Custodial Remand'. In 2013 I received an MA in Criminology (Distinction) from QUB. My MA dissertation explored the function prison plays in Western society using a framework of political economy, and was short-listed for the Howard League 'Sunley Prize'. As a mature student, I completed my undergraduate degree with the Open University (OU) over the span of a decade and two children, graduating with a BA Honours in Criminology and Psychological Studies in 2012. My final two pieces of work with the OU focused on the phenomenology of single parenthood, and the effects of mass incarceration. Whilst commencing the OU degree with the aim of achieving single Psychology Honors, participation in Criminology and Social Psychology modules diverted my interest from individual Psychology, to Sociological understandings of 'crime' and harm.

I joined the Samaritans in 2005, and shortly after began visiting what was then the Hydebank Wood Women's Prison and Young Offenders Centre (YOC) as part of the Samaritan's Prison Support team, providing emotional support to prisoners. I continued this work over the following decade. The experience of listening to prisoners' stories was foundational in my decision to undertake PhD research in this area. As Samaritans, we are privileged to support people in crisis, within our ethos of confidentiality, non-judgementality and self-determination, yet there was a personal tension in bearing witness to both the social injustice exhibited by the criminalisation of marginalised populations and the harms inflicted by imprisonment, within the limited capacity of the organisation to enact structural and institutional change.

My PhD research, based on original empirical material, uses a critical feminist methodology to examine the gendered experience of custodial remand in Northern Ireland. The small number of women imprisoned in Northern Ireland are marginalised within a predominately male prison estate, which is physically compounded by their geographical location within the male site of what is now the Hydebank Wood College and Women's Prison. The thesis considers that many women are held in custodial remand not because of the severity of their criminal offence, but due to their socio-economic marginalisation and psychological vulnerabilities, and the perceived risk their circumstances pose to their bail in the community. An element of judicial decision-making in the use of remand is the positioning of the prison as the default setting in the face of a lack of community alternatives, in conjunction with the 'gender responsive discourse' that prison estates have adopted which facilitates this process (Russell and Carlton, 2013). The durability of the institutionalised prison process is such that it has the ability to absorb and incorporate the ideals of reform, without implementing meaningful change (Carlton and Seagrave, 2013). The pains of remand imprisonment (Gibbs, 1982) compound the existing harms and trauma of the female remand prisoner's life whilst the processes of imprisonment extend their socio-cultural and economic marginality (Baldry, 2010). This research puts forward that many women on remand exist in a 'space in-between', surviving on a continuum of liminal marginality that stretches from their social environment before prison, through the temporal and spatial vacuum of the remand regime within the prison, extending to the transitional space of the post-release setting.

In addition to my PhD research I am also involved in a research project at QUB School of Law, interrogating the Northern Ireland Prison Service and its recent emergence from a three year 'prison reform' process, and I am a British Academy funded member of "The Voluntary Sector in Criminal Justice Research Network" Early Career Researcher Mentoring Scheme. Within the School of Law, I am the External Engagement Officer for the Gender Justice and Society Network, and a member of the Human Rights Centre and I have arranged a number of events in this capacity; a seminar with the Northern Ireland Prison Ombudsman in response to the use of solitary confinement in the region, a day of workshops on 'the Innocence Project' Griffith College in conjunction with the NI Human Rights Festival, and a panel, 'Human Rights and Womanhood: issues facing women in Northern Ireland' for International Women's Day (IWD) in conjunction with local activist group, 'Reclaim the Agenda'. I am a founding coordinator of the Irish Postgraduate Prison Research Network which arranged a number of workshops across the island of Ireland on the topics of methodology and ethics of prison research, and research grants and funding processes. In addition, I was on the organising committee for the 7th Annual Postgraduate Criminology Conference (QUB 2015) and I am a moderator of a number of online research network groups; PhD and Early Career Researcher Parents, Postgraduate Prison Research Network and the British Society of Criminology Postgraduate Community.

Activism, Organisational Work and/or Professional Membership
As mentioned above, I have been a volunteer with Samaritans' Prison Support since 2005. During the years 2011-2014 I was in post as the Branch Prison Support Officer, coordinating our branch's delivery of services to prisons in the greater Belfast area, setting up and maintaining listener peer support schemes, and holding weekly support and supervision meetings with prisoner volunteers. From 2014-2016 I was a Regional Prison Support Officer for Ireland, supporting branches in their provision of service across the island of Ireland, and coordinating Samaritans' regional provision with the Northern Ireland Prison Service (NIPS) and the Irish Prison Service (IPS), and currently I am the Regional Prison Support Officer for Northern Ireland. I also sit on the executive committee of Northern Ireland Association for the Care and Resettlement of Offenders (NIACRO) and a number of regional suicide prevention groups. In addition, I am a member of People Before Profit, a grassroots activist group and political organisation across Ireland and have campaigned with them against the closure of mental health centres and women's hostels, as well as in support of women's reproductive rights and marriage equality in Northern Ireland. As mentioned above, I have coordinated an event for IWD in conjunction with feminist activist group Reclaim the Agenda, which included raising the issue of women's imprisonment in Northern Ireland. As I approach the end of my PhD research my hope is to disseminate my research further within activist communities with the aim of raising locally the prominence of prison abolition, and the plight of imprisoned women in particular. This is imperative at a time when women are still being imprisoned on a campus with young males, yet whilst Department of Justice plans are in motion for a long-promised new prison site for women, this development is likely to increase carceral capacity and must also be resisted.

Selected Works
McNaull, G. (forthcoming 2017) 'Post-Corston Reflections on Remanded Women's Experiences in Northern Ireland' in Moore, L., Scraton, P. and Wahidin, A. (eds) *Women's Imprisonment and the Case for Abolition: Critical Reflections beyond Corston*, London: Routledge

McNaull, G. (2016) 'Review of: Criminal Justice in Transition: The Northern Ireland Context McAlinden A.M and Dwyer. C (Eds.)' in *Howard Journal of Criminal Justice*, Volume 55, No.4 pp 537-540

Killean, R., Stannard, J., McNaull, G., Beigi, S., Born, A., Johnston, S., O'Malley, G. and Watters, J. (2016) *Review of the Need for Stalking Legislation in Northern Ireland* Queen's University Belfast [online] Available from: http://www.niassembly.gov.uk/globalassets/documents/justice/stalking-inquiry/qub-law-school.pdf (accessed 18th April 2017)

16

Women's Rights and Legal Consciousness in Bolivia: A Socio-Legal Ethnography

Ashley S. F. Rogers

> The woman from the country has not expected such difficulties: the
> law should always be accessible for everyone, she thinks...
> (Kafka, 1915[1])

Introduction

Socio-legal research has a long tradition of examining the relationship between law and society and has presented many fascinating insights into legality, legal consciousness and the meaning of law (Engel and Yngvesson, 1984; Bumiller, 1992; Merry, 1990; Nielson, 2000, 2004; Cowan, 2004; Harding, 2011). All of these however, tend to be situated in the global north. Halliday and Morgan (2013) highlight that there is very little legal consciousness research engaging with different countries in the global south. Therefore, this chapter introduces my doctoral work on legal consciousness in the Pluri-national State of Bolivia, in South America. Law, for the purposes of this research, is considered to be "situated at the intersection of life and theory" (Flood, 2005: 34), and my research seeks to explore both theoretically and empirically the relationship between women's rights, legal consciousness, and subjectivity in the high altitude city of La Paz.

Bolivia, an ethnically and legally plural landlocked country, presents a unique context within which legality and legal consciousness can be examined. Its rich social, cultural and political history is steeped in resistance – to national and international subjugation, colonialism, and environmental concerns – spanning hundreds of years (see: Klein, 2003;

---

[1] The gender in the quote has been changed from man to woman to reflect the context of my research. Kafka's 'Before the Law' was a story I regularly thought of when hearing women's narratives of law in Bolivia.

Postero, 2006). Much of the oppression experienced has been cultural, subjugating indigenous peoples and women. This has often been manifested through politics, which meant that for Bolivia, the year of 2006 marked an important political, social and legal shift. In this year that the majority of Bolivians celebrated the electoral victory of the first indigenous president, Juan Evo Morales Ayma. What is fascinating about Morales and his party, the Movimiento al Socialismo (MAS), is that it emerged as a social movement, and social organisations and movements from the countryside therefore form this political party. My research is situated in the changing landscape of Bolivian law and society since Morales came in to power.

Morales and the Legal Changes

Morales has now been the longest standing president in Bolivia's history. The concept of 'change' has been central to the MAS party's political campaign, and Morales has certainly been quick to implement changes in Bolivia. These have included the nationalisation of key industries, the development of a cable car system in the administrative capital of La Paz that has transformed the lives of many living on the periphery of the city, and an improvement in the country's economic status. The most notable changes for my research are the legal ones. This includes the development of a New Constitution in 2009 and the transition from a nation state to a pluri-national state – granting greater autonomy to indigenous communities and recognising customary forms of law. These changes reflect a commitment to decolonisation and place Bolivia's complex and diverse population at the heart of politics.

Women's rights have also been expanded in the Constitution, and there is continued pressure from women's movements and organisations that strive to emphasise the need to address particular gender issues. It was women's rights in particular that sparked my interest in the changing legal and political landscape in Bolivia. It should be pointed out here that whilst I had initially intended to investigate the opportunities and challenges for women of finding a platform within and across two different legal frameworks, collective rights and individual rights, this changed after my first few weeks in Bolivia. The research shifted to focus on one particular legal change that was hailed as a great achievement for women's movements – the 2013 Comprehensive Law to Guarantee Women a Life Free From Violence (Law 348).

Methodological Approach

It is in the recent aftermath of the establishment of Law 348 in March 2013 that I began my ethnographic fieldwork. Between October 2014 and October 2015, I lived in La Paz, often considered to be the highest de facto capital city in the world, at an altitude of 11,975ft. This hectic and noisy urban location provided a backdrop of sacred mountains and moon-like landscapes, beneath which was an explosion of colourful indigenous and non-indigenous cultures and traditions. It is a diverse and complex setting within which to explore the meaning of law in women's everyday lives. As I witnessed researchers arriving in La Paz and immediately leaving for the countryside, I decided to stay[2]. It was often suggested that women in the city knew about their rights, and could report violence if they wanted to. Focus tended to be on indigenous women in rural settings, yet my decision to stay led to the revelation that knowledge of the law and an ability to denounce violence and access justice in La Paz was not easy.

The 'field' in Bolivia had many sites. I conducted participant observation in a women's centre in the heart of La Paz, hereby referred to as Casa de las Brisas. I also attended public meetings, events, protests and marches, and conducted informal, narrative interviews with Bolivian women in order to explore the presence and meaning of law in their lives. These were further supplemented with more formal interviews with civil society organisations (CSOs) and government institutions, inspired by Nielson's (2014) "law in motion" approach. Doing this, I sought to move socio-legal research and legal consciousness studies out of the formal legal spaces of courts and police stations and into everyday life in a location that had yet to be explored in such a way.

Law 348 and Legal Consciousness

Every day in La Paz alone, there are approximately 100 cases of violence against women[3]. The creation of Law 348 criminalises this violence and for the first time recognises the crime of femicide. To deal with these crimes,

---

[2] For an exploration of encounters with law in rural Bolivia, I recommend the work of Goodale (2009).

[3] There is no systematic collection of data in Bolivia in relation to violence against women, and therefore figures are rarely accurate. The Special Police Force Against Violence though estimate that they receive 100 cases daily. http://www.lapublica.org.bo/al-toque/la-paz/item/527-la-paz-y-el-alto-encabezan-en-cantidad-las-denuncias-por-violencia-intrafamiliar

a dedicated police unit has been established, although the performance of which is already heavily criticised with institutional sexual violence already raised as an issue (Enlaces Bolivia, 2017). These legal changes recognise the gendered aspects of violence and highlight women as "standing alone in relation to the state" and "as legal subjects no longer mediated by their embeddedness in family relationships" (Merry, 2003: 353). It offers new legal and criminological vocabularies within which experiences of violence can be framed. Discussions of violence are no longer just constrained within the private sphere, and in fact violence is now recognised as a public concern. Oppressive, patriarchal ideas and attitudes are being increasingly challenged. Although this presents the changes as a success, there remains a long way to go.

Through an exploration of legal consciousness I am able to highlight the implications of the law and the narratives that exist, which make it meaningful in practice as opposed to in text. In text, the law is commendable. Legal consciousness does, to some extent, incorporate legal knowledge and awareness (Sarat, 1977), but it is also about the way that women use the law, talk about it, resist it or accept it. Drawing in particular on the work of Merry (1990, 1995, 2003 and 2006) and Ewick and Silbey (1998), the concept of legal consciousness is central to my theoretical framework which draws together theory, method and practice. It allows the exploration of the more subtle encounters with law in every day life and the ways that law and legal discourses have come to shape women's conceptions of themselves and their relationship with society. Therefore it highlights the interactive and mutually constitutive relationship between law and society, through the lens of "human action and social constraint" (Ewick and Silbey, 1998: 38).

Resistance, Space and Civil Society Organisations

Given that there was a conscious shift in my work to explore experiences and legal encounters outwith the criminal justice system, this research presents important patterns of resistance that can be seen to cross temporal-spatial boundaries. The emphasis on the connections between personal narratives and biographies, and larger social situations and histories becomes increasingly apparent. This reveals the influence that law has on women's lives and the way they frame their rights, even if they have never had any formal interaction with it. In relation to resistance, the role of CSOs are also highlighted as being important spaces for encountering law, as they are not only contributors to knowledge, understanding, subjectivity and resistance (see: Ward and Green, 2016), but they also present and construct forms of legal consciousness.

My work emphasises the opportunities and challenges that exist for resistance through relationships between women and CSOs. These organisations are often considered to occupy a space somewhere between individual women, the state and law. As Blandy and Sibley (2010: 278) point out, "law and space actively constitute society, while being themselves continually socially produced". In Bolivia, CSOs are not only important spaces for resistance, they also act as translators of the law (Merry, 2006). Merry and Levitt's (2009) work on the vernacularisation of rights is used to highlight the importance of this 'in-between' space.

Resistance in my research is not *against* the law, as it has tended to be in a lot of other socio-legal studies and thus fitting neatly in to Ewick and Silbey's (1998) cultural schemas of legal consciousness. In fact, Law 348 has been a welcomed legal change. Women are advocates of the law. Instead then, resistance is expressed in relation to the poor implementation of the law and the legal institutions, which further reinforce oppressive, hetero-patriarchal[4] attitudes of society. This in turn affects women's ability to mobilise the law and access justice. Whilst CSOs establish, organise and strengthen the discursive spaces around patriarchy and *machismo*[5], they also play an important role in securing political space for "voices and interests that mainstream preferences and projects tend to overlook or marginalise" (Iglesias and Valdes, 1998: 515). Yet many women are still dissatisfied at their inclusion in these organisations, often considering their role as being one of a 'show-and-tell' nature to further organisational aims as opposed to help them as individuals. The on-going struggles for recognition – in all social spheres – is then not only against violence but against the attitudes that have constructed violence as a norm and as a part of everyday life to be endured by Bolivian women.

---

[4] Thanks to another European Group member, Hannah Wilkinson for introducing me to this term.

[5] *Machismo* is a Spanish term, which can be related to notions of patriarchy, hypermasculinity and aggression. In Bolivia, similar to the work of Freidric (2013) in the context of Ecuador, machismo is often expressed as an inherent part of culture, used to explain violence against women. In this way, it can be considered to be to the detriment of the social, political, and economic dimensions of violence, and the normalization of it, through cultural explanations that rest upon this term.

Emancipation or Regulation

Legal, economic, political, and social structures in Bolivia are stacked against women. Halliday and Morgan (2013) suggest that a complex legal consciousness exists whereby a gaming approach is adopted, strengthened by a faith or belief in legality that goes above or beyond the law. Women in Bolivia support this analogy. A very complicated and unjust legal system is revealed, where access to justice is considered as a game, luring women in with the promise of using rights to gain protection and justice. Yet they continue to advocate for and have faith in the law. This faith is firmly tied to the emancipatory and often mythical nature of the ideational visions that law can invoke whereby "an illusion of law as a source of power disconnected from other power structures in society" exists (Bumiller, 1988: 10).

Women in Bolivia receive very little assistance in their attempts to access justice through Law 348. Mobilising it requires money. Completing papers requires money. Maria Galindo from Mujeres Creando, an influential women's rights organisation in La Paz, spoke passionately during a public event in September 2015 condemning violence against women, stating that "the police ask for money for anything, to move themselves[6]". When Law 348 was constructed in Bolivia, the guaranteed 'freedom' from violence in its title did not appear to be conditional on resources, yet access to resources, and in particular money, is one of the greatest obstacles for women who want to denounce violent behaviour. Given the structural conditions of society, whereby women are often financially dependent on their husbands - and where husbands or other family members are often the perpetrators of violence - they are at a disadvantage before the debilitating legal game begins.

The legal system is constructed in a way that women find exhausting and disempowering. The notion of a system often suggests some form of order or organisation, and yet this does not appear to be the way that women experience the law in Bolivia.

> I mean I live fleeing, I flee to save my life, I don't know, I have like a necessity to live. I fled that day [the last day of violence experienced]. I fled earlier. I returned. I started the lawsuits. I came here [to La Paz] and pressed charges. I went to the doctor, to the

---

[6] Translated from Spanish

> police, to other institutions, to groups of women, to NGOs, return
> to the police, to the courts, to the Defensoria[...]I am exhausted
> (Ariana, Casa de las Brisas, July 2015) [7].

Ariana's narrative of violence and the law typifies the experiences of many women that I encountered during my fieldwork. The speed at which she spoke, and her rapid repetition of the word "I" not only reflected the chaos of the system and the need to move quickly, but also the fact that she was alone. The lack of support for women, combined with the complicated legal process itself, tends to isolate and disempower them. Alongside this, women at Casa de las Brisas were very aware of victim-blaming attitudes which drew more attention to their behaviour than to the criminal behaviour of the aggressor. At times it meant that conceptualising themselves as 'victims' was met with resistance, yet an identification with, and adoption of this label, is necessary in order to initially access and mobilise the Law 348. Therefore, as women engage with the language of rights and legal frameworks, they are engaging with emancipatory illusions of a future where law represents justice and empowerment (Santos, 2002), but a very unjust and disempowering system is revealed beneath. Exploring women's narratives reveals the power of the law to construct and reconstruct women's identities and subjectivities.

The Right Kind of Victim

Legal change does not, of course, automatically produce social change. Although it could be suggested that Law 348 emerged from below, as a counter-hegemonic form of law (Santos, 2002), it appears that it could be considered here to have become another form of hegemonic regulation – drawing attention to forms of women's behaviour that are deemed to be undesirable in society. An example of this occurred when a young woman was killed outside of one of La Paz's nightclubs.

> Yes but did you hear she was drunk?!" said one of the staff members at the women's centre. "I thought something wasn't right about that case, *and* she was flirting with other men that night, too. She was obviously trying to make [her boyfriend] angry. He is from a good family, you know. They are good people.

---

[7] Translated from Spanish

Contrasts are constructed between acceptable and unacceptable female behaviour based on gender stereotypes and patriarchal views, presenting the victim as partly responsible. Victim blaming is not uncommon in Bolivia, nor across the world, yet as the discourses around the woman's death came to be more enveloped in such language, the understanding of a victim shifted. Ideas of what it means to be a 'victim' become saturated with the infiltration of victim blaming discourses, which fix themselves firmly to the identity required to access the law. Making sense of women's narratives of law by "setting them within larger frames of significance" (Geertz, 1983: 232) therefore reveals the broader social, cultural and institutional challenges within which women must navigate.

Going Forward

Social change will hopefully take place, but currently what this legal transition of Law 348 could be considered to have done, is to reinforce the status quo in Bolivian society by promoting impunity, due to the failure of the legal system. Patriarchal and oppressive opinions and perceptions of women are currently embedded within institutions established by the law, and through which the law can be accessed. When law is pushed through existing structures of society without due attention, it excludes women's individual experiences and understandings, and disregards the power of law to construct, and be used to construct, subjectivities – whether they be in line with mainstream gender ideas, or marginalised alternative subjectivities (see: Butler, 1999). Ideas of violence are presented in legal terms and it is within the definitions and language of the law that women's experiences must now fit. The myth of law then, is in the ability to present visions of justice through its symbolic power, and at the same time condone and contribute to the attitudes and ideologies that are the cause of violence against women.

Through an exploration of legal consciousness and subjectivity, the full weight of the stereotypes and patriarchal attitudes that have justified violence against women are revealed. It is here that both the game of law and the myth of law come together to further (re)construct, regulate, and reinforce various subjective positions that define, limit, and structure women's choices. As Merry (1995: 20) points out, "the law provides a place to contest relations of power, but it also determines the terms of the contest". Women are not passively accepting these terms. They are resisting the oppressive forms of power through street protests, events, marches, and the use of art and social media everyday. In the words of an inspirational Bolivian woman I have come to know: "I believe we are witnessing an important and new Latin American wave of feminism, so watch closely!" (see: Luna Sanz 2017).

Acknowledgements

I would like to thank the ESRC for funding my research, as well as my supervisors at the University of Stirling, Professor Samantha Punch and Dr Bill Munro, for their expertise and guidance. I would also like to thank the European Group for the Study of Deviance and Social Control for their interest, enthusiasm and support in relation to the development of my research. Above all else, I would like to thank the many individuals and organisations in Bolivia that provided me with their stories and experiences of law, amongst others. I will always stand in solidarity and support with Bolivian women.

References

Blandy, S. and Sibley, D. (2010) 'Law, Boundaries and the Production of Space' *Social and Legal Studies Volume* 19, No. 3 pp 275-284

Bumiller, K. (1988) *The Civil Rights Society: The Social Construction of Victims* Baltimore: John Hopkins University

Butler, J. (1999) *Gender Trouble: Feminism and the Subversion of Identity* London: Routledge

Cowan, D. (2004) 'Legal Consciousness: Some Observations' *The Modern Law Review* Volume 67, No. 6 pp 928-958

Engel, D. and Yngvesson, B. (1984) 'Mapping Difficult Terrain: 'Legal Culture', 'Legal Consciousness', and Other Hazards for the Intrepid Explorer' *Law and Policy* Volume 6, No. 3 pp 299-307

Enlaces Bolivia (2017) 'Director de la FELCV de La Paz es enviado a la cárcel por acoso sexual a una policía', *Enlaces Bolivia* 6 April 2017 Available from : http://www.enlacesbolivia.com/9177-Director-de-la-FELCV-de-La-Paz-es-enviado-a-la-carcel-por-acoso-sexual-a-una-policia#sthash.Wjc87bIR.dpuf (accessed on 6th April 2017)

Ewick, P. and Silbey, S. (1998) *The Common Place of Law* Chicago: University of Chicago Press

Flood, J. (2005) 'Socio Legal Ethnography' pp 33-48 in Banakar, R. and Travers, M. (eds) *Theory and Method in Socio-Legal Research* Portland: Hart Publishing

Freideric, K. (2013) 'Violence Against Women and the Contradictions of Rights-in-Practice in Rural Ecuador' Special Issue: Violence against Women in Latin America. *Latin American Perspectives Volume* 41, No. 1 pp 19-38

Geertz, C. (1983) *Local Knowledge: Further Essays in Interpretive Anthropology* New York: Basic Books

Goodale, M. (2009*) Dilemmas of Modernity: Bolivian Encounters with Law and Liberalism* Stanford: Stanford University Press

Halliday, S. and Morgan, B. (2013) 'I Fought the Law and the Law Won? Legal Consciousness and the Critical Imagination' *Current Legal Problems* Volume 66, No. 1, pp 1-32

Harding, R. (2011) *Regulating Sexuality: Legal Consciousness in Lesbian and Gay Lives* London: Routledge

Iglesias, E. M. and Valdes, F. (1998) 'Religion, Gender, Sexuality, Race and Class in Coalitional Theory: A Critical and Self-Critical Analysis of Latcrit Social Justice Agendas' *Chicano-Latino Law Review* Volume 19, No, 1 pp 503-588

Klein, H. S. (2003) *A Concise History of Bolivia* Cambridge: Cambridge University Press

Law N° 348 (2013) *La Ley Integral Para Garantizar a Las Mujeres una Vida Libre de Violencia*, Estado Plurinacional de Bolivia Available at: http://www.migracion.gob.bo/upload/l348.pdf

Luna Sanz, M. B. (2017) ¿Estamos ante una nueva Ola del Feminismo? *La Migraña*: La Paz

Merry, S. E. (1990) *Getting Justice and Getting Even: Legal Consciousness Among Working-Class Americans* Chicago: University of Chicago Press

Merry, S. E. (1995) 'Resistance and the Cultural Power of Law' *Law and Society Review* Volume 29, No. 1 pp 11-26

Merry, S. E. (2003) 'Rights Talk and the Experience of Law: Implementing Women's Human Rights to Protection from Violence' *Human Rights Quarterley* Voume 25, No. 2 pp 343-381

Merry, S. E. (2006) *Human Rights and Gender Violence: Translating International Law into Local Justice* Chicago: University of Chicago Press

Merry, S. E. and Levitt, P. (2009) 'Vernacularisation on the Ground: Local uses of Global Women's Rights in Peru, China, India and the United States' *Global Networks* Volume 9, No. 4 pp 441-461

Nielson, L. B. (2000) 'Situating Legal Consciousness: Experiences and Attitudes of Ordinary Citizens about Law and Harassment' *Law and Society Review* Volume 34, No. 4 pp 1055-1090

Nielson, L. B. (2004) *License to Harass: Law, Hierarchy and Offensive Public Speech* Princeton: Princeton University Press

Nielson, L. B. (2014) 'Thinking Law: Thinking Law in Motion' *Brazilian Journal of Empirical Legal Studies* Volume 1, No. 2 pp 12-24

Postero, N. G. (2006) *Now We Are Citizens: Indigenous Politics in Postmulticultural Bolivia* Stanford: Stanford University Press

Sarat, A. (1977) 'Studying American Legal Culture: An Assessment of Survey Evidence' *Law and Society Review* Volume 11, No. 3 pp 427-88

Santos, B. S. (2002) *Toward a New Legal Common Sense: Law Globalisation and Emancipation* Cambridge: Cambridge University Press

Silbey, S. (2005) After Legal Consciousness, *Annual Review of Law and Social Science* Volume 1, pp 323 – 368

Ward, T. and Green, P. (2016) 'Law, the State, and the Dialectics of State Crime', *Critical Criminology* Volume 24, No. 2 pp 217-230

Extended Biography

Research

In 2007, I graduated from the University of Stirling, Scotland, having completed my honours degree in Criminology and Sociology, which sparked a keen interest in crimes of the powerful, state crime, resistance and human rights. This interest can be attributed to the work of Green and Ward (2004) and their text *State Crime: Governments, Violence and Corruption*. My undergraduate dissertation focused on the United Nations definition of genocide, and I argued that whilst the situation during that time in Darfur, Sudan, was not being defined as genocide by the UN, that it indeed should have been. After spending some time travelling across Eastern and Southern Africa, I became increasingly interested in notions of legality and in particular with human rights law. In 2009-2010, I completed a Masters at the University of Glasgow in Human Rights and International Politics. It is here that my interest in Bolivia began, inspired by the lectures and work of Dr Mo Hume, and at a time of legal transitioning with the establishment of the New Constitution. My Masters thesis was a feminist analysis of *Indigenous Movements and Globalisation: Collective Identity as a Counter-Hegemonic Tool*.

Although I remained in higher education as a Teaching Assistant at the University of Stirling, I did not return to formal education myself until 2012, when I was awarded a 1+3 scholarship from the Economic and

Social Research Council through their socio legal stream of funding. I continued my work on legality with my thesis entitled *Escribanos: The Making of the Colonial Subject*, examining the construction of and relationship between law and subjectivity. I completed my Masters in Applied Social Research with distinction and an award for my thesis in 2013.

In October of the same year I began my doctorate, seeking to explore women's rights, legal consciousness and subjectivity in the context of Bolivia. Whilst this research began more broadly on women's rights legal frameworks, when I began my twelve months of ethnographic fieldwork in 2014, my research became more focused on gender-based violence and legal transitions in this area. It engages with notions of resistance, the spatial aspects of law, power, identity and subjectivity. Most importantly, it highlights the relevance and value of legal consciousness as a framework for exploring experiences of law using ethnographic methods.

I believe that my methodological and theoretical approach could be employed in other settings too, in order to uncover the relationships that women have with the law in order to draw attention to the structural conditions of society, which produce, promote, and reinforce gender-based violence.

Activism, Organisational Work and/or Professional Membership

As a member of the Scottish Centre for Crime and Justice Research, I have a range of research interests, knowledge and skills. I take a critical criminological approach to my research, and outside of my work in Bolivia I have also been involved in issues relating to people seeking asylum and refugees - in particular with Unaccompanied Asylum Seeking Children (UASC). This began during my time volunteering at the Scottish Refugee Council (SRC) in between my two Masters programs and has continued with my involvement in projects at the University of Stirling (funded by the Carnegie Trust) exploring the needs of UASC in Scotland and the practical challenges that Local Authorities face.

I have also continued my interest and work with civil society organisations – an interest that really only emerged through my doctorate fieldwork. I have recently been involved in a British Academy/Leverhulme funded research project exploring how a re-invigorated 'public sphere' might shape conceptions of social justice and active citizenship in Scotland.

I am also a member of the *Socio Legal Studies Association*, *Postgraduates in Latin American Studies*, and the *European Group for the*

Study of Deviance and Social Control. I have taken an active role in each of these, presenting my work at conferences and becoming more involved in events organisation, mental health and wellbeing activities and journal editing. Having a professional background in events, marketing and management, has also equipped me with the skills and interests in attending and organising numerous academic events including a day focused on the challenges of field research that are rarely discussed in published work, entitled *Reflections from the Field*, held at the Faculty of Social Sciences, University of Stirling, in 2016.

Future Aspirations

With my doctorate research due for completion in 2017, and teaching experience accrued since early 2009, my future aspirations include different avenues of continuing to work in academia. One option is securing funding for post doctorate research to continue my work on the relationship between law and society, and in particular contributing to legal consciousness and socio-legal studies. I also aim to continue my involvement with and support for Bolivian women's rights movements and groups that fight to improve the implementation of law against violence and access to justice.

Given my range of interests in relation to Criminology, as well as an emerging interest in global sociology, I aspire to continue my work in these areas through both research and teaching by securing a lectureship. In particular, I hope to promote ethnographic methodologies to explore constructions of the legal subject and highlight the importance of deconstructing and exploring relationships between individuals, society, and law, particularly in relation to crimes of the powerful and gender.

Selected Works

Rogers, A. (2017) *Access to Justice and Legal Consciousness in Bolivia*, Socio-Legal Studies Association Annual Conference, University of Newcastle, 6th April 2017

Rogers, A. (2017) *Legal Consciousness, Gender Violence and the Development of Social Movements,* Invited Guest Speaker at Research Seminar Series, Abertay University, 16th March 2017

Rogers, A. (2017) *Global Social Science: Practical Challenges and Ethical Dilemmas in Latin America*, Invited Guest Speaker for the Scottish Centre for Crime and Justice Research, University of Glasgow, 10th March 2017

Rogers, A. (2016) Legal Consciousness and Subjectivity: Women's Rights and Violence in Bolivia, *University of Stirling Research and Enterprise Blog*, University of Stirling

Rogers, A. (2016) *Women's Rights, Legal Consciousness and Identity in Bolivia*, European Group for the Study of Deviance and Social Control annual conference, Portugal, September 2016

Rogers, A. (2016) *Reflections on a Year of Fieldwork in La Paz, Bolivia*, Reflections from the Field Symposium, University of Stirling, 5th April 2016,

Contact Details
Email: ashleysarahfrances@gmail.com
Twitter: @rogers_ashley1

17

Resistance from Within: Early Findings from a Study on Youth Justice Practitioner's Experiences of Policy

Adam Scott

Introduction

Calls for penal system revolutionary reform have formed the foundations for abolitionists, where aims toward utopian ideals provide an earnest response to a failing system. However, the image of an assumed system that is ubiquitously punitive may only serve to provide a convenient untruth. In this chapter, I propose that pockets of resistance against the crime control paradigm exists within practitioner circles, where a dystopian ideal may in fact limit our ability to recognise revolutionary factions from within the system. This chapter traces some initial observations from an ongoing study into practitioners' experiences of understanding and delivering youth justice policy, with a specific focus on how Restorative Justice (RJ) is interpreted and used as a method for justice interventions. This chapter will argue that critical thinkers have been preoccupied with 'resetting' the justice agenda from outside of the field and as a result may have neglected to acknowledge a revolution from within. Contrary to popular critical narratives, some justice practitioners may resist or even transcend occupational cultures of violent power. For example, Sim (2008) reflected on a 1976 study at Glasgow's Barlinnie Special Unit highlighting a minority of prison officers that had deviated from the *status-quo* culture of masculinity, hostility and violence that ratified a retributive response to prisoners. Instead, some officers displayed empathy and understanding towards the needs and stories that individuals presented. And though within the academy, there has been a critical response to stereotypical views of offenders, Sim (2008) highlights that a sanitised view of justice professionals (prison officers in this case) reflecting state violence has become normalised. To have a default theoretical understanding of justice professionals as being the docile embodiment structurally allows for a level of convenience in scholarly theorisation. This chapter will be split into 3 sections. Firstly, it will contextualise RJ within youth justice. Secondly, the landscape of youth justice and the professionals assigned to carry it out will be framed using Pierre Bourdieu's theory of *habitus*, *field* and *capital*. Thirdly, it will draw upon 3 themes that I have observed during my time in the field that highlight ways that practitioners manage power within the paradoxical field of a Youth Offending Team (YOT).

A critical approach towards justice practitioners within the environment of youth justice arguably shifts the justice paradigm and how it must be analysed. YOT's were born from New Labours' attempts to divert young people away from traditional justice paths using a managerialistic approach, where policies could reflect those processes that 'worked' and that were informed by 'evidence-led' research (Muncie, 2006). In a 'what works' approach driven by an understanding of risk factors, and where risk existed, YOT's would intervene (Newburn and Crawford, 2003). A pragmatic approach to crime control saw a bifurcation of youth justice policy, that addressed the welfare concerns surrounding incivility through risk management, and RJ that retained some prevailing ideologies, whilst retaining the impetus of accountability and responsibility, and therefore evading any 'populist condemnation' of being soft on crime (Muncie, 2006). Early intervention strategies, predicated by actuarial processes of calculating risk, coordinated practitioners and programmes of RJ to steer and 'correct' any young person who may show signs of an offending future. Such a system has been designed to prevent a young person from being ensnared by a failing justice system (Newburn and Crawford, 2003). The fact that such a process has been implemented suggests that the justice system acknowledges itself as a failure, creating interventions and the means to divert young people away from being ensnared by it and reducing the opportunity for it to do harm. Thus, RJ and the YOT practitioner become symbolic of a criminal justice antithesis that is to rebuke problematic punitive justice with the acknowledgement that deeper social problems are correlated with offending behaviour. However, rather paradoxically, they are still designed to sit within the structures of the wider justice system.

Without becoming embroiled in a critical discussion surrounding RJ, I will use a standard set of universalisms regarding its practice. RJ proponents suggest that it is an inclusive process that seeks to put right the harms caused and where the voices and needs of the victim, offender and community are heard. Through personal exchanges, understanding and forgiveness can take place bringing about a deeper understanding of each other's position and thereby leaving the process with closer social bonds than before (Zehr, 2005; Johnstone, 2001). The problem arises when RJ, a methodological approach foundered in empathy, forgiveness and inclusion, is expected to run seamlessly within, and fostered by, a justice system geared towards isolation, labelling and punishment. As Copson (2016) points out, emerging utopian responses that offer genuine alternatives often become little more than an extended arm of the current system, and therefore do little to challenge accepted justice discourses, rendering the potential merits of RJ to be potentially neutralised by the system it is situated in.

For Copson (2016), to realise utopian ideals, a shift in discourse is necessary. The language of crime and criminal justice inhibits critical theory from moving beyond the parameters of existing power structures and instead arguably only serves to replicate them. Instead, a reframing of crime must head towards a *zemiological* approach of analysing harms. Utopian theory offers little to challenge the rhetoric of criminal justice however, it is through a shift in how knowledge is produced surrounding crime, instead responding to harm, that 'realistic utopias' may be realised within the current system. This offers 'a new starting point' for the way crime is conceptualised and responded to, rather than a recycling of failed narratives. RJ fits the mould of such a new beginning, steeped in critical thinking to reimagine how crime is framed however, it becomes abated when RJ is framed as a post justice, administrative diversion process, to reduce the headcount into the justice system, within the crime control paradigm.

The concept of habitus and field provides a lens to explain how YOT practitioners have embodied utopian ideals whilst maintaining their interests within the field of criminal justice. For Bourdieu (1984), there is context and structure behind the decisions of 'actors' in how they respond to stimulus. Action is a product of both internal and external factors where actors make both conscious and subconscious decisions, and reactions to the world around them. An individual's habitus is difficult to articulate; it is part of an individual's being, and is only brought to their attention when that habitus is questioned by different forms of habitus. Habitus is formed through deep rooted socialisations, and provides what Bourdieu calls *'a feel for the game'*, where habitus is constructed over time to form an internalised history. Habitus allows an individual to navigate the social world around them, within their native environments. Habitus is played out and reproduced unconsciously "without any deliberate pursuit of coherence" (Bourdieu, 1984: 172) requiring no concentration and enables an individual to participate as an 'insider'. Peoples' tastes, morals and values have been culturally engrained over a long period of time and are reinforced by the world around them.

Whereas habitus affects action subconsciously as part of an actor's socialised view of the world, field, or multiple fields, affect action externally. A field is a "semi-autonomous, relatively bounded sphere of action in which people, groups, and organisations struggle with and against each other" (Page, 2013: 153). Bourdieu (1984) argued that there are numerous fields (such as the academic field and the justice fields) that enable actors to understand the parameters of the acceptable social action. There are field specific rules and regulations, these are the basic values and assumptions that Bourdieu calls *doxa*, the knowledge of which enable actors to improve or maintain their position within the field. Within the field, the resources that enable an actor to thrive are known as *capital*. An actor can gain capital by successfully negotiating and completing actions that hold high value within that field.

Bourdieu (1984) argues that certain actors have a natural 'feel for the game' within a field, they are naturally able to gain capital, and this is entrenched within their personal habitus and how that is translated in the field. An individual's ability to perform well in a field is dependent upon their habitus and on their position that they hold within the hierarchy of the field. Fields also react to external powers, and interplay with other fields. Macro-level forces such as governance, politics and economics may impact upon the field. However, for Bourdieu (1984), fields will act very much like a 'prism', in that those external forces that impede upon the logic of the field are dealt with by refraction. Some of these influences are deflected away, whilst others are absorbed but are distorted to fit with the current logic of the field. What emanates is a distorted version of the original influence that has been manipulated to fit with the logic in place. Fields may evolve over time as actors change from within and external forces begin to have an impact, however, the more established a field is, the more it will retain its autonomy against such forces.

Bourdieu (1984) provides a framework from which to explain key observations I have made in how the complexity of the YOT field, itself a small field, is conjoined to many other fields, as is expected with multi-agency/discipline environments. For YOT officers their task and their environment is surrounded by juxtaposed relationships, not only in their approach, but also within their physical environment, or their field. Whilst the goal is to meet the underlying social needs of young people through multiagency partnerships, these partnerships and office spaces are filled with contrasting cultural and practitioner aims from education, social work and health that focus on welfare. The youth justice field is based upon critical theory that crime is intrinsically connected to wider societal harms. The justice field remains a large presence where language and methods are still inherently linked to the wider systems of justice, and there is always a practitioner justice occupancy of the YOT field with active and seconded police officers employed within the YOT, as well as regular interaction between YOT practitioners and justice representatives. Whilst in the field I observed three key themes that highlight how external justice pressures are refracted, absorbed and manipulated within the YOT field: the Maverick; the Governor; and the Director.

1-The Maverick

The purpose of the YOT is ultimately to engage and manage young people, therefore, I saw those whose habitus lay within an acute ability to build a rapport with young people and engage them in a way which would hold capital among their peers. My observations saw that individuals who engaged well with the young people were of a particular disposition, that face to face engagement was more important than the administrative processes that should follow. The administrative processes, such as risk assessments, report writing and court letters are seen as fundamentally important by those in positions of leadership and within the wider justice framework. These components make up the actuarial, quantifiable, and bureaucratic response of a policy that aims to calculate social ills and whether they have been 'rectified'. I call these individuals 'mavericks', because they remain (on the most part) autonomous from external justice pressures, refracting any logic that administrative processes can displace an ability to effectively communicate in the physical presence between colleagues and young people. Individuals who sit within this theme obtain their capital from gaining a deeper qualitative 'feel' for their work, that emotions and human interactions cannot be quantified or calculated.

2-The Governor

Then there are those that embody those strategic policies by rigidly reaffirming correct procedure and by ensuring that they directly reflect the expectations of administrative justice. 'Governors' achieve capital in the wider justice setting by completing administrative tasks and taking pride in being recognised for excelling within their bureaucratic remit. This was visible in the field where some individuals would have certificates and accreditations clearly visible, detailing that they were knowledgeable on restorative techniques, risk assessments, or youth work. In one conversation with a governor I had asked if a YOT practitioner may change behaviour away from the field. The governor explained that they should remain a practitioner at all times and stay within the accepted moral code/law regardless of situation or environment. Governors aim to gain capital by being thorough in their administrative duties and gain capital through embracing the dichotomy of youth work with administrative governance.

3-The Diverter

The YOT field is based upon the acknowledgement that their fundamental role is as a response to justice measures and ultimately to divert young people away. Although each practitioner is working, in premise, to divert young people from criminal justice, I observed individuals discussing cases where their sole focus was on shielding the young person from criminal justice practitioners, such as the courts or the police. In one case, a young person had admitted to a practitioner that he had intentions to commit sexual assault. Following this, the practitioner had a discussion with a senior manager in handling this case. The objectives were clear, and they were to ensure that the young person did not progress further into the criminal justice system. Little time was spent discussing or unearthing why the young person wanted to commit the crime, or how to stop it, no discussion was raised to the possible danger the targeted victim faces. Instead, the focus was solely on the task of ensuring the young person did not improve on their recorded criminal career. I found this to be a recurring theme, where a primary focus is given to ensuring that the young person is steered clear of criminal justice interactions. Here capital is gained, or at least the practitioners' position within the field is retained, by doing their basic role of diverting young people from justice.

Practitioners would regularly show elements of all three themes, and exploit naturally overlapping fields of welfare and justice to retain or improve their capital. Importantly, there were examples of those whose habitus made them excel as mavericks, and others as governors, however, they all used techniques as diverters to maintain their position within the YOT field. What was particularly evident was that in terms of RJ, the governors seemed to hold capital as they were deemed to reflect the administrative approach to RJ. Practitioners would consult those governors who held RJ capital for affirmation that their strategies were indeed 'restorative'. Invariably, the governor would acknowledge the 'restorativeness' of a project so long as it involved some form of community reparation, apology, or victim liaison. The YOT field reflects a bifurcated youth justice, whereby practitioners are able to gain capital through a rejection of criminal justice measures and display an ability to address deeper welfare concerns. Whilst, at the same time practitioners can find capital in adhering to those administrative processes that ensure that YOTs remain intrinsically linked to the crime control paradigm.

Conclusion

Though these are initial findings, they highlight that Criminology may need to better equip itself to uncover more potential fractures of power. It is ideologically convenient to assume a seamless path of violence from policy formulation through to delivery. To assume that justice professionals are docile actors who embody an extended arm of state violence holds a similar naivety as the Lombrosian assumption of the 'born criminal'. These early findings have highlighted that in one particular setting practitioners that do enact government power may restrict it to the context of professionalism in their administrative duties and workplace dialogue in search of organisational capital. Practitioners display a 'feel for the game' when diverting from traditional justice, and often will have a natural habitus of showing understanding and humanistic empathy towards young people. This is reminiscent of the observations of Sim (2008) who argues that prison officers maintain a humane empathy towards prisoners despite the intense masculine and violent culture. In the case of the YOT, there is a certain external justice pressure, however, the YOT field may largely protect practitioners' natural habitus of empathy and understanding in dealing with conflict. This protective environment arguably makes it more likely that they can retain their occupational habitus and refract those violent pressures from the wider justice system.

It must be reiterated that these are early findings, though they do highlight the complex nature of the practitioner. Like any subject of social enquiry, motives behind action are complex and are therefore worthy of further investigation. At this point I return to Copson (2016: 91) who argues that academic theorising and criminal justice needs a new 'starting point', I suggest that this may be an example of such a new starting point, where some practitioners are able to reframe criminals as victims of social harm.

References

Bourdieu, P. (1984) *Home Academicus* Palo Alto, CA: Stanford University Press

Copson, L. (2016) 'Realistic Utopianism and Alternatives to Imprisonment: The ideology of crime and the utopia of harm' *Justice, Power and Resistance: Foundation Volume*, pp 73 – 96

Johnstone, G. (2011) *Restorative justice: Ideas, values, debates 2nd ed* New York: Taylor & Francis

Muncie, J. (2006) 'Governing Young People: Coherence and Contradiction in Contemporary Youth Justice' *Critical Social Policy* Volume 26, No.4 pp 770-793

Newburn, T and Crawford, A. (2003) *Youth Offending and Restorative Justice: Implementing Reform in Youth Justice* Devon: Taylor & Francis.

Page, J. (2013) 'Punishment and the Penal Field' in Simon, J. and Sparks, R. (eds) *The Sage Handbook of Punishment and Society* London: SAGE Publications pp 152 – 166

Sim, J. (2008) 'An Inconvenient Criminological Truth: Pain, Punishment and Prison Officers' in Bennett, J., Crewe, B. and Wahidin, A. (eds) *Understanding Prison Staff* Devon: Willan Publishing pp 187 – 212

Zehr, H. (2005) *Changing lenses: A new focus for crime and justice 3rd ed* United Kingdom: Herald Press (VA)

Extended Biography

Research

I completed a BA (Hons) in Criminology with Psychology at Hull University in 2007 going on to complete an MSc in Criminology at Leeds Metropolitan University in 2012. In 2010, I had taken a role as a Support Worker in Leeds working within young people's homes for 'Looked After Children' which saw my academic interests turn to youth justice. Shortly after this I took a position with Wakefield Youth Offending Team working as part of a pilot scheme that implemented the *Youth Restorative Disposal*. This looked to divert first time, low level offending children away from criminal justice measures and instead intervene with Restorative Justice. This experience would ultimately shape my research interests and as I saw statistically, the positive affect the pilot had upon reducing first time entrants into the criminal justice system.

In 2014, I decided to continue with my studies in the form of a PhD with a sole aim of showcasing my experiences within the YOT as an exemplary model of justice. In 2015, I began my position at Liverpool john Moores University as a Graduate Teaching Assistant, and since this point my research aim has become somewhat *skewed* by Critical Criminology. An enlightening period saw my focus shift from an emphasis in showing why my practitioner experience was 'better', and instead I began to question why this model may be less harmful to young people. In doing so, I have identified both the need for administrative Criminology but also the absolute need for Critical Criminology to provide the guide for policy formulation. A Critical Realist perspective has drawn me towards questioning the legitimacy of policy that has its routes within critical theory, but is distorted within the administration, and then ultimately how these policies are enacted and understood by those charged with their delivery.

At the time of writing, I am in my third year of fulltime PhD study. On reflection of my short research career I can see that what I once saw as my research interests (Restorative Justice and Youth Justice) are merely the vessels which I have used to hopefully dig deeper into the relationship (or lack of) between critical ideologies, administrative policy formulation, and policy delivery.

Following the completion of my PhD, I aspire to continue to bridge the gap between policy and practice, and indeed, the gap between policy and ideological interpretations of the social world. My aim would be to continue to do this within the academic environment, however, I would also welcome opportunities to work directly with those organisations that advise, formulate and implement policy to address social ills.

18

Addressing the Collateral Damage of Fast Fashion: the Perception of Social Harm and the Possibility of Consumer Agency

Katja Simončič

Introduction

This chapter addresses social harm induced by consumerism within the garment industry, more precisely, the negative societal consequences of fast fashion. In an effort to find a way of minimising these externalities, special attention is given to the public perception of the social harm concept and the notion of consumer agency. The text is a brief presentation of my research in its nascent phase.

The pursuit of the 'good life' that can only be achieved through the practice of consumerism has become the prevalent global narrative, aspired to by the vast majority of humans, regardless of nationality, ethnicity, gender, religion, or class. The dominant contemporary neoliberal ideology mandates not only that consumption is good, but that it is necessary for the 'health' of our economies and, moreover, an equivalent to freedom (Szeman and James, 2010). Its violently harmful consequences that have manifested themselves in an unsustainable exploitation of global resources and an inhumane exploitation of workers are simply 'business as usual', hidden in the opaque process of production, that often takes place too far away for anyone to care.

When asked directly "would you rob a bank?" and "would you buy a t-shirt if you knew it was made by a child in inadequate conditions?" most people would probably answer both questions with a resounding "no" While the majority of people indeed would not rob a bank, a large percentage of consumers are aware of the possibility that a piece of clothing they desire was made unethically[1], but they ignore that

---

[1]The term ethical fashion is open to interpretation, since what individuals consider as ethical depends on cultural and social factors and is thus subjective. In the context of this

knowledge and buy it regardless. The issue evokes Hannah Arendt's (1963) theory on the banality of evil contending that evil does not always result from the acts of monsters but can occur as a consequence of mere non-thinking on the side of ordinary citizens. The relevance of the idea that such non-thinking can be as dangerous as intentional harm serves as an argument for an exploration into the causes of moral indifference evident in the discrepancy identified above. In an effort to contribute to a, hopefully, more responsible form of consumption and consequently a reduction in social harm, my research aims to stimulate action by encouraging the debate on the need for a shift in the perception of the social harm concept.

The hypothesis motivating this debate is that consumption would become more responsible, resulting in the reduction of social harm if social harm was perceived as negatively as, for example, crime in the public sphere. The perception of social harm, which serves as the key concept of this research is examined within the phenomenon of fast fashion, i.e. the massive and swift production and consumption of cheap and stylish clothing (Cachon and Swinney, 2011).

Rationale

This section specifies the main reasons as to why it is worth considering a campaign for a change in the perception of social harm in society: the universality of the issue, the irrational status of social harm as 'normal', the unsustainability of current levels of production and consumption and the possibility of consumer agency.

In the span of a lifetime every human being is a victim of some or other harmful event that (criminal) law does not address, labelled simply as 'normal', 'routine', an 'outcome of the market economy', 'an accident' or a 'mistake' (Hillyard *et al.*, 2004). At the same time, we all participate, as consumers, in the production chain that inflicts harm to others and the environment and we again accept those consequences as standard. Yet, within Criminology, these questions remain side-lined. Non-critical criminologists maintain a narrow focus on the harm that falls within the scope of legal definitions of violence allowing for the denial of a whole range of other activities and processes that have vast physical and psychological consequences for those exposed to them (Cohen, 2013).

---

chapter, the term stands for a process of production that has neither a negative impact on the people involved in it nor on the environment.

The fact that all humans are victims as well as perpetrators of social harm indicates a universal relevance of the social harm concept and justifies the need to accord it greater academic attention.

Article I. In the USA 14,000 deaths a year occur as a result of murder (Uniform Crime Reports, 2011), 300,000 people die due to white-collar crime (Cedric, 2016)[2] while air pollution causes 200,000 early deaths each year (Chu, 2017). Looking at the numbers alone, one would imagine that people attribute greater severity to the last two, yet, the answer is not that straightforward. While the public perception of these types of harms has indeed grown more negative in the last 40 years, citizens are still more concerned about murder and street crime than of the impact criminal, let alone legal, acts of the rich and powerful might have on their lives (Cedric, 2016). Likewise, people claim to be more concerned about the environment (Pew Research Centre, 2010), yet, they seem to do little about it as consumption of new clothing (Wicker, 2016) and greenhouse gas emissions caused by human activities increase (US Environmental Protection Agency, 2017). There is a common understanding, that while criminal harms merit the response of the State, disapproval from the general public and widespread media coverage, other social harms that are not criminalised do so to a much lesser extent. The current value system in our society that prioritises criminal harms over other social harms must be put under greater academic scrutiny.

The central concern fuelling this research is that many of those who have the ability to, do consume too much and disregard the collateral damage that it causes. The priorities of fashion consumers have changed dramatically in the last 30 years; we shop in larger quantities, more frequently (Hobbes, 2015) and expect to get more for the money we are willing to spend (de Klerk and Tselepis, 2007). In the early 1990s, brands produced two to four new fashion collections a year, which were aligned with the seasons and planned months in advance (Hobbes, 2015). Today, complete flexibility is required, with several new items of clothing designed and manufactured every week (Bhardwaj and Fairhurst, 2010).

According to the Global Footprint Network[3] (2017), in order to replace the resources human beings are using and to offset our waste, an

---

[2]The number of white collar crime victims indicated above includes a wide spectre of injuries: workers injured at work or poisoned by toxic chemicals, citizens exposed to toxic waste and deadly forms of pollution and consumers that have suffered from inadequate products, addictive substances and below average health services (Cedric, 2016). For more see: Herbert and Landrigan (2000); Kramer (1984); Reiman and Leighton (2015).

[3]Global Footprint Network is a research organization that addresses the global

equivalent of 1.6 planets would be needed. The fashion industry, producing over 100 billion items of clothing annually, with 60% ending up as waste within a year (ibid) is the second largest global industry polluter (EcoWatch, 2015).

The damage is, however, not limited to the environment. Garment workers are often exposed to human rights violations and discriminatory practices such as unfair pay, forced labour, child labour, violations of women's rights, unreasonable working hours, dangerous working conditions, discrimination, and the absence of trade unions (Stotz and Kane, 2015). The fashion industry is one of the largest inflictors of slave labour (EcoWatch, 2015). Women, who represent 68 per cent of the workforce in the clothing industry, are particularly vulnerable to various forms of violence and sexual harassment. They often work long and unpredictable hours, receive wages even lower than enslaved men, and have limited access to maternity leave (International Labour Organisation, 2014)

The responsibility for inadequate working conditions and environmental damage created by the garment industry evidently lies on the shoulders of big brands and local factory owners who exploit low standards of worker and environmental protection. Furthermore, blame can be attributed to the governments of the countries of production, that fail to institute stricter standards or, even more commonly, fail to enforce the law that is in place (Hobbes, 2016). Digging deeper in an effort to allocate accountability, according to Haug and Busch (2016) the list of actors expands to include market regulators[4], supplier regulators,[5] consumers, mediators,[6] designers, marketers, producers, suppliers, and workers.[7]

---

management of natural resources by using the Ecological Footprint metric, which compares human demand on nature to what the planet can renew. See: http://www.footprintnetwork.org.

[4]Under "market regulators" Haug and Busch (2016) "understand national and cross-national institutions defining laws and regulations for the local consumer market in relation to production, marketing use of suppliers and product materials".

[5]Under "supplier regulators" Haug and Busch (2016) understand "national and cross-national institutions defining laws and regulations for the production area in focus" (often developing countries).

[6]Under "mediators" Haug and Busch (2016) understand magazines, news media, activist organizations, etc.

[7]Haug and Busch (2016) point out that workers, suppliers, and governments, in developing countries have very little ability to act against the harmful effects of the fashion industry. They argue that fast fashion providers and producers are not able to afford to produce

Even though the consumer is neither the most responsible nor the most forceful actor in the production of social harm in the garment industry (Robins, 2012), the power consumers might possess when acting collectively is an important consideration. Research, however, shows a clear inconsistency between the concern for ethical issues that fashion consumers claim to feel and their actual consumer patterns (Joergens, 2006). According to Ehrich and Irwin (2005), one of the reasons for the attitude-behaviour gap is that many consumers intentionally avoid learning about unethical practices in the garment production processes in order to protect themselves emotionally. Niinimaki (2010) finds that cost, style, quality, a continuous desire for new clothing and compatibility with one 's existing wardrobe, all contribute to the fact that the number of ethical shoppers remains low. Furthermore, the meaning of clothing goes well beyond its functional role, as clothes have always been a venue for expressing one's individuality (ibid) and a way of seeking the acceptance of others (Kaiser, 1990). Lastly, it might be as simple as: "aesthetics trump ethics" (Joy *et al*, 2012: 286). Ethical or ecological fashion is still often understood as shapeless and not stylish as the term eco-fashion frequently brings up the memory of hippie environmental movements of the 1960s and 1970s (Welters, 2008). Since ethical fashion builds on the idea of sustainability and long-term use it does indeed clash with the constantly evolving term 'fashionable'.

Nevertheless, numerous authors contend that consumers do not have to be pawns of governments, transnational, and multinational corporations (TNC and MNC) and their lobbies, but can actively exercise their consumer agency and participate in the changes brought about by globalisation (Eckhardt and Mahi, 2004).[8] Miller (1995) states that today, the larger part of added value created by the workers is reflected in lower prices for the consumer, rather than in larger profit margins for the capitalist. Changes in retail in the late 20th century largely occurred as a response to the existing demand, indicating that the power to dictate the terms of production has shifted to the consumers.

---

clothes to fair standards. The authors are wary of placing too much responsibility on the shoulders of consumers on account of the fact that fashion is largely targeted at young people who often cannot offord to buy ethically produced clothing.
[8]See also: Wilk (1990), Miller (1996)

Concluding Thoughts

While Hannah Arendt's concept on the banality of evil originally applies to Adolf Eichmann and ordinary German citizens, who, under Nazism, worked according to the rules of the existing system and by doing so caused massive harm to the Jewish people, an illustrative contemporary example of moral indifference is the massive consumption of cheap[9] clothing. Continuous consumer demand for newer and cheaper fashion items is inextricably linked to the exploitation of natural resources and the destruction of the environment, and harms to garment workers in the countries of the Global South.

Undeniably, the principal perpetrators of Nazi horrors were the architects and engineers who envisioned the system, yet, one wonders, as Hannah Arendt did, as to why so few ordinary citizens revolted. Arguing that consumers could possess the power to steer change should neither be understood as a stance for a neoliberal "individualisation of responsibility" for collective problems (Bevir and Trentmann, 2007: 232) nor an absolution of the responsibilities of trans national corporations and states (Ethical Fashion Forum, 2013). In light of the projection that the equivalent of two planet Earths will be needed to sustain us by 2030 if we do not start producing and consuming more responsibly (Global Footprint Network, 2017), we should seek to identify all those responsible and look everywhere for possible effective changes.

Acknowledgements

I want to thank my mentors, Dr Aleš Završnik and Dr Renata Salecl for their thoughtful guidance and constructive criticism of my work. Furthermore, I want to thank all of my colleagues at the Institute for Criminology at the Law Faculty in Ljubljana for the opportunity to engage with them in a lively debate on a daily basis. I am extremely grateful for the trust and freedom to explore the issues I am fascinated by.

---

[9] Cheap solely for the consumer, as the *real* price is paid is by those lower in the production chain.

References

Arendt, H. (1963) *Eichmann in Jerusalem: A Report in the Banality of Evil* London: Penguin

Bevir, M. and Trentmann, F. (2007) *Governance, Consumers and Citizens: Agency and Resistance in Contemporary Politics* New York: Palgrave Macmillan

Bhardwaj, V. and Fairhurst, A. (2010) 'Fast Fashion: Response to Changes in the Fashion Industry' *The International Review of Retail, Distribution and Consumer Research* Volume 20, No.1 pp 165-173

Cachon, G. P. and Swinney, R. (2011) 'The Value of Fast Fashion: Quick Response, Enhanced Design, and Strategic Consumer Behavior' *Management Science* Volume 57, No. 4 pp 778-795

Cedric, M. (2016) 'Violent Street Crime Versus Harmful White-collar Crime: A Comparison of Perceived Seriousness and Punitiveness' *Critical Criminology* Volume 24, No. 1, pp 127-143.

Chu, J.M. (2017) 'Study: Air Pollution Causes 200,000 Early Deaths Each Year in the U.S' *MIT News* [online] 29th August Available from: http://news.mit.edu/2013/study-air-pollution-causes-200000-early-deaths-each-year-in-the-us-0829 (accessed 23rd February 2017)

Cohen, S. (2013) *States of Denial: Knowing about Atrocities and Suffering*: John Wiley & Sons

De Klerk, H. M. and Tselepis, T. (2007) 'The Early-adolescent Female Clothing Consumer: Expectations, Evaluation and Satisfaction with Fit as Part of the Appreciation of Clothing Quality' *Journal of Fashion Marketing and Management: An International Journal* Volume 11, No. 3 pp 413-428

Eckhardt, G. M. and Mahi, H. (2004) 'The Role of Consumer Agency in the Globalisation Process in Emerging Markets' *Journal of Macromarketing* Volume 24, No. 2 pp 136-146

EcoWatch (2015) 'Fast Fashion Is the Second Dirtiest Industry in the World, Next to Big Oil' [online] 17th August Available From: http://www.ecowatch.com/fast-fashion-is-the-second-dirtiest-industry-in-the-world-next-to-big--1882083445.html (accessed 23rd February 2017)

Ehrich, K. R. and Irwin, J. R. (2005) 'Wilful Ignorance in the Request for Product Attribute Information' *Journal of Marketing Research* XLII pp 266–277

Ethical Fashion Forum (2013) 'Value Chain Call to Action' [online] Available from: http://source.ethicalfashionforum.com/digital/value-chain-call-to-action-1st-Draft (accessed 23rd February 2017)

Global Footprint Network (2017) 'Ecological Footprint' [online] Available from: http://www.footprintnetwork.org/our-work/ecological-footprint/#worldfootprint (accessed 23rd February, 2017)

Haug, A. and Busch, J. (2016) 'Towards an Ethical Fashion Framework' *Fashion Theory* Volume 20, No. 3 pp 317-339

Herbert, R. and Landrigan, P. J. (2000) 'Work-Related Death: A Continuing Epidemic' *American Journal of Public Health* Volume 90, No.4, pp 541-545

Hillyard, P. Pantazis, C. Tombs, S. and Gordon, D. (2004) *Beyond Criminology: Taking Harm Seriously* London: Pluto Press

Hobbes, M. (2015) 'The Myth of the Ethical Shopper' *The Huffington Post* [online] Available from: http://highline.huffingtonpoxrticles/en/the-myth-of-the-ethical-shopper (accessed 23rd February 2017)

International Labour Organisation (2014) 'Wages and Working Hours in the Textiles, Clothing, Leather and Footwear Industries: Issues Paper for Discussion at the Global Dialogue Forum on Wages and Working Hours in the Textiles, Clothing, Leather and Footwear Industries' Geneva: ILO

Joergens, C. (2006) 'Ethical Fashion: Myth or Future Trend?' *Journal of Fashion Marketing and Management: An International Journal* Volume 10, No. 3 pp 360-371

Joy, A., Sherry Jr, J. F. Venkatesh, A. Wang, J. and Chan, R. (2012) 'Fast Fashion, Sustainability, and the Ethical Appeal of Luxury Brands' *Fashion Theory* Volume 16, No. 3 pp 273-295

Kaiser S. (1990) 'The Social Psychology of Clothing: Symbolic Appearances in Context' Second Edition New York: Macmillan

Kramer, R. C. (1984) 'Corporate Criminality: The Development of an Idea' *Corporations as Criminals* pp 13-37

Laine, A.L. (2015) "Integrated Reporting: Fostering Human Rights Accountability for Multinational Corporations" *The George Washington International Law Review.* Volume 47, No.3, pp 639 - 667

Maniates, M. F. (2001) 'Individualisation: Plant a Tree, Buy a Bike, Save the World?' in *Global Environmental Politics* Volume 1, No. 3 pp 31-52

Maniates, M. and Meyer, J. M. (2010) *The Environmental Politics of Sacrifice* Cambridge, MA: MIT Press

Miller, D. (1995) 'Chapter 1: Consumption as the Vanguard of History' pp1-52 Miller (ed) (1995) *Acknowledging Consumption* London: Routledge

Miller, D. (1996) 'The Myth of Cultural Erosion' pp 153-65 in R.W. Belk, N. Dholakia, and A. Venkatesh (ed) (1996) *Consumption and Macromarketing* Cincinnati, OH: Southwestern

Niinimäki, K. (2010) 'Eco-clothing, consumer identity and ideology' *Sustainable Development* Volume 18, No. 3 pp 150-162

Pew Research Center (2010) 'Growing Concern Over Environment Problem' [online] Available from: http://www.pewglobal.org/2007/06/27/global-unease-with-major-world-powers/256-3/ (accessed 23rd February, 2017)

Reiman, J. and Leighton, P. (2015) *The Rich Get Richer and the Poor Get Prison: A Reader* Boston: Routledge

Robins, J. E. (2012) 'Slave Cocoa and Red Rubber: ED Morel and the Problem of Ethical Consumption' *Comparative Studies in Society and History* Volume 54, No. 3 pp 592-611

Stotz, L. and Kane, G. (2015) 'Facts on The Global Garment Industry' *Clean Clothes Campaign Available at* https://cleanclothes.org/resources/publications/factsheets/general-factsheet-garment-industry-february-2015.pdf

Szeman, I. and James, P. (2010) *Global Local Consumption* London: SAGE

Uniform Crime Reports (2011) [online] Available from: http://www.fbi.gov/about-us/cjis/ucr (accessed 23rd February 2017)

US Environmental Protection Agency (2017) 'Climate Change Indicators: Greenhouse Gases' [online] Available from: https://www.epa.gov/climate-indicators/greenhouse-gases (accessed 23rd February 2017)

Welters, L. (2008) "The Natural Look: American Style in the 1970s" *Fashion Theory* Volume 12, No. 4, pp 489–510

Wicker, A. (2016) 'Fast Fashion is Creating an Environmental Problem' *Newsweek* [online] 1st September Available at: http://europe.newsweek.com/old-clothes-fashion-waste-crisis-494824?rm=eu (accessed 23rd February, 2017)

Wilk, R. (1990) 'Consumer Goods as Dialogue About Development: Research in Progress in Belize' *Culture and History* Volume 7, pp 79-100

Extended Biography

Research

My drive to study law is underpinned by a desire for change. I have always been interested in issues related to social justice, development, sustainability and in finding ways to reduce inequality. My first real opportunity to deal with these topics in depth was my undergraduate thesis titled "International Development Cooperation in Light of Inadequate Development of Recipient Countries". It addressed the issue of ineffectiveness of International Aid that has been flowing to the African continent in the last 60 years and presented an analysis of the forms of aid and of the reasons behind the presumed inefficacy as well as a set of suggestions to improve the effectiveness of the system.

During my period of undergraduate study I realised that my primary interest was not in learning about the existing Law, but rather in learning about local and global issues that legal solutions could address and potentially solve. After working as a trainee at the Institute for International Law and International Relations at the Faculty of Law for six months, I thus enrolled in the International Development Studies MSc program at the University of Amsterdam. Sceptical of the concept of Aid 'given' to the coutries of the Global South by the countries of the Global North, from the beginning I was fascinated by the agency of the poor in the developing world. In light of their eagerness to improve their lives as well as the tremendous structural obstacles they face, I was interested in the possibilities that the poor have to lift themselves out of poverty through entrrpeneurship. I spent July and August 2014 in Cebu, the Philippines, researching the engagement of local entrepreneurs in the booming service outsourcing industry and the obstacles they face in setting up small and medium size business in that specific sector.

After graduating in January 2015 I returned to Slovenia and co-organised an event called SIXPO-Ljubljana Social Innovation Expo, that encouraged young individuals to create entrepreneurial ideas with a social impact. I wanted to put the knowledge I gained conducting empirical research in the Philippines to good use and, furthermore, learn more about social entrepreneurship in Slovenia.

In October 2015 I obtained a position at the Institute of Criminology at the Law Faculty in Ljubljana where I currently work as a junior researcher and pursue a PhD in Criminology. In an effort to combine my interests in social justice with Criminology I set out to explore harmful actions of transnational corporations and the concept of social harm in particular. The fact that criminology adresses and condemns certain harms and neglects others contributes to the distorted perception that social harm is 'normal' and reinforces the myopic belief that the only answer to it is the criminalisation of harmful activities and the expansion of the criminal justice system (Hillyard *et al.*, 2004).

Studying social harm, I first took interest in "land grabbing"; i.e. the appropriation of extensive amounts of land that has been taking place mainly in the countries of the Global South and could be understood as a form of 21st century colonialism. My second major research focus has been the consumer, who contributes to the harm caused by consumerism, yet can also be considered a victim of it. The logic fueling my interest has been, again, the possibility of agency individuals have to actively participate in forming a society that meets their needs. Additionally, the phenomenon that I have been looking at more closely is fast fashion', the massive production of cheap clothes and an evident source of social harm in the form of inadequate workers rights protection, polluted environment (Laine, 2015) and time erosion for the consumer (Worldwatch.org, 2016). My next step within the research this reserachwill be a more in-depth investigation of the role transnational corpoartions and the state play in the reproduction of social harm.

In the next four years I will be, aside from my PhD focus, conducting research in Poland, China, Italy and Morocco on the topics of place-making and consumerism in the context of Trans-making, a Horizon 2020/MSCA-RISE project. In light of the fact that consuming and encouraging people to consume have become central activities in the public space, the rationale for my research is the hypothesis that reclaiming the public space from corporations and marketing agencies can open up the possibilities for greater participation of citizens in the public sphere and consequently a more equal and inclusive society.

Activism, Organisational Work and/or Professional Membership
During my undergraduate studies at the Law Faculty in Ljubljana I engaged in volunteer work with Amnesty International Slovenia and the Asylum home for refugees and spent a semester working at the Government Office for Integration at the Mnistry of the Interior, as a part of a Legal Counselling program for foreigners and refugees organised by my faculty. My work with refugess continued in my role as a trainee at the Peace Institute, the leading Slovenian Institute for Contemporary Social and Political studies in 2015. At the Institute I researched migration and freedom of speech issues and conducted an empirical study on the way administrative officials implement the principle of protection of parties' rights.

Selected Works
Simončič, K. (2013). Mednarodno razvojno sodelovanje v luči pomanjkljive stopnje razvoja držav prejemnic pomoči: (diplomska naloga) (Undergraduate dissertation)

Simončič, K. (2014). Philippine-Owned SMEs in the Service-Outsourcing Sector: Research on the Opportunity for Indigenous Entrepreneurship in the Service Outsourcing Industry in Cebu, the Philippines (Graduate dissertation)

Cvikl, L., Mihelj Plesničar, M., Simončič, K., Završnik, A. (2015) Weekly Data Collection on the Situation of Persons in Need of International Protection: Slovenian National Report (Report, European Union Agency for Fundamental Rights)

Kogovšek Šalamon N., Simončič, K. (2015) Učinkovita interpretacija načela varstva pravic strank v upravnem postopku (Article, Javna Uprava, Letn. 51, št ¾ (2015), str. 73-94).

Contact Details
Email: katja.simoncic@yahoo.com
Linkenin: si.linkedin.com/in/katjasimoncic

19

Neutralising Deviance: The Legitimation of Harm and the Culture of Finance in the City of London

Alex Simpson

Introduction

This chapter draws on overarching themes that emerged out of an ethnographic study of harm and deviance in the City of London's financial services industry. Taken from my PhD thesis, the findings consider issues of morality and justice in the organisation of economic life. In the context of widening material, social and economic inequality, the project asked, *how economic agents within the financial services industry actively [re]produce a culturally embedded and dominant system of market behaviour?* This led to three key findings; [1] an ethnographic understanding of the City of London as a bounded enclave of wealth, privilege and success, organised around a self-serving set of rule-systems and cultural practices; [2] the ways in which individual financial actors internalise the market through the legitimising capital of speed, intelligence and discipline; [3] how financial action, as a set of social arrangements, tapers individual notions of social responsibility by exalting the monetary unit and neutralising the production of social harm. Examining organisational practice and normalised social deviance, the findings lead to a deeper understanding the relationship between finance and society as well as speaking to the way in which market ideology exists as a 'world making power' (Bourdieu, 1987) that involves the capacity to impose a legitimate vision and its divisions on a social world.

While the events of the 2008 financial crisis recede into the past, as a society, 'we' continue to feel its widespread social, economic and political effects (Dinerstein *et al*, 2014). The logic of 'the market' continues to intermesh the economic logic of austerity with social responsibility, ensuring that the poorest and most vulnerable pay the highest price (French and Leyshon, 2010; Joseph Rowntree Foundation, 2012; Peck, 2012). To prop the failing banks, the UK Treasury pumped in £566 billion, amounting to 89 per cent of its assets, into the financial services industry (National Audit Office, 2011).

Creating a public crisis out of a banking crisis, the outcome wedded us all involuntarily to the City's high-stakes game of risk. While crises, economic or otherwise, are usually defined by change and the demise of past unstable conditions, the 2008 financial crisis accelerated a far-reaching ideological programme of 'more market' (French and Leyshon, 2010). The consequence has been almost ten years of further privatisation, welfare cuts and the unshackling of the market institutions from the regulatory controls of democratic governance – a process that has increased levels of harm and suffering throughout society (Peck, 2012; Pemberton, 2015).

By focusing on the City of London, the project critically explores constructions of harm and deviance within systems of financial action and seeks to explain its cultural legitimisation. The actions explored as part of this study may not be defined in law as 'criminal', yet there remains a moral imperative to further understand the structures of power and cultures of neutralisation that, in Sykes and Matza's (1957) use of the term, continue to produce well-told effects of social, economic and political harm onto society without sustained levels of critical reflection. Drawing on an ethnographic approach, the data is drawn from a three-tiered mixed method, incorporating fourteen months of non-participant observation, photographic representation utilising over 130 photographs, and 27 in-depth interviews. The findings explore the descriptions, explanations and evaluations that individuals attach to their social experience to collectively construct a bottom-up vision of financial life within the City of London.

Space, Power and the City of London

Ethnographic observation of the practices and actions within the City of London led to an understanding of its symbolic function as an expressive field of power. As a spatial, technological and social environment, the City is a bounded and unified system of financial action that espouses a dominant vision of 'the market' as a deliberately abstract and benevolent social system. It is a spatial system that uncritically accepts the 'truth' of competition and the 'virtue' of profit. The City's instantly recognisable skyline offers a sense of identity and 'ownership' for Londoners and the UK – the benign names of the skyscrapers, such as the 'Gherkin' or the 'Walkie-Talkie', being part of a carefully managed strategy. It is a projection of the City that needs to be challenged and viewed as part of an intergenerational statement of market dominance. Layers of history and, with it, legitimation are etched onto City's topographical landscape to engender a coherent structure of 'oneness', 'wholeness' and 'greatness'. Together, the spatial organisation of the City stands as a 'reservoir of symbolic power' (Wacquant and Bourdieu, 1993) and serves as a very real reminder of who is responsible for the wealth and success it generates. In turn, this produces and maintains a symbolic boundary of inclusion and exclusion.

Within this environment, the abstractions of the market are reduced, in a solid and tangible sense, to impinge on minds and bodies of individuals who work within this space. At the centre lies the symbolic construction of the bank – the principal producer and funder of the City's collective wealth. Here, the speed and the flow of financial market practice is mapped out through an interconnecting web of technological tools of communication. Through the web of technology, individuals are able to extend their reach beyond the physical confines of the trading room and are exposed to the universal demands of global capital. The bank is the social arena that provides the social context for financial action. Here, actors engage in a competitive struggle for distinction organised around a strategic display of authority and prowess. A universal acceptance of the force of competition binds together the financial workforce and internalises the market's speed and flow as a force of progress and development.

The relational vision of financial action comes together to establish and maintain a common affiliation of material and spatial exclusivity. As an enclave of wealth, privilege and success, the City's status is legitimised through its relation to power that divorces it from wider social interests of non-economic or monetary value. It is a reading of social space that situates cultural deviance within a bounded environment of financial market action; one that reproduces a negotiated and self-serving system of moral judgement, structured by the force of competition, profit and growth.

A 'Super Subset of Individuals': Internalising Market Speed, Intelligence and Discipline

Examining the field of finance leads to a critical evaluation, through in-depth interviews, of the shared beliefs, ideologies and symbolic valuation of cultural resources that function within the City. Together, these contribute to the production of power and establish a dominant financial market framework. The never-ending trial of competition reduces financial action to a game of survival. Those who succeed in this ritualistic expression become part of a 'separate, sacred group' (Bourdieu, The State Nobility: Elite Schools in the Field of Power, 1996) who capitalise on their exclusivity and adherence to values of the financial market. Specifically, this leads to the embodiment of speed, intelligence and collective discipline – legitimising systems of market capital.

Within the financial marketplace, individuals compete to hone in on and control the rapid fluctuations of finance market action. Recognising and rewarding a sacrificial commitment to the financial market, individuals construct a collective ability to 'feel the market' as a 'rooted essence' running through their body. The ritual of competition forces the exclusion of the weak, reducing financial action to a zero-sum competition and survival. Despite the chaos and upheaval of competition, the financial market takes on a Malthusian 'natural order' or 'positive check' that, even after the 2008 financial crisis, serves to ensure that it is only the strong and most able who survive. It is a process of natural selection that leaves only an elective elite who are defined by their ability to internalise the speed, intelligence and discipline of the financial market.

Embodying speed and flow of the financial market becomes marker of cultural distinction that separates insider financial experts from commonplace outsiders. The distinction establishes a hierarchical demarcation of experience that prioritises financial efficacy over broader issues of social responsibility. Yet, competition establishes a destructive internal battle in which weakness becomes a market imperfection to be exploited. Insecurity, vulnerability and paranoia are rife within the City. Within market action is a powerful sensory and addictive thrill, one that masks the inherent harmful destructive and sacrificial character of financial life. A sacrificial commitment to the financial market, displayed through long hours, heavy drinking and embracing the intense pressure of ceaseless competition, establishes a dominant system of discipline. Discipline compels individuals to transform the negative and restraining practices of financial life into a system of embodied, material and institutional empowerment. Moreover, it transforms financial harm into a legitimised form of symbolic recognition and common affiliation.

Whereas capital, particularly cultural capital, is usually thought of in relation to socially desirable traits (such as intellectual acumen in the university setting or emotional responsiveness in the healthcare system) in the financial field speed, discipline and intelligence each manifest through a prism of individualist competition and survival. In this manner, intelligence is turned into a weapon that is used to exclude, instil vulnerability and exploit other actors in the field in the pursuit of profit. Together, speed, discipline and intelligence are a ruling and embodied system of cultural capital through which agents of economic life embody the financial market system as well as reconcile individual sacrifices or wider social incompatibilities. Here, harm production is de-stigmatised through a relationship to power and, as a taken-for-granted part of financial efficacy, becomes part of normal financial practice.

[Re]structuring Perceptions of Deviance and Harm in the City of London

The final analysis relates to evaluating the role of harm and deviance in the cultural formation of practice in the City of London. The relational and situation understanding of financial life within the City of London serves to create understandings of the social world that determine individual chances of success or failure as well as establishing what is judged to be 'reasonable' or 'unreasonable'. The result is a culturally and spatially situated understanding of harm and deviance. Constrained by the legitimising framework of financial action, certain harmful practices may not acquire the distinction of deviance so long as the negative costs are externalised beyond the immediate sphere of reference. In other words, by maintaining the integrity of the market (i.e. by not engaging in criminal acts of fraud, deception or insider trading), social and economic harm is legitimised as part of financial life if the harm and destruction of financial affect impact alternative – or marginalised – social spaces.

Such social disconnection is crystallised around a dominant financial 'way of being' in which individuals adapt and limit their frame of reference to the social world. The ill-defined 'real economy' forms the basis of all commodities, financial instruments and services that are bought and sold through the financial marketplace. However, individuals retain no underlying interest in the community itself – that is to say, us. Interest is limited to exposure to price. 'We' then are removed from the collective gaze of financial actors and are, in turn, atomised through asymmetrical contracts of debt that are being bought, repackaged and sold on in a never-ending cycle of financial violence. In the manner of Polanyi (2001 [1944]), our true value is expressed as a monetary value or as a commodity. Everything else remains tangential. The dominance discourse of finance that is pervasive throughout the City dismisses harms that result as an inevitable function of market engagement; these expressed as 'friction costs' or 'collateral'. Moreover, the discourse of complexity that runs through finance underpins this re-structuring which compartmentalises the inverse relationship between finance and society. The result is a fundamental social detachment in which the logic of competitive interest does not extend beyond the sphere of the self. Divorced from underlying issues of social wellbeing not recognised by the financial market, risk and recklessness becomes legitimised in the pursuit of profit.

As a set of social arrangements, financial action tapers individual notions of social responsibility by exalting the monetary unit and, in the process, [re]shape and [re]define the boundaries of moral efficacy. Out of this competitive struggle emerges a 'logical' and 'moral' system of market domination – legitimised further by its close proximity to the broader field of power – that restructures the perceptions and interests and the dominant field. Acts of social deviance become established as a normative way of life, despite the manifestation of social harm, since the costs are relocated beyond the immediate field of the self and are pressed onto a marginalised cultural field. This leads to a relational and situated cultural understanding of the ways in which harm and deviance are neutralised and transformed into a legitimate system of profit making.

Conclusion

The findings point to a relational understanding of social deviance and the legitimisation of social harm. In the context of the field of finance, by way of cultural and symbolic association, many of the practices of financial life are not viewed by their perpetrators to be deviant at all. Acts of social deviance and harm creation can be legitimised by the dominant field of finance as it filters the perceptions of a given social setting. A common adherence to the moral and legitimising cultural framework of the market serves to normalise competitive pursuit of profit.

Engendering a myopic focus, the financial market becomes a 'natural' force of social cohesion, productivity and intellectual strength. It is through displays of intellectual acumen and sharpness that a range of products and services are created, bought, repackaged and sold on through the matrix of market interaction. Tied up within these products are very real world social outcomes whose interests and experiences are played out beyond the field of financial life. However, their only inherent value is in an exposure to price and the propensity for capital gain (be it economic or cultural). Beyond this proxy valuation of price, all harms that may be pressed onto the social lives and experiences embedded within these products is legitimised by the 'terms of the game' as laid out by the dominant field of finance. In other words, the close relational proximity shared by the field of finance and the broader field of power mean that acts of harm production can appear to be a 'natural', 'inevitable' or 'inconsequential' friction of financial activity.

Acknowledgements

Throughout the three years of the project and beyond, so many people have given me so much help in so many wonderful and unexpected ways that it would be impossible to thank them all. If it were not for the support of my supervisors, Gareth Millington and Rowland Atkinson, then this project would never have been. Similarly, the support of the European Group has been truly amazing throughout. Finally, it would be remiss if it did not thank Dawn Stephen and Yvonne Jewkes who have been brilliant in their guidance as I continue my academic development in Brighton.

References

Bourdieu, P. (1987) 'What Makes Social Class? On the Theoretical and Practical Existence of Groups' *Berkley Journal of Sociology* Volume 32, pp 1-18

Bourdieu, P. (1996) *The State Nobility: Elite Schools in the Field of Power* Cambridge: Polity Press.

Dinerstein, A., Schwartz, G. and Taylor, G. (2014) 'Sociological Imagination as Social Critique: Interrogating the 'Global Economic Crisis'' *Sociology* Volume 48, No. 5 pp 859-868

French, S. and Leyshon, A. (2010) '"These F@#king Guys": The Terrible Waste of a Good Crisis' *Environment and Planning* Volume 42 No. 11 pp 2549-2559

Joseph Rowntree Foundation (2012) Financial Crisis, Five Years On: The Poorest Pay the Price. [Online] Available From: http://www.jrf.org.uk/blog/2012/08/financial-crisis-five-years-poorest-pay-price (accessed 25 June 2013)

National Audit Office (2011) The Comptroller and Auditor General's Report on Accounts to the House of Commons London: HM Treasury.

Peck, J. (2012) 'Austerity Urbanism: American Cities Under Extreme Economy' *City*, Volume 16, No. 6 pp 626-655

Pemberton, S. (2015) *Harmful Societies: Understanding Social Harm* Bristol: Polity Press

Polanyi, K. (2001 [1944]) *The Great Transformation* Second Edition. Boston, MA: Beacon Press

Sykes, G. and Matza, D. (1957) 'Techniques of Neutralization: A Theory of Delinquency' *American Sociological Review*, Volume 22, No.6 pp 664-670

Wacquant, L. and Bourdieu, P. (1993) 'From Ruling Class to Field Power: An Interview with Pierre Bourdieu on La noblesse d'Etat' *Theory, Culture and Society* Volume 10, No. 3 pp 19-44

Extended Biography

Research

I am a Senior Lecturer in Criminology at the University of Brighton, having joined in September 2015. My research interests focus on a range of issues, including the criminology of harm, elite social deviance, cultural marginalisation and cultural economy. I also have a keen interest in qualitative research methods, including ethnography, photographic representation and elicitation, critical discourse analysis and in depth interview techniques. I was awarded my PhD from the University of York in 2015. Supported by an ESRC studentship, the thesis is an ethnographic exploration of the culture of finance and the neutralisation of deviance within the City of London. This research project is a profile of inverted social deviance that creates a sociological snapshot of the organising interests and ideologies functioning within spaces and institutions of global finance. Engaging in the everyday routines, expectations and assumptions of economic actors embedded within the financial services industry, the study contributes towards an enhanced understanding of how the cultural sensibilities that underpin a market based reality perpetuate gross social and economic inequalities through the shifting of negative market costs on vulnerable sections of society. Leading to a critical evaluation of the organising ideologies and taken-for-granted assumptions that function within the City of London, the principal findings detail the relational struggles, strategies and vested interests that dominate the field of finance life.

Currently, I am part of a four-person research group at the University of Brighton that is preparing an ESRC bid which examines the role of debt amongst young adults and the impact which it has in relation to future opportunity. I have also worked on a British Academy funded project based at Brunel University which was an ethnographic study of class-based experiences of dirt and dirty work. Other previous research experience includes a discourse analysis of the politics of representation and recognition for culturally marginalised groups following the 2011 London riots, notions of memory and home for migrant communities as well as an exploration of symbolic expressions of religiosity in the home. Prior to undertaking my PhD, I was awarded a Distinction in Globalisation and Development from Warwick University in 2012 as well as a First Class degree in Sociology from the University of Leicester in 2010. I have been part of a four-person organising committee for the post-graduate study group, NYLON, and I continue to be a regular member of its post-doctorate group, NYLUM. This is international intellectual working group which was set up by Richard Sennett and Craig Calhoun to connect students and academics with a shared interest in culture and qualitative research methods.

Future Aspirations

Future research developments include expanding on my PhD to focus on the way market practice impacts on other social sites outside of the City of London. In particular, this includes an unfolding project that explores the ways competitive sport prepares and perfects financial actors for the corporeal rigours of financial market action. This is organised around a focused ethnography of a north London cycling club, the members of which predominately work in the City of London. The focus on cycling, in this context, offers an innovative exploration of a particular class and gendered ritual, predicated on competitiveness, aggression and prowess. Developing themes of masculinity and performativity in the context of finance, the project explores the deeply entwined cultural practices of finance and club cycling and, in doing so, unpacks the way sport functions to produce the dominant masculinist disposition and 'hardened body' that is 'fit for work' and 'fit for play'.

Selected Works

Simpson, A. [expected 2017] *'Consecrating the Elite: Culturally embedding the financial market in the City of London'* in T. Geelan, M. Gonzalez Hernando and P. Walsh (eds) *From Financial Crisis to Social Change: Towards Alternative Horizons,* London: Palgrave Macmillan.

Hughes, J. Simpson, R. Slutskaya, N., Simpson, A. and Hughes, K. (2016) *'Beyond the Symbolic: A Relational Approach to Dirty Work through a Study of Refuse Collectors and Street Cleaners'* in *Work, Employment and Society,* Volume 31, No. 1, pp 106-122

Simpson, A., (2016) *'The Big Short is a Perverse Robin Hood Parable – in which King John Wins' The Conversation,* [online] https://theconversation.com/the-big-short-is-a-perverse-robin-hood-parable-in-which-king-john-wins-54422

Simpson, A. (2015) *'A Four-Step Process to Studying the Field through the City of London' Current Research on Cities* Volume 51, pp 96-105

Simpson, A., Slutskaya, N. Hughes, J. and Simpson, R. (2014), *The Use of Ethnography to Explore Meanings that Refuse Collectors Attach to their Work' Qualitative Research in Organizations and Management* Volume 3, No. 9, pp 183 – 200

Contact Details

Email: ats130@gmail.com
Twitter: *@a1exsimps*

20

Deafening Attempts to Silence: Critically Exploring the Deaths of Patients Detained in Psychiatric Detention

Carly Speed

"Valuing the View from Below": Introducing the Issue

This chapter is based upon ongoing doctoral research into the deaths of patients detained under the Mental Health Act in England. The issue of deaths in psychiatric detention is a persistent issue. Historically, statistics related to the deaths of 'lunatic asylum' patients were not collected on a national basis. However, statistics related to individual asylums indicated the problematic nature of the issue. An example of this was the West Riding of York Pauper Lunatic Asylum, where between 1819 and 1840, there were 2,739 admissions with 868 deaths (Lancet, 1840: 732). Contemporarily, with statistics now gathered on a national basis, the Care Quality Commission (CQC, 2016: 52) stated that between 2011 and 2016 there were 1,202 deaths of detained patients in England. Of these, 102 deaths were due to an "unknown cause", 200 were as a result of "unnatural causes" and 900 were attributed to "natural causes" (ibid: 52). However, this was an issue referred to by Hardy (2013: np) who argued that "death by natural causes does not necessarily mean it was not preventable". This was a point also stressed by Legal Practitioner Seven who, when being interviewed for this research, noted that "deaths could be as a result of natural causes but these deaths were often preventable and involved just as many failings an unnatural deaths".

This chapter outlines ongoing research aimed to undertake a critical analysis of deaths in psychiatric detention from those with first-hand experiences of the issue. Key to the research was developing a critical understanding of how various official "regimes of truth" (Foucault, 1977: 208) have promoted the subjugation and silencing of various different subordinate knowledges, thus attempting to disqualify them. In turn, they are dismissed as "nonconceptual, as insufficiently elaborated, naive knowledges" (Foucault, 2003a: 7). This research focuses on "valuing the view from below" (Stubbs, 2008: 8), thus "ensuring that voices and experiences of those marginalised by institutionalised state practices are heard and represented" (Scraton, 2007: 10). Therefore, the research utilises several different data collection methods which aims to align closely with the theoretical underpinnings of the research and allowed subjugated voices and knowledges to be heard. The first of these methods was archival research. Accessing files at The National Archives (TNA), local archives, and newspaper archives allows for an understanding to emerge related to the historical treatment of patients, their families and advocates. Following on from this, online campaign websites were examined. These websites were established by bereaved families following the death of their relative in psychiatric detention and chronicle the efforts of their families in obtaining justice and accountability. Finally, in order to examine the contemporary picture related to deaths in psychiatric detention, the research gathered the experiences of bereaved families, legal practitioners, coroners and a member of parliament, through interviews and questionnaires.

Through these various different data collection methods, a number of key themes emerged and these themes were apparent in both the historical and contemporary data. The first of these was the control over patients along with their families and advocates, in both life and death. This linked to another theme of the research: that of the extensive attempted silencing of these groups. The blaming of patients, families and advocates was also referred to endlessly throughout the research. This further linked with the next theme of the prolific official denial of responsibility and accountability related to any wrongdoing, again in both the life and deaths of patients. This official denial of accountability and responsibility was particularly prevalent in the inquest and investigation processes following the deaths of detained patients. The final theme of the research was the continuous challenge, contestation and resistance demonstrated by patients, families and advocates (for further discussion indicating other key findings of the research please see: Speed, 2017a and Speed 2017b).

This chapter will now focus on one of the key findings of the research detailed above, the attempted dismissal and silencing of patients, families and advocates, in both life and death. It is not the case that following death, detained patients suddenly become subjugated and marginalised. In life, this was often the official response to them, as this chapter will demonstrate. Therefore, despite the fact that the research focused on the deaths of patients and the aftermath of these deaths, it was vital to also understand the response to them in life in order to comprehend the origins of the silencing and subjugation that they are subjected to in death.

Attempts to Silence the Voices of Patients, Families and Advocates

In Life
In 1938, a patient wrote to the Home Secretary detailing the abuse he had received in the mental hospital he was housed within. For the patient, his experience within the hospital was so bad that he stated that he would prefer capital punishment (TNA, 1933-56). An internal investigation found no evidence corroborating the claims made by the patient and instead the focus was deflected on to the complainant himself, with the staff at the hospital claiming that the patient had been aggressive towards them (ibid). This deflection of attention away from any official wrongdoing was also apparent between 1975-78 when the relative of a psychiatric patient wrote continuously to the authorities regarding allegations concerning the treatment his relative had received as a patient (TNA, 1975-78). The correspondence alleged that the abuse of his relative was widespread by various members of staff and the abuse had "filled [the patient] with fear and terror", which had "totally degraded her inhumanly" (ibid). For the family, the system was an "18th century charade" (ibid). However, an inquiry into the allegations instead focused attention onto the relative who it was alleged had "contributed to" the issues being examined within the inquiry (ibid).

Ex-patients sharing their experiences has assisted in challenging the secrecy surrounding the response to patients. Pole-Jones detailed her time in a psychiatric unit during the 1970s. She stated that she was given ten times the dose of a particular medicine per day than a large man should take (Gray, 2006: 20). She also alleged that upon asking the staff for water they would "make me plead and beg for the water. They used to do the same thing with food. They used to throw it at me and make me grovel on the floor for it" (ibid: 22). For Pole-Jones, the staff "tried to force you into a position where you have to acknowledge that you are wrong" (ibid: 22). John O'Donoghue, another individual who shared his experiences as a patient in the 1970s and 1980s, argued that being a patient meant that he had "a destiny that isn't mine but which has been assigned to me. I'm marked by events, by comments from others and files I have no right to see" (O'Donoghue, 2012: 98).

Regarding more contemporary experiences, Family Member Two, when interviewed, noted how their family had written numerous letters to the hospital where their relative was detained, detailing their concerns regarding their relative being actively suicidal. The family stated that they "never received a single reply". Their relative later did go on to take their own life and upon informing the coroner that they had tried to warn the hospital, the hospital trust representative "completely refuted the fact that numerous letters had been sent to them". This was also reflective of comments made by Legal Practitioner Eight who said that when working with bereaved families, they would often share copies of the letters they had sent to hospital trusts, which had received no reply or replies which "dismissed or downplayed their concerns [...] concerns that were actually, in hindsight, extremely valid".

In Death
Following the deaths of individuals in police and prison custody these cases are passed externally for independent investigation. However, following the deaths of patients detained under the Mental Health Act, there is no equivalent independent investigation system, meaning that the hospital trust in charge of the care of the deceased at the time of their death investigate their own potential failings. This, for INQUEST, reflected a "glaring disparity" between the official response to the deaths of detained patients, in comparison to the deaths of those in police and prison custody (INQUEST, 2015: 5). Participants in the research persistently indicated their dismay at the lack of an independent investigation system and this was summarised by Family Member Three who questioned "how can you really justify investigating yourself over something as serious as a death?" As Legal Practitioner Seven noted, "of course you would minimise wrongdoings and divert attention away from your own failings".

The battles faced by bereaved families following the death of their relative in psychiatric detention was demonstrated by the family behind Campaign A who chronicled their fight for justice and accountability on their website. During the time that their relative was detained, the family alleged that she was assaulted, prescribed inappropriate levels of powerful drugs and had been "seriously neglected [...] on a systemic basis". Following her death, the family found it "shocking" and "appalling" to learn that detained patients do not have the same safeguards as prisoners or those in police custody should they die. Therefore, the family aimed to "get things changed, once and for all, so that no family ever has to go through the tragedy that we have". However, this quest for justice and accountability was hindered when they found that the coroner overseeing their case felt that it was "not worth proper consideration" and with "aggression imbued throughout a rushed verbal judgement [...] he refused to look at my family once". This mirrored the experiences of Family Member Three, who noted how the coroner assigned to their case "glossed over our concerns" and if their barrister "hadn't continually challenged every point then we would have walked out at the end [of the inquest] none the wiser". Similarly, for the family behind Campaign C, the inquest, rather than providing answers, "served to bring more questions". Therefore, in aiming to simply "find the truth" (Campaign G) following the death of their relative, families and advocates experience "doors being closed in your face, left, right and centre" (Family Member Three). As a family member behind Campaign F noted, "I can't understand why the battle for accountability and justice should be so hard". However, despite the hurdles placed in their way, families such as those involved with Campaign E "continue [their] fight for the people that now have no voice".

Concluding Thoughts

Foucault attacked the idea that state institutions and their practices have become more enlightened and humanitarian (Foucault, 2003b). This research also questions this, through critically analysing the continued suppression, subjugation and silencing of patients, along with their families and advocates over decades and, in some cases, centuries. It was therefore unsurprising that the CQC (2016: 6) noted that they had found "little or no improvement in some areas that directly affect patients [and] their families". As the family behind Campaign D argued, "how many more must die before action plans actually get actioned and when will things actually change?"

The issues displayed within this research demonstrate a continued lack of official regard for patients, families and advocates, whilst also critically examining how dominant power structures have attempted to silence any resistance and challenge. The research questions why there are such sustained efforts to silence and discredit the voices and experiences of these groups and why the dominant voices in this area, such as hospital trusts, are so keen to exploit their ability to utilise their power to "operate beyond public scrutiny and thus accountability" (Tombs and Whyte, 2003: 4). However, this research has also demonstrated that despite the subjugation and marginalisation they face, patients, families and advocates have contested the restraints placed upon them and these contestations were as apparent in the 18th century as they are today. This has resulted in alternative truths and knowledges emerging that have directly challenged dominant voices in this area. Therefore, these groups have successfully navigated the attempts to silence them at every turn. An attempted silencing that is truly deafening.

Acknowledgements

Thank you to all of the individuals who took part in this research. Taking the time to talk in such depth regarding your experiences was very much appreciated. Thank you also to Professor Joe Sim, Dr Victoria Cooper and Dr David Scott for your ongoing support. Thanks too to Samantha Fletcher for your kind comments on this chapter. Finally, thank you to Liverpool John Moores University for covering the cost of my tuition fees whilst also funding the archival research.

References

CQC (2016) *Monitoring the Mental Health Act in 2015/16,* Newcastle upon Tyne: Care Quality Commission

Foucault, M. (1977) *Discipline and Punish,* London: Penguin Books

Foucault, M. (2003a) *Society Must be Defended,* London: Penguin Books.

Foucault, M. (2003b) *Madness and Civilization*, Abingdon: Routledge

Gray, P. (2006) *The Madness of Our Lives: Experiences of Mental Breakdown and Recovery,* London: Jessica Kingsley Publishers

Hardy, L. (2013) *'Deaths of Detained Patients-An Independent Investigation?'* (Online) 29th July Available From: http://www.pannone.com/media-centre/blog/medical-negligence-blog/deaths-sectioned-patients-%E2%80%93-independent-investigation. (Accessed: 28th January 2017)

INQUEST (2015) *Deaths in Mental Health Detention: An Investigation Framework Fit For Purpose?* London: INQUEST

Lancet, The. (1840) *Volume the First Edited by Thomas Wakley*, London: George Churchill

O'Donoghue, J. (2012) *Sectioned: A Life Interrupted,* London: John Murray Publishers

Scraton, P. (2007) *Power, Conflict and Criminalisation*, London: Routledge

Speed, C. (2017a) 'As Little Regard in Life as in Death: A Critical Analysis of Subjugation and Accountability Following Deaths in Psychiatric Detention' *Illness, Crisis and Loss,* Volume25, No.1 pp 27-42

Speed, C. (2017b) ''They Cannot Speak Anymore-We Will Make Their Voices Count': Critically Examining Deaths in Psychiatric Detention' in Atkinson, K, Huber, A and Tucker, K (eds.) *Voices of Resistance: Subjugated Knowledge and the Challenge to the Criminal Justice System*, Liverpool: Centre for the Study of Crime, Criminalisation and Social Exclusion

Stubbs, J. (2008) 'Critical Criminological Research' in Anthony, T. and Cunneen, C. (eds.) *The Critical Criminology Companion*, Annandale: Hawkins Press

The National Archives (1933-56) Offences with Respect of Ill-Treatment of Patients by Staff of Institutions (MH 51/411) London: TNA

The National Archives (1975-78) Bolton Area Health Authority: Inquiry into Allegation Concerning the Treatment of Patients (In Particular Mrs Sarah Elizabeth Ashton) in the Psychiatric Department, Bolton General Hospital (MH 160/1157) London: TNA

Tombs, S. and Whyte, D. (2003) 'Introduction: Scrutinizing the Powerful: Crime, Contemporary Political Economy, and Critical Social Research' pp 3- 45 in Tombs, S. and Whyte, D. (eds) *Unmasking the Crimes of the Powerful* New York: Peter Lang

Extended Biography

Research

Whilst undertaking my degree in Criminology at Liverpool John Moores University, a topic that was of particular interest to me was deaths in custody. For that reason I decided upon the self-inflicted deaths of prisoners in England and Wales as a dissertation topic. Here, I gathered data from legal practitioners, academics and the team at INQUEST. During correspondence with INQUEST, it became apparent that the deaths of patients detained under the Mental Health Act was an extremely neglected area in relation to critical research. Therefore, following completion of my degree, I then went on to undertake a Master's degree in Critical Social Science, also at Liverpool John Moores University. The thesis focused on the deaths of detained patients and was shortlisted for the Howard League John Sunley Prize in 2014. As part of this research, data was gathered from legal practitioners who had represented bereaved families. There were numerous areas that a one year Master's degree could not address and therefore the research was continued at doctoral level, thus allowing an increased amount of data to be gathered through varying methods and differing participant groups, as discussed within this chapter.

Whilst undertaking my doctoral research, I assisted with the Equality and Human Rights Commission's inquiry into the deaths in custody of those with mental health problems. The Commission's interest in this topic was reflective of the growing concern related to deaths in custody. Despite this, the deaths of detained patients has remained a largely hidden issue and it was therefore important to share the findings of my various pieces of research as widely as possible. Therefore, I have presented the research at various conferences, most notably as a keynote speaker at the 42nd Annual Conference of the European Group for the Study of Deviance and Social Control. Other conference presentations have included the British Society of Criminology Conference and the National Deviancy Conference.

Future Aspirations

Upon completion of my doctoral studies, I aim to continue teaching Criminology. Teaching alongside my studies has enabled me to share my research with my students and a large percentage of them have chosen to focus on deaths in custody within their assessments. Assisting others in learning about such an important topic will undeniably promote increased understanding and awareness of the issue of deaths in psychiatric detention. Furthermore, researching deaths in psychiatric detention will not cease upon completion of my doctoral studies. I aim to continue to conduct research in this area, particularly around the historical data that has been neglected for so long, in addition to continuing to present and publish my findings as widely as possible.

Selected Works

Speed, C. (2014) 'Making the Invisible Visible: A Critical Analysis of Deaths in Psychiatric Detention' in *European Group for the Study of Deviance and Social Control,* Summer Newsletter II, 38-42

Speed, C. (2014) 'Degradation and Death: Psychiatric Detention in England and Wales' in *European Group for the Study of Deviance and Social Control,* Autumn Newsletter III, 17-21

Speed, C. (2017) 'As Little Regard in Life as in Death: A Critical Analysis of Subjugation and Accountability Following Deaths in Psychiatric Detention' in *Illness, Crisis and Loss* Volume 25, No.1 pp 27-42

Speed, C. (2017) 'Deaths in Psychiatric Detention', in Morley, S. Turner, J. Corteen, K. and Taylor, P. (eds) (2017) A *Companion to State Power, Liberties and Rights.* Bristol: Policy Press

Speed, C. (2017) ''They Cannot Speak Anymore-We Will Make Their Voices Count': Critically Examining Deaths in Psychiatric Detention' in: Atkinson, K. Huber, A.R. and Tucker, K. (eds.) *Voices of Resistance: Subjugated Knowledge and the Challenge to the Criminal Justice System*, London: EG Press pp.91-101

21

Subverting 'Crime Diagnosis': the Deconstruction of Social Dangerousness in Biographical Tales of 'Mentally Ill Offenders'

Luca Sterchele

Crime and 'mental illness': an introduction

The relationship between crime and 'mental illness' has been central in Criminology since its emergence. In numerous writings from the Italian School of Criminology exponents, criminal behaviour is explained as strictly connected to psychological disorders (although defined in a pretty naïve way): for example, Garofalo (1885: 8) wrote that the 'criminal' is characterised by "psychological anomalies and inveterate habits", and Cesare Lombroso pointed out the anti-social personality of the 'born criminal', deeply affected by a 'moral insanity' (Lombroso, 1876). In the same years, numerous criticisms to those theories arose. One of the most influential is one by Tarde (1885) who strongly criticised Lombroso's theories, arguing that madness is a product of civilization and that the definition of 'criminal behaviour' is strictly connected to the social organisation in which it is embedded.

Since then, those theories related to the 'born criminal' have been rejected by a number of scholars and their scientific inadequacy has been widely shown (for an overview see: Hester and Eglin, 1999 [1992]; Melossi, 2002). Nevertheless, it is possible to see their still-strong influence in some aspects of the study of the 'criminal issue', and in the subsequent forms of penal responses adopted. In these respects, the case that I want to study here is paradigmatic; what happens when a 'mentally ill' person commits a crime? What kinds of explanations are given of his/her behaviour? What is the penal reaction to these acts?

The Deconstruction of a *dispositif*: a Brief Index of the Chapter

In this chapter I introduce a research project aimed to provide an answer to those questions, to analyse the legal implications deriving from it and, whether it may be appropriate, to move toward further critiques of the penal reaction that is deployed. I will start this chapter with a brief explanation of the legal framework in which this case study is embedded, and of the institutional management of 'mentally ill offenders'. I will then present the empirical framework for the research, which seeks to collect life stories from those classified as 'mentally ill offenders'. The purpose of this is to restore the multidimensionality of their personalities that has been flattened by the psychiatric diagnosis, which following the hypothesis of this work acts as a Foucauldian *dispositif*; and to counteract the positivist rigidity of the direct connection that is still made between 'mental illness' and criminal behaviour.

Revolving Doors: 'Mentally Ill Offenders' and the Italian Penal System

The Italian penitentiary order is based on a 'double track'[1] logic: on the one hand, for 'responsible' subjects (seen as being able to make decisions and to understand the meaning of their behaviour) there is the penalty; on the other, for 'non-responsible' subjects (considered devoid of free will and understanding) there is the 'security measure'[2]. The subjects considered not responsible for the action they committed, cannot be punished with the same system bestowed on 'responsible subjects'[3]. It is, following Foucault, a *revolving door system*: "in terms of the law, when pathology comes in, criminality must go out" (Foucault, 2003: 32). Nonetheless the judge, counselled by a psychiatrist, may consider them as 'socially dangerous', and enforce on them a 'security measure': this, unlike the penalty, is aimed at ensuring 'social safety' while treating the supposed illness of the offender, removing their 'criminal essence' (Mantovani, 1992).

The 'mentally ill offender' thus faces a particular path: until recently, the 'security measure' would have been spent in a Forensic Psychiatric Hospital[4], for an undetermined period of time. With the recent law

---

[1] Sistema del "doppio binario".

[2] 'Misura di sicurezza'.

[3] This is not to say that the treatment of those considered 'non-responsible' is exempt from any associated harm, as it will be clear in the following pages.

81/2014 things have apparently changed: the subject, grossly simplifying, should now be hospitalised in smaller facilities headed by the Ministry of Health[5] or taken into custody by local psychiatric services. This transformation, although representing a good opportunity to definitively overcome an institution "ignoble for a civil country"[6], it is not the solution to all the problems. Since the penal code has not been amended, the risk of a "labels reform" is always around the corner (Miravalle, 2015). Moreover, the evaluation of 'social dangerousness' is still central in the process of application of the 'security measure'. This evaluation is based on a number of factors that are juridical, medical and social: it is at the intersection of those forms of knowledge and power that it is possible to still find alive the figure of the 'insane criminal'.

Being 'socially dangerous': Essentialisation and Neutralisation of the 'lunatic criminal'

The 'security measure' has a strongly positivistic nature: as demonstrated before, it is not a punishment for an act but a neutralisation of the dangerousness of its perpetrator's personality. In the reconstruction made by Foucault (1975) it is possible to see how this mechanism arises directly from a crisis in the punitive system elaborated by the reformers: rational punishment becomes impossible when the crime is perceived as deeply irrational. As argued by Castel (1976:40):

> L'équilibre des délits et des sanctions s'inscrit dans un système rationnel parce que le criminel est responsable de ses actes. Le fou pose un problème différent. Aucun lien rationnel n'unit directement la transgression qu'il accomplit et la répression qu'il subit. Il ne saurait être sanctionné, mais il devra être traité. Sans doute le traitement sera-t-il souvent une sorte de sanction. Mais [...] elle doit être justifiée par la rationalisation thérapeutique[7].

---

[4] Ospedale Psichiatrico Giudiziario.

[5] Those structures, called Residenze per l'esecuzione della misura di sicurezza (Rems), are meant to be different from Forensic Psychiatric Hospitals in a number of features: the maximum number of beds available in one structure is strongly reduced (max. 20 beds), the internal staff will be composed only of health professionals (while before the *polizia penitenziaria* was appointed for surveillance, exactly as in normal prisons) and a maximum length of stay is established (correspondent to the maximum of the penalty that would have been bestowed if the subject was considered 'responsible').

[6] As it has been defined by the President of Republic at the time, Giorgio Napolitano.

[7] "The equilibrium of crimes and punishments is inscribed in a rational system because the

It's in this terrain of crisis that psychiatry can become grafted into the penal system (Foucault 1978; Campesi 2008), producing different effects. On the one hand, the field of application is extended to petty offences (Venturini, 2010: 151), outplacing the most 'problematic patients' of the territorial psychiatric services to penal structures, somewhat in line with the trend to *prisonfare* showed by Wacquant (2009; 2010). From these considerations the double role that psychiatry is called to play in those cases appears clearly:

> Il fatto risulta evidente nell'alleanza originaria della psichiatria con la giustizia. Lo psichiatra, nell'espletamento del suo mandato professionale, è contemporaneamente medico e tutore dell'ordine [...]. Gli è cioè riconosciuto il diritto di mettere in atto ogni tipo di sanzione attraverso l'avallo che gli dà la scienza, per un arcaico patto che lo lega alla tutela e alla difesa della norma (Basaglia, 1976: 20)[8].

On the other hand the psychiatric diagnosis gives a reconstruction of the patient's life story, re-reading it through the lens of the pathological. The role of the psychiatric classification is:

> to repeat the offense tautologically in order to register it and constitute it as an individual trait. Expert psychiatric opinion allows one to pass from action to conduct, from an offense to a way of being, and to make this way of being appear as nothing other than the offense itself, but in general form, as it were, in the individual's conduct (Foucault, 2003: 16).

It is in this productive work of subjectivation, in the construction of the socially dangerous subject that the diagnosis works as a *dispositif*: the narrative produced about the mentally ill offender recalls the

---

criminal is responsible for his own behavior. The 'lunatic' poses a different problem. There are no rational connections linking directly the transgression he made and the repression to which he's subjected. He won't be sanctioned, but he will be healed. Of course, the treatment will often be a sort of a punishment. But this will be rationalised as a therapy" (translation by author).

[8] "The fact appears clearly in the native alliance between psychiatry and justice. The psychiatrist, in his professional mandate, is contemporarily a clinician and an enforcer. He has the right to put in practice every type of sanction through the legitimation given to him by science, for the archaic path that binds him to the defense of the norm" (translation by author).

Subverting 'crime diagnosis'

unpredictable and fearsome figure of the "furious lunatic" (ibid), and invokes the need of neutralising his constituent violence. In this sense the attitude towards the mentally ill offender can be considered as an illustrative example of the "criminology of the other" (Garland, 2001), and the penal reaction to his acts as a kind of "Feindstrafrecht" (Jakobs, 1985).

Can madness speak? Biographical tales as practices of resistance

The project presented here rises from a necessity to oppose the specific representation of the 'insane' that was outlined in the previous pages: this portrayal, in fact, is often extended far beyond the cases of criminal behaviours, generally connecting 'madness' with violence in a wider context (Fiorillo and Cozza, 2002). The purpose is to deconstruct the figure of the 'socially dangerous' individual, enabling him/her to produce his/her own alter-hegemonic narrative. This, in hypothesis, would permit criticism of both the inherent positivism that underpins the psychiatric reconstruction of crime and the specific representations that depict mentally ill persons as 'inherently dangerous' (*ibid.*), thus leading to a dismantling of the legitimacy of the 'security measure'. It could be relevant to explicitate, at a more general level, that the main theme underlying all the work is based on a specific political issue, well clarified in the paraphrase of a famous work by Spivak (1988): "can *madness* speak?"

In the empirical part of this work, life stories of so called 'mentally ill offenders' sectioned in forensic psychiatric institutions have been collected, using biographical interviews. This method is particularly appropriate for our purposes for many reasons: first of all, it permits retracing the institutional route that the subjects have traversed (between sanitary centres, hospitals and also prisons), showing both the interplay between institutions with different 'missions', and the way in which each one of those contributes to the construction of their subjectivity. Following Roberts (2002:171), we see how "identities are formed and develop in relation to spatial, organizational and other types of structures": biographical methods, in this sense, are particularly suitable to the diachronic analysis of the evolution of exclusion processes of marginalisation (Chamberlayne *et al*, 2002; Sbraccia, 2007).

The approach followed, moreover, assumes particular relevance if we consider the biographical production of the subjects in relation to the diagnostical one: as previously seen, the diagnosis vertically reconstructs their life through a pathologising narrative, reducing them to nothing more than their 'illness' and their 'crime'. By contrast, the biographical tale could restore the multidimensionality of the subject's existence. As Fassin (2007:238) noted:

> Against the positivism of a clinical approach that reduces illness to being only an object, with a diagnosis and a prognosis, in short, that reduces it to pathology, their interpretation [of social scientist studying illness experiences] was attentive to the patient's perspective and restored its rights to the processes of subjectivization that in the end turn the illness into an experience.

The reconstruction of life stories can thus be seen as a revival of experiences and forms of un-spoiled identity (Goffman, 1963), able to overturn the effects of the diagnostical *dispositif* and the subsequent process of subjectivation. This would make possible, in a certain sense, to restore the possibility of the 'voice' of 'mentally ill' persons, that is a central part of this work:

> Voce confusa con la miseria, l'indigenza e la delinquenza, parola resa muta dal linguaggio razionale della malattia, messaggio stroncato dall'internamento e reso indecifrabile dalla definizione di pericolosità e dalla necessità sociale dell'invalidazione, la follia non viene mai ascoltata per ciò che dice o vorrebbe dire (Ongaro and Basaglia, 1982: 139)[9].

A first person tale by 'mad criminals' can thus be seen as a way to emancipate the speech of 'mentally ill' persons from specialistic interpretations. Reconstructing and narrating biographical stories means creating a space in which the voice of 'madness' returns to be 'hearable' for what it says, regaining the power to speak for itself. Moreover, this could give us the opportunity to hurl a critical gaze toward the offence made by the subjects, disrupting the direct relation between their pathology and the crime they committed, and thus dismantling the basis of the legitimacy of a neutralising mechanism such as the security measure.

---

[9] "A voice confused with misery, indigence and delinquency; a speech muted by the rational language of illness; a message torn apart by internment and made incomprehensible by the definition of dangerousness and the social necessity for invalidation; madness is never listened to for what it says or would like to say".

Biographical Approach and the Risk of "Psychologism"

It is important, as Ferrarotti (1981) pointed out, to avoid any kind of "psychologism" in the interpretations of the biographies: there is a high risk, using this methodology, to fall into the individual without considering structural and power relations that are central in their life and representations. This is an important and significant warning: there is an awareness that this research will not necessarily lead to the production of narratives that are different or oppositional from the dominant one. It is important to consider, in this sense, that the interviewed subjects are not autonomous and isolated beings, and that the place in which they live, the relations in which they are embedded, and other more or less structural factors are playing a central role in the 'production of their story'. The ideal type of subject that we are going to interview will probably present some specific features: they will be sectioned in a particular structure, that is controlled by strict surveillance that is extended far beyond physical compresence; they will know that their refusal of or opposition to the therapy and diagnosis is often seen by the medical personnel as a mark of their pathological state; they will maybe come from a long period of institutionalisation, that is particularly deleterious for their self-determination (Goffman, 1961; Basaglia, 1965). Given those problems (and many others) there is thus a high probability of a reproduction of the 'hegemonic narrative' and even of an avoidance of certain arguments (even though the avoidance to talk about some events may be considered, in some way, a proper form of alter-narrative). It is possible, in other words, that the biographical tale produced by the subject is just a reproduction of the portrayal that the institution has made of him/her: this could happen both for instrumental purposes of the subject, or simply because they introjected the dominant representation of the 'unconscious criminal' that has been made of them.

Space and Narratives: an Ethnographic Study of Power Relations

It is certainly difficult to prevent this from happening, but it is possible to avoid mis-interpretations if we keep considering the centrality of power relations and their subjectivising effects. As Plummer (2007: 402) remembers:

> Life stories and the 'memories' they bring with them always have a latent political structure: people tell their stories – or do not tell

> their stories – in conditions that are not entirely of their own making within a circuit of power. Some people can elaborate long and detailed stories: others are silenced. Some are always being heard, others never. The understanding of the ways in which people come to tell their stories – and what they say and cannot say, and even how they say it – must be seen as an important part of the politics of the ethnographic project.

An ethnographic attention to the relations between inmates, operators, doctors and eventually guards[10] will in these respects represent a central part of the study. Considering the strong influence exerted by this power network in which subjects are embedded, it could be useful to produce comparative work: reconstructing biographies of people that are similar by profile, but retained in different institutions, will help to clarify the role exerted by the specific context in the production and reproduction of certain types of narratives.

In conclusion, it is argued that the reconstruction of a number of biographies of 'mentally ill offenders' retained in forensic psychiatric institutions would permit to reach a double purpose: to deconstruct the deterministic connection that is often made between 'mental illness' and 'crime' whenever the two elements appear together, contrasting the representation of the 'mentally ill' as inherently dangerous and the penal reaction that is thus deployed; and to create the conditions under which 'madness' could produce its own discourse in first person, regaining voice and the right to speak for itself.

References

Basaglia, F. (1976) *La maggioranza deviante: l'ideologia del controllo sociale totale*, Torino: Einaudi

Basaglia, F. (1981) *Scritti I: 1953-1968. Dalla Psichiatria Fenomenologica all'esperienza di Gorizia*, Torino: Einaudi

Campesi, G. (2008) 'L'individuo pericoloso. Saperi criminologici e sistema penale nell'opera di Michel Foucault' pp 121 – 142 in *Materiali per una storia della cultura giuridica*, No.1, il Mulino: Bologna

Castel, R. (1976) *L'ordre psychiatrique: l'âge d'or de l'aliénisme*, Paris, Les Editions de Minuit

---

[10] That are still present in the external perimeter of the structures

Subverting 'crime diagnosis'

Chamberlayne, P. Rustin, M. and Wengraf, T. (eds) (2002) *Biographies and Social Exclusion in Europe: Experiences and Life Journeys,* Bristol: Policy Press

Fassin, D. (2007) *When Bodies Remember: Experiences and Politics of AIDS in South Africa*, Berkeley: University of California Press

Ferrarotti F. (1981), *Storia e Storie di Vita*, Roma e Bari: Laterza

Fiorillo G.P. and Cozza M. (2002) *Il Nostro Folle Quotidiano: indagine sulla rappresentazione della follia e della malattia mentale*, Roma: Manifesto Libri

Foucault, M. (1978) 'About the concept of the "Dangerous Individual" in 19th Century Legal Psychiatry' *Journal of Law and Psychiatry* Volume 1, No.1 pp 1-18

Foucault, M. (1975) *Surveiller et Punir: naissance de la prison*, Paris: Gallimard

Foucault, M. (2003) *The abnormal: lectures at the College de France 1974-75*, London: Verso

Garland, D. (2001) *Culture of Control: Crime and Social Order in Contemporary Society*, Chicago: Chicago University Press

Garofalo, R. (1885) *Criminologia: studio sul delitto, sulle sue cause e sui mezzi di repressione*, Torino: Fratelli Bocca

Goffman, E. (1961) *Asylums: Essays on the Condition of the Social Situation of Mental Patients and Other Inmates*, New York: Anchor Books

Goffman, E. (1963) *Stigma: Notes on the Management of Spoiled Identity*, New York: Simon & Shuster

Hester, S. and Eglin, P. (1999) *Sociologia del crimine*, Lecce: Manni Editore; for the first edition see: Hester S., Eglin P. (1992), *A Sociology of crime*, New York: Routledge

Jakobs, G. (1985) 'Ierung im Vorfeld einer Rechtsgutsverletzung' *Zeitschrift für die gesamte Strafrechtswissenschaft De Gruyter*, No.97, pp 751-785

Lombroso, C. (1876) *L'uomo delinquente*, Milano: Hoepli

Mantovani, F. (1992) *Diritto Penale: parte generale*, Padova: CEDAM

Melossi, D. (2002) *Stato, Controllo sociale, Devianza: teorie criminologiche e società tra Europa e Stati Uniti*, Milano: Bruno Mondadori

Miravalle, M. (2015) *Roba da matti: il difficile superamento degli Ospedali Psichiatrici Giudiziari*, Torino: Gruppo Abele Edizioni

Ongaro, F. and Basaglia, F. (1982) *Salute/Malattia: le parole della medicina*, Torino: Einaudi

Plummer, K. (2007) 'The call of Life Stories in Ehtnographic Research' pp. 395-406 in Atkinson P. Coffey A., Delamont S., Lofland J. and Lofland L. (ed) *Handbook of Ethnography*, London: Sage Publications

Roberts, B. (2002) *Biographical Research*, Buckingham, Philadelphia: Open University Press

Sbraccia, A. (2007) *Migranti tra Mobilità e Carcere: Storie di Vita e Processi di Criminalizzazione*, Milano: Franco Angeli

Spivak, G. (1988) *Can the Subaltern Speak? Reflections on the History of an Idea*, New York: Columbia University Press

Tarde, G. (1885) 'Le type criminel' pp 593-627 in *Revue Philosophique* Volume 19

Venturini, E. (2010) *Il folle reato: il rapporto tra la responsabilità dello psichiatra e la imputabilità del paziente*, Milano: Franco Angeli

Wacquant, L. (2009) *Punishing the Poor: the Neoliberal Government of Social Insecurity*, Durham: Duke University Press

Wacquant, L. (2010) 'Crafting the Neoliberal State: Workfare, Prisonfare and Social Insecurity' *Sociological Forum*, Volume 25, No.2 pp 197-220

Extended Biography

Research

I began my university studies at the Università di Padova in 2010. As an undergraduate student in Communications, mainly interested in Journalism, Cinema and Music, I soon became fascinated by some Sociological issues. It was thus after taking some courses in Sociology and a year spent at the University of Strathclyde in Glasgow, that I got my Bachelor degree: my thesis was based on a comparison between Italian prison conditions and those of England and Wales. I continued my studies in Sociology and Social Research at the Università di Bologna: in that period, I conducted research in a Forensic Psychiatric Hospital in Reggio Emilia, which sought to analyse the profiles of the people that resided there before the final dismantling of the institution, planned for the following year (2015). This research became the empirical background of my Master's thesis, which I wrote under the supervision of Sandro Mezzadra and Giuseppe Mosconi. One of the main results obtained was the display of the imbalance, in the institutional practice, between the declared purpose of healing and the concrete practice of punishing. In doing this work I deepened my interest in the work of Franco Basaglia and the movements of deinstitutionalisation, that are still central topics in my studies.

I am now a PhD student in Social Sciences at the Università di Padova, in the department of Philosophy, Sociology, Pedagogy and Applied Psychology: as it is possible to see from the chapter I have presented, my work is aimed at studying the ways in which so-called 'mentally ill offenders' can counteract the reduction of their behaviour and personality made by the psychiatric diagnosis. This is aimed both at understanding how and to what extent 'madness' can regain the right to speak for itself, and if the criminal act of the 'mentally ill' can be explained in a more critical way, against the forensic psychiatric reductionism.

Together with my PhD project, I'm working on two other small research projects that are still in a very embryonic stage. The first one is regarding a methodological reflection about using Visual Methods in studying custodial institutions. I think in fact that the 'public' potential of these methods can be fruitfully used to raise awareness about some issues regarding these places. It is not only about denouncing the conditions under which the everyday life of a number of people is lived behind the walls of the institution; it is also a good way to show the small practices of coping and resistance that inmates put into practice to make those conditions more bearable.

The second work is based on a reflection about the concept of "dual diagnosis"[11]: this is a very frequent judgement. It is particularly difficult in fact, when drug addiction and mental illness appear together, to understand the relations between the two. When I did my research in the Forensic Psychiatric Asylum of Reggio Emilia I found that approximately 75% of the inmates were ascribable to that category. So I'm now wondering: given the overcoming of those institutions, and the consistent reduction in beds available in restrictive facilities, what is going to happen? It may be of course that some of those subjects will be hospitalised in sanitary structures or local communities; but it is licit to think that for the most problematic of those the un-balance between the 'mental illness' and the drug addiction may be solved in favour of the latter, leading to incarceration in particular prisons. I have not yet started to work on this hypothesis, but I'm seeking to begin work soon with the collection of some data, and hoping to have the work done by the end of the year.

---

[11] It is a category used to indicate the co-occurring of mental illness and substance abuse problems: it is particularly problematic, since it is not clear if there is any causality between the two, neither the possible direction of it (even though a number of theories tried to establish it).

Activism, Organisational Work and/or Professional Membership
In January 2016 I moved to Barcelona, where I had an internship at the Observatorio del Sistema Penal y los Derechos Humanos, under the supervision of Iñaki Rivera Beiras. While I was there, I followed both the activities of the Observatorio and some classes of the specialisation degree in Sociologia Juridico Penal at the Universitat de Barcelona. In 2016, I intensified my already existing activism for Associazione Antigone, becoming an Observant for the Emilia Romagna Region. With this still ongoing activity I from time to time visited some penal institutes within the region, in order to inspect various features. This activity also became an important opportunity for my work, making it possible to do some 'ethnographic' research (although really limited) and to maintain an awareness about what was going on in the regional prison system.

Since December 2016, I am also a member of the organising group of the first-level specialization degree in Critical Criminology, organised both by Università di Padova and Università di Bologna, and a collaborator of the research group Slan.G (Slanting Gaze on Social Control, Labor, Racism and Migration).

Contact Details
Academic profile: https://unipd.academia.edu/LucaSterchele
Email: luca.sterchele@libero.it; lucaksterchele@gmail.com;
LinkedIn: https://it.linkedin.com/in/luca-sterchele-820aa246

22

Foucault and the City:
Conceptualising Social Control Over Urban Space

Maryja Šupa

"A work, an object, a piece of architecture, a photograph, but equally a crime or an event, must: be the allegory of something, be a challenge to someone, bring chance into play and produce vertigo" (Jean Baudrillard, 2005).

Introduction

My research started out as a personal theoretical curiosity: although Foucault has never focused explicitly on the city as a central object of his works, what was his take on urbanity, especially beyond the well-known works such as *Discipline and Punish* (1991) or *History of Sexuality* (1978)? And how useful could these insights be in interpreting issues of social control as they unfold within, over and through urban space? The relevance of this question is simple: space cannot be escaped unless one is asleep, in a coma, or dead. The city threads together the fabric of everyday life and is layered into the experiences of social class, age, gender, race and many others. In contrast to institutional settings, social control over urban space concern the majority rather than a minority and offers insights into how different forms of power – both from above and from below – interrelate.

These considerations brought me to the next question, namely, what are the useful methods of conceptualising social control in the city? To address both the visible and invisible aspects of power, I chose three dimensions: the physical structure of an urban neighbourhood, the legal regulation of public space at the national and municipal level, and the semiotic landscape created by public signage. Besides the obvious analysis of legal documents, my main research methods were observation and photo-documentation, yielding a rich pool of qualitative data. I conducted the study in Lukiškės, a centrally-located neighbourhood in the city of Vilnius, Lithuania, typical for the city because of its contrasts. The space of 0.4 square kilometres contains a maximum-security prison, the parliament, several ministries, residential housing, the national library, a high-rise office complex, semi-defunct research institutes and a public square notable for contested collective memories, all framed by a river and desolate green interstices.

Foucault and the City

Although Foucault never developed a comprehensive theory of urban development, both the city and specific spaces situated within it were always close to the surface of his arguments about power, knowledge and subjectivity. One of the earliest and most exclusively spatial texts, *On Other Spaces, Heterotopias* (Foucault, 1984), presents three key points defining his spatial stance. First, while some spaces discussed as heterotopias in the piece, such as ships, exist "outside society" and are thus conducive to transgression, others are established to contain transgressive individuals, an idea later extensively developed in *Discipline and Punish* (Foucault, 1991). Thus, the functions and uses of space are contradictory, and neither total control nor total liberty is possible or enforceable as the ultimate urban condition. Second, lived space is defined as "relations among sites" rather than a collection of physical structures. Thus, to understand urban power relations one must analyse the network of multiple built structures in a larger area, rather than single buildings. Third, Foucault outlines "inviolable" oppositions, such as private and public, work and leisure, cultural and useful spaces. These oppositions have since been redefined, contested and colonised, introducing ever greater ambiguity into the interpretation of spatial categories.

Urban space also serves as a staging ground for the three modalities of power put forward by Foucault throughout his work: sovereignty, disciplinarity and biopolitics. While sovereignty is the primary power modality in pre-modern societies, disciplinarity and biopolitics emerge in the modern state-subject relation. Foucault stresses that the modalities do not supersede each other directly, but, rather, coexist in varying degrees of domination depending on the context. *Security, Territory, Population* (Foucault, 2007) brings power and space together by describing the specific traits of disciplinarity and biopolitics as they are applied to (urban) space. Disciplinary power aims for the perfection of disciplined individual bodies, acts on artificially created spaces such as prisons or hospitals, involves the construction of such spaces, effectively encloses and isolates, endorses total surveillance, and focuses on the present (Foucault, 2007). Meanwhile, biopolitical power aims to preserve life and ensure the "quality" of the population, acts on natural or pre-existing spaces, involves the regulation of such spaces, effectively expands and promotes circulation, seems to happen out of its own accord and incorporates the future into the present by measures such as risk prevention (Foucault, 2007). The spatial characteristics of disciplinarity and social control often seem to be opposites. However, rather than working counter to each other, in reality they have proven to frequently reinforce each other or to cover separate domains without much interference. It is notable, also, that these two modern power modalities echo contemporary shifts in social control, namely, its punitive and actuarial turns, debated critically by criminologists (Cohen, 1985; Garland, 2001). This framework, used to interpret the practices of social control over urban space, reveals tensions experienced by the everyday subject.

My search for the dimensions along which to conceptualise social control in urban space and within which to trace disciplinarity and biopolitics, led me to three research fields which have been actively developing during the past two decades. First, the field of critical urban studies and numerous other disciplines which focus on the significance of space for everyday experience and late modern social issues (Borer, 2006; Gieryn, 2000; Hayward, 2004; Soja, 2003). The inherent physicality of space suggests that certain characteristics of physical structure tell a local story of use, counter-use, control, and compliance or resistance. Second, legal geography stresses the mutual co-constitution of law and spatial structures, and their interdependence (Braverman *et al*, 2014; Bennett and Layard, 2015; Delaney, 2015). Thus, to understand physical space, one must also understand the ideal-type or utopian representations of the same space conveyed by legal documents. Third, the emergent concept of semiotic landscapes (Jaworski and Thurlow, 2010; Laitinen and Zabrodskaja, 2015; Zabrodskaja and Milani, 2014) focuses on the visual, textual and material forms of public signage to explain how power relations are woven into the fabric of urban communication. It is significant because public signage presents both formal and informal, administrative and local meanings embedded in urban everyday life.

Physical Structures and Power Relations

The physical space of the research area is diverse in terms of building age, density, and mixed-use functions. This diversity greatly contributes to the fact that it is impossible to impose on the neighbourhood a uniform, consistent strategy of social control. New structures are planned into the existing neighbourhood grid. Thus, disciplinary aspects of physical space (such as access limitations, containment by fences or walls, transparency, surveillance, degree of decrepitude) are highly individual at and around each built structure. The three largest contained areas in the neighbourhood include the prison compound, the church and the school, all walled and fenced. All three belong to the classical disciplinary institutions, in contrast, for example, to the parliament and other governmental institutions, which may be easily approached and touched. The whole neighbourhood is traversable by foot, and the perspective is frequently interrupted by irregular building shapes and jagged corners. While the notion of public space initially implies that it is publicly accessible, the visual field is occupied with many glimpses of private and restricted spaces. That in itself creates a dominant power relation: colonising the visual field by being *visible*, yet staying *unknowable*. These disciplinary aspects are pre-determined and supported by the biopolitical agendas of urban development, territory planning and risk prevention.

From the perspective of biopolitics, its main agenda is the organisation three interspersed flows circulating through urban space: people, goods, and money. Their movements are based on a temporal axis. Daytime brings greater openness and access to commercial premises because that is what contributes to the circulation of goods and money. Populations circulate through the neighbourhood with a temporal rhythm: the mass of residents' exchanges places with employees and transients during the daytime and returns for the night. Their circuits are put into motion by the disciplinary obligation of work. Thus, disciplinary and biopolitical practices give way to each other in a periodic breath-like pattern.

A publicly discussed case illustrating the interplay of power modalities is Lukiškių square. Historically, it has been a site of contrasting functions, housing the main food market and infectious diseases ward in the 19th century, as well as the circus or the gallows at other times (a comprehensive history of the area is presented by Jogėla *et al*, 2008). During the Soviet era, it was home to Lenin's statue and since its demolition in 1990 has become a site of contested memories and uses. In the past 27 years, numerous refurbishment projects have been proposed, to attain the official goals of commemorating liberation fights and national identity, offering yet another biopolitical discourse of death-oriented memory to honour the population's survival potential. Many proposals featured changing the ample green areas (arbitrarily used for picnics, sports and children's activities) to planes of concrete or stone, emphasising the prevalence of the state function, and rapid circulation of passers-by, whose behaviour is disciplined by eradicating the means for uncontained, unprescribed and unpredictable spontaneous use.

Legal Dimensions of Social Control

An analysis of national and municipal legislation regulating conduct in public space has revealed a rhetorical difference in their clauses. National administrative and penal codes are worded as lists of actions that procure consequences, while municipal rule-sets are formulated as lists of both prohibited and obligatory actions. Both document categories possessed prominent keywords, permuted throughout the clauses in various metaphorical forms. In the national legislation, the emphasis was on *public calm* and *public order* as an overarching value that must be enforced and defended within urban public space. Notably, the two terms are never defined in any of the documents that have been analysed. Besides introducing a legal grey area (how loud a shout is necessary to disturb public calm?), such ambiguity serves not so much as a tool for determining offences, but rather a vision of the ideal population: perpetually orderly, perpetually calm, as if these traits reflect the population's natural, desirable state of being.

Meanwhile, many of the municipal rules were emphasising *order* and *cleanliness* of the urban environment. Although the terms seem to express a concern with the aesthetic state of the urban landscape, in reality some of the clauses in these rules are directed against specific populations rather than physical disorder. Examples include a prohibition to play sports in undesignated spaces, or to give and receive alms, or to dry laundry over open balcony rails. In contrast to national legislation which is concerned with more general forms of conduct and describes only actions, the municipal rule-sets describe in detail many possible circumstances and variants of an action, for example, meticulously listing all the surfaces inside apartment blocks where scribbling or posting notes is prohibited: walls, floors, doors, window panes, and elevators...

Thus, the national legislation is more expressive of the biopolitical agenda, while the municipal legislation (being, in theory, closer to the subject) reflects disciplinary goals. It is also apparent that selective enforcement of these norms is rife in the city, because urban space is too complex to control each minute rule. Besides their (not so successful) function as a set of norms, the legal documents may be read more readily as a non-literary utopia. If each and every rule were enforced, everyday life in the city would become a tightly controlled and rigid world. Little space would be left for consensual decisions by members of communities living or working in specific local spaces and their personal responsibility to each other.

Tracing Social Control in Public Signage

Public signage encompasses both the physical and the symbolic realm, and depending on authorship, form, and contents may be placed at different points on the continuum between legality and transgression, formal and grassroots origins. It is quite rigorously regulated both in terms of contents, such as advertising rules, and in terms of form, where municipal rule-sets especially are rigorous about the appropriate places, types and materials to be used for public communication.

Spatial knowledge is produced by administrative signage – street names and house numbers which separate and divide the urban fabric into individual structures. They create a public mental map, provide a frame of reference to talk about the city, and, thus, in a disciplinary fashion, govern the mind depending on the position of the body in space. Another form of disciplinary content represents and targets conduct (un)desired in a specific space, such as visual symbols that prohibit smoking, littering, or alcohol consumption. In biopolitical interest, a significant proportion of public signage – primarily traffic lights and traffic signs – directs and promotes the circulation of pedestrian and vehicular populations. Another ample category includes shop and office signs, advertising, and shop window promotions which serve not only to attract and direct a potential flow of consumers but also promote the circulation of goods and money.

Besides graffiti, legally criminalised forms of public communication include posted announcements, drawings, memorial wreaths and other forms of small-scale urban media. A significant proportion of illicit public signage reproduces the same biopolitical or disciplinary goals as its official counterpart: directing consumer flows in the case of illegal advertising, or regulating conduct, for example, by informal indications of parking space ownership, or a warning to beware of falling icicles. Such formally illicit forms of public signage are seldom prosecuted by law enforcement or complained about by the public. Only those forms of communication that fall beyond the dominating biopolitical and disciplinary discourses are actively marginalised as unpleasant or disruptive. These are tags, graffiti, slogans, stickers, and other expressions whose contents represent knowledge created by the author-subject rather than imposed on other subjects. This is knowledge rooted in personal mundane experiences, such as tags of nicknames, observations about everyday life, or public social commentary.

Conclusion

Urban space is a complex expression of power relations. Walking around the city, digging through spatial legislation and the extent of its actual enforcement, reading into licit and illicit public signage reveals the tensions and contradictions of social control over and through urban space. Many of these tensions may indeed be interpreted as measures of disciplinary or biopolitical logic. However, It is not the actual sorting into categories such as disciplinarity or biopolitics that is valuable, but rather seeing how various physical and discursive forms interplay, reinforcing or cancelling each other out to create the possibilities and impossibilities, the unique experiences of everyday life in different cities.

My research was limited to a single neighbourhood in a single city. Other districts and other cities may tell a different story of how social control is configured in urban space. The Foucauldian framework of analysis offers a direction, a possibility of reading urban space to understand how its organisation reflects contemporary strategies of social control, the underlying motivations, and the defining characteristics of spatial conducts and counter-conducts.

Acknowledgements

This chapter is a summary of the main findings of my doctoral thesis, defended in 2016 at Vilnius University, Lithuania. I would like to thank my advisor, Prof. Aleksandras Dobryninas, for his patient guidance, feedback and engagement with my work. Agnė Girkontaitė has been a supportive buddy at the best and worst of times, and always had a spark of sociological imagination at hand. In the last days of completing the thesis, Jurga Bakaitė kept my sanity ticking, and Veronika Urbonaitė–Barkauskienė offered a most supportive proof-reader's eye. Mr.

Nežinomas has lent me the camera for taking hundreds of photos in the research area; I owe him a couple of beers. Finally, a lion's share of thanks goes to Tomas Verbaitis.

References

Baudrillard, J. (2005) *The Intelligence Of Evil or the Lucidity Pact* Oxford: Berg

Bennett, L. and Layard, A. (2015) 'Legal geography: Becoming spatial detectives' in *Geography Compass* Volume 9, No. 7 pp 406–422

Borer, M. I. (2006) 'The Location of Culture: The Urban Culturalist Perspective' in *City & Community* Volume 5, No. 2 pp 173–197

Braverman, I. Blomley, N. Delaney, D. and Kedar, A. (2014) 'Introduction: Expanding the spaces of law' pp 1–29 in Braverman, I, Blomley, N., Delaney D. and Kedar, A. (eds) *The Expanding Spaces of Law: A Timely Legal Geography* Stanford: Stanford University Press

Cohen, S. (1985) *Visions of Social Control: Crime, Punishment and Classification* Cambridge: Polity

Delaney, D. (2015) 'Legal geography I: Constitutivities, Complexities, and Contingencies' in *Progress in Human Geography* Volume 39, No. 1 pp 96–102

Foucault, M. (1978) *The History of Sexuality: The Will to Knowledge* New York: Pantheon Books

Foucault, M. (1984) 'On Other spaces, Heterotopias' in *Architecture, Mouvement, Continuité* Volume 5, pp 46–49

Foucault, M. (1991) *Discipline and Punish: The Birth of the Prison* London: Penguin Books

Foucault, M. (2007) *Security, Territory, Population: Lectures at the Collège de France 1977-1978* New York: Picador

Garland, D. (2001) *The Culture of Control: Crime and Social Order in Contemporary Society* Chicago: The University of Chicago Press

Gieryn, T. F. (2000) 'A Space for Place in Sociology' in *Annual Review of Sociology*, Volume 26, pp 463–496

Hayward, K. (2004) *City Limits: Crime, Consumer Culture and the Urban Experience* Portland, OR: Routledge-Cavendish

Jaworski, A. and Thurlow, C. (2010) 'Introducing semiotic landscapes' pp 1–40 in Jaworski, A. and Thurlow, C (eds) *Semiotic Landscapes: Language, Image, Space* London, New York: Continuum

Jogėla, V., Meilus, E. and Pugačiauskas, V. (2008) *Lukiškės: Nuo priemiesčio iki centro (XV a. – XX a. pradžia)* Vilnius: Lietuvos istorijos institutas

Laitinen, M. and Zabrodskaja, A. (2015) 'Dimensions and Dynamics of Sociolinguistic Landscapes in Europe' pp 11–25 in Laitinen, M. and Zabrodskaja, M. (eds) *Dimensions of Sociolinguistic Landscapes in Europe: Materials and Methodological Solutions* Frankfurt am Main: Peter Lang

Soja, E. W. (2003) 'Writing the city spatially' in *City* Volume 7, No.3 pp 269–280

Zabrodskaja, A. and Milani, T.M. (2014) 'Signs in Context: Multilingual and Multimodal Texts in Semiotic Space' in *International Journal of the Sociology of Language* Volume 2, pp 1–6

Extended Biography

Research

I studied Information Science for my Bachelor's degree, but switched to Sociology for my Master's. I fell in love with reading, writing and researching enough to defend a PhD in Sociology supervised by Prof. Aleksandras Dobryninas, a Criminologist, in 2016. All of the studies were completed at Vilnius University, Lithuania.

In addition to my studies, I have been employed as a freelance researcher for two projects at the Civic Society Institute in Vilnius, Lithuania, collecting and analysing data about civic education in schools and facilitation of collaboration between governmental institutions and NGOs.

I have also volunteered for *Mokslo pieva*, an informal interdisciplinary team of senior and junior researchers, to organise problem-based workshops for students and a week-long data-crunching summer school. During these activities we encouraged students to work together in teams of different disciplines and experience levels, to learn from each other as well as tutors, to solve real-life problems with real-life data, and achieve results in a limited timeframe. These have been very rewarding moments of working with interesting people and seeing the actual impact that sincere teaching may make.

My research inspiration comes from a fascination with cities and how they work, spaces shared with hacker and punk subcultures, 15 years of reading science fiction, and watching the world go by.

Future Aspirations

I hope to tackle two topics in the near future:

1. **Reconfigurations of urban childhood experiences:** Children comprise a specific population group that often remains voiceless but is rarely framed as excluded. I am interested in the changing opportunities for children to interact in the city and with the city, and to use urban space, as well as implicit and explicit imposition of social control on these practices. The initial stage of this research could focus on a comparison of Soviet and Post-Soviet childhood experiences in Vilnius and other post-communist cities.
2. **Public representations of harmful conduct:** Frequently the Lithuanian media presents issues such as addictions, reproductive health (including homebirth, fertility treatment, or abortions), and youth subcultures as harmful conduct. These images form a significant part of the broader public discourse around regulation and norm-setting. What, then, are the public representations of non-criminal or victimless transgressions, and what do they reveal about the relationship between the state and its subjects, tendencies towards social blaming or social empathy, and solutions of controversial policy-making debates?

Selected Works

Šupa, M. [Forthcoming] 'Biopolitics and Disciplinarity in the Legislation of Conduct in Public Spaces of Vilnius' *Juridica International*

Šupa, M (2016) *Physical, Legal and Discursive Aspects of Social Control in Urban Space: The Case of a Centrally Located Neighbourhood in Vilnius* Doctoral thesis Vilnius: Vilniaus universiteto leidykla

Šupa, M. (2015) 'Mapping Practices of Social Control: A Foucauldian Analysis of Urban Space' *Kriminologijos Studijos* Volume 2, pp 82–123

Šupa, M. (2014) 'Cultural transformation of Critical Criminology' *Sociologija: mintis ir veiksmas* Volume 1, No. 34 pp 146–167 (in Lithuanian)

Contact Details

Email: maryja.supa@kf.vu.lt

Research Gate: https://www.researchgate.net/profile/Maryja_Supa

23

From "Amused Tolerance to Outrage"[1]: A Critical Analysis of the Framing of Child Sexual Abuse is within Institutional Sites

Katie Tucker

Introduction

The current focus upon institutional abuse and 'grooming' in England has provided a watershed moment in the history of responses to child sexual abuse (CSA) and has led to the expansion of media, legal, official, and political debate surrounding the problem and the required solutions. This chapter outlines on-going research into contemporary public discourses on CSA in England. By performing an analysis of public discourse, between 2010-2015, this research critically considers these debates through a document based analysis. The research focuses upon four central institutional sites highlighting the development of 'talk and text' surrounding the problem of CSA and the necessary responses. The focus upon these institutional sites enables a consideration of how CSA has been framed in this period and how, as a result, dominant understandings of CSA have shifted within this specific historical context. The research contributes to on-going scholarly debates regarding the understanding of, and subsequent responses to, CSA, and aims to have an impact on policy responses.

Institutional Sites and CSA

This research centres around four institutional sites. Institutional sites are those from which discourse is produced and legitimised (Foucault, 2002).

---

[1]In a recent commentary Professor David Pilgrim (2014) highlighted the way in which CSA was framed during the mid-20th Century and how there has been a shift in dominant attitudes in these terms. This chapter explains how the ongoing research will develop that analysis.

The sites in focus in this project are the law, the media, politics, and official discourse. Although this choice of sites is not exhaustive (academic discourses, social media debates, and fictional representations among other contributions could also be considered), these four have been central in the time frame under analysis, and their importance is echoed within the existing literature.

The analysis of all sites against the backdrop of recent scandals and consequent police operations (Jimmy Savile and Operation Yewtree, and the Rotherham and Rochdale CSA scandal alongside other high profile cases of CSA[2]) is time-limited and concentrates on the period of 2010-2015. This five-year period allows for this research to examine the extent to which, in this pivotal historical moment, feminist analyses of CSA, have influenced (or not) the evolution of public discourses in this context. All data within the analysis is currently publicly available, and is to be subject to a Foucauldian discourse analysis through a Feminist poststructuralist lens.

The importance of the law in defining the problem of CSA has been a prominent concern of reformers and feminist activists since the 19th century. The work of Carol Smart (1976, 1999, 2000) and other feminist scholars (Angelides, 2004; Cowburn and Domenelli, 2001; Howe, 2008) has exposed the historical struggle between reformers and the law to (re)define child/adult sexual relationships. Historically, legal discourse has failed to distinguish sex/gender differences, viewing both as inherent and omitting the social aspects at play that reinforce gender inequality (Belknap, 2014: 8). The law, with its silencing and disqualification techniques (Ballinger, 2000), also serves to consistently 'other' the victims of sexual abuse (Walklate, 2008). Building upon this body of feminist research, one of the key concerns of this project is the extent to which victims' perspectives on CSA have been included within legal discourses in the chosen time period.

---

[2] Jimmy Savile was an English radio DJ and television personality. He was posthumously (after subsequent official inquiries), found to have abused over 450 children between the years 1955-2010. Operation Yewtree was the large-scale Metropolitan Police investigation into CSA beginning in 2012 initially into accusations made against Savile, which then led to the investigation and arrests of 19 other high profile men.

The vast cases of CSA and Child Sexual Exploitation (CSE) in Rochdale and Rotherham were committed by those involved in so called 'grooming gangs' firstly in Rotherham in 2010, and later in Rochdale in 2012. These cases put the issue of CSA firmly back on the public agenda in the UK due to the sheer number of victims and the social divisions of race and religion being central to the framing of CSA by all institutional sites.

The media has been long identified as a significant site for the production of discourse on CSA (Atmore, 1998; Bell, 2002; Cowburn and Dominelli, 2001; Hayes, 2014; Kitzinger, 2004, 2011; Nava, 1988). The central concern here lies with the ability of the media to shape dominant understandings of the problem and affect the direction in which policy is developed (Davidson, 2008; Warner 2009). This critique accords with feminist work in the UK that has pointed to the media-driven emphasis on 'the paedophile' and associated risk from 'strangers' as the main characteristics of dominant discourses on CSA (Bell, 2002). From a feminist perspective, the media have historically masked the relevance of hegemonic masculinity in men's involvement in CSA (Cowburn and Dominelli, 2001) and this 'de-gendering' is reproduced through media sources which present legal discourses as unproblematic, common sense, and scientific. The media have also historically, served to define CSA as a 'public' problem understood through the notion of 'stranger-danger', and thus have deflected attention away from the risk of CSA within the 'private' domain (Jewkes and Wykes, 2012; Kitzinger, 2011). While there is undoubtedly an importance to social media discourses on CSA in the period in question, the analysis in this section focuses on the coverage of CSA in news media reports produced within 2010-2015. This focus is justified due to the central importance of traditional news media (newspapers and television news) in bringing the issue of CSA to the fore during this period.

CSA has, arguably become a more significant political issue following recent scandals not least because of the historical involvement of politicians in the perpetration and cover-up of the sexual abuse of children (Browne, 2014). Political discourse on CSA has expanded significantly since 2010 as politicians have sought to explain and respond in varying ways to the problems of the past and present. The apparent shift in political culture around the problem of CSA – as Pilgrim (2014) puts it, from an '"amused tolerance' to 'outrage'" – requires substantive analysis to consider how the public discourses in this context have shifted in line with this cultural change. Pilgrim (2014) highlights that historically, senior officials have turned a blind eye to the abuse of children classifying paedophiliac tendencies as part of the institution reserved for political patriarchs. The culture surrounding the depiction of young girls and women as 'groupies' and the famous (or infamous) band members and DJ's subjected to these 'throws of adolescent passion' in the 1970's and 1980's adds to the 'amused tolerance' of child sexual exploitation and abuse (ibid). It is also apparent contemporaneously, given the outcome of police investigations such as Operation Yewtree (2012), that Savile and other high profile individuals demonstrated somewhat 'accepted' sexual norms of the mid-20th Century that were not only tolerated but also consciously covered-up. Political responses to both the Rotherham and Rochdale cases and Operation Yewtree have been subject to critique by academics as well as media commentators (Browne, 2014; Gallagher, 2014; Greer and Maclaughlin, 2013; Middleton, 2015). However, there is a need to subject the political discourses produced in this period to a systematic critical analysis. In interrogating the contemporary *political landscape of CSA* (Reavey and Warner, 2003), the study considers how this issue has been discursively framed in this field, as well as highlighting connections between these four institutional sites.

Official policy discourses have also potentially had a significant impact on recent public discussions around CSA. The period in focus here has seen a flurry of activity in the policy arena with a range of new policy documents and reports produced by government departments, committees, public bodies, and third sector organisations. Each seeking to contribute to the wider debate on the problem of CSA, and the development of responses in the aftermath of recent high profile cases (Home Office, 2010, 2014, HM Government, 2015; All Party Parliamentary Group (APPG) on Child Protection and NSPCC, 2014; The Sexual Violence Against Children and Vulnerable People National Group (SVACV), 2013; Jay, 2014; Gray and Watt, 2013; Children's Commissioner for England, 2015). These reports, along with others, are subject to analysis to consider the contours of the policy debate as well as the relationship between policy discourse and that produced in the other institutional sites in focus here. The need for analysis of official discourse produced in the period 2010-2015 is due to the apparent impact this discourse has already had on public debates about CSA, as well as the on-going impact it will undoubtedly have on policy developments from 2015 onwards. The on-going Independent Inquiry into Child Sexual Abuse (IICSA) is heavily influenced by both policy and previous inquiries produced 2010-2015 and these past inquiries (and their failures) are key in setting the terms of this current inquiry. Even with the previous inquiries and subsequent implementation of various recommendations the IICSA continues to fail in its aims to;

> Identify institutional failings where they are found to exist, to demand accountability for past institutional failings, to support victims and survivors to share their experience of sexual abuse, and

to make practical recommendations to ensure that children are given the care and protection they need (IICSA, 2016).

CSA Through a Feminist Poststructuralist Lens

Feminist work has sought to understand, and respond to, CSA and it is here that this research presents a novel contribution. It is feminism that is the point of origin for contemporary discourses on CSA (Scott, 2001). Feminist campaigning resulted in parliamentary legislation and eventually the 1885 Criminal Law Amendment Act of which changed the age of consent from 13 years old to 16 years old (Jackson, 2000: 12). This legislation remains the foundation for the 21st century approach to CSA outside of the family (Smart, 1989, 2016). These changes to the law, and the implementation of the National Society for the Prevention of Cruelty to Children (NSPCC) in 1884 were in response to societal concerns surrounding juvenile prostitution and more widely, the 'moral state of the nation' (Jackson, 2000, 2015, see: Smart, 1989, Richardson and Bacon, 1991). The dominance of conservative ideas about the family has proved extremely problematic for feminist advances into CSA as this private and 'safe' sphere as defined in public discourse is always positioned in contrast to the public and 'dangerous' sphere of society; keeping CSA a 'secret' offence (Cowburn and Dominelli, 2001).

This document-based research employs a feminist poststructuralist theoretical framework. Poststructuralism refers to a theory, or a group of theories, "concerning the relationship between human beings, the world, and the practice of making and reproducing meanings" (Belsey, 2002: 5) and the common factor in poststructuralist analyses of social organisation, social meanings, power and individual consciousness is *language* (Weedon, 1997). Michel Foucault's work, and fundamentally his understanding of *power* (see: Gordon, 1980), has provided a key influence over poststructuralist ideas, and feminist poststructuralist work has taken up, and developed, key ideas from Foucault's work to explore and contest gendered power relations (Howe, 2008; Peci *et al*, 2009; Weedon, 1997).

The feminist poststructuralist framework employed within this research is directly informed by the work of Foucault. Although he did not articulate a feminist position, and in fact it could be argued that he did not prioritise gender at any point in his work, Foucault's focus on the 'Other' both models and supports the un-silencing of which feminism has highlighted during the last fifty years (Ashe, 1987). It is his ideas around truth, power, discursive formations, and discourse (Foucault, 1977, 1981, 1990, 1991, 2002) that are central to and may be utilised within a feminist analysis of public discourses on CSA in England from 2010-2015. Discourses are ways of constituting knowledge, of talking about, a specific topic or subject at a given historical moment, and the focus in this research lies with the ways in which CSA has been discursively framed. The analysis of legal, media, political, and official discourses seeks to understand the positionality of the author, the intended audience, and the circumstances under which the text was produced (Waitt, 2005) whilst considering the interrelations between the four institutional sites.

Feminist poststructuralist work is best understood as "a mode of knowledge production which uses poststructuralist theories of language, subjectivity, social processes and institutions to understand existing power relations and to identify areas and strategies for change" (Weedon 1997: 40). Due to the focus of feminist poststructuralism on the historical positioning of power and its unstable and conflicting meanings it is well suited to undertake an analysis of CSA. The very definitions of CSA have been constantly conflicted throughout history; legally, socially, and politically. Feminist poststructuralism allows for a consideration of the extent to which dominant understandings of CSA are reliant upon overarching notions of what is considered to be 'normal' in terms of child-adult relationships, child protection and arguably, childhood itself. Considering the notions of a 'normal' family as a site of struggle, this research remains consistently critical of the constructions of 'normality' as it is this discursive construction that allows for CSA to be hidden from view. It is hidden because both the perpetrators and victims are represented as 'abnormal', as separate from the ideal of 'family', therefore constructing a dominant discourse where survivors and victims are blamed.

The method utilised within this research is a Foucauldian discourse analysis. Foucauldian discourse analysis at its most basic level involves a "careful reading of texts, always with a view to discover discursive patterns of meaning, contradictions and inconsistencies" (Gavey, 1989: 467) and more broadly allows us to focus on "the role of discourse in the (re)production and challenge of dominance" (Van Dijk, 1993: 249). This method asks its followers to undertake an analysis of language and texts (both spoken and written) in order to identify discursive practices within them (Willig and Stainton-Rogers, 2008: 91), allowing for discourse to be prioritised and for a full engagement within the struggle to have CSA recognised as a social and gendered issue.

In *The Order of Discourse* (1981) Foucault argued that we should not see discourse as only a set of statements with a similar purpose, but that we should see their existence as due to a complex set of practices, which help to keep some in circulation whilst excluding others. Those discourses which are side-lined may give us more insight into CSA than those thrust upon us by various institutional sites. It is not only what is heard and (re)produced that is important for a Foucauldian analysis, but also what is *unsaid* (Woodak and Myer, 2009) and it is here the relationship between theory and method may be fully appreciated. Feminist poststructuralism also asks for the researcher to question why certain things are articulated within discourse and to also consider what is *excluded* (Howe, 2008).

Conclusion

On this basis, the research explores how CSA is put into discourse by exposing and analysing what has been included and what has been excluded in public discourse during the five years to the end of 2015. The convergences and distinctions between the four institutional sites are mapped to explore the development of dominant discourse(s) on CSA. A Foucauldian discourse analysis of CSA from 2010-2015 must seek to problematise the ways in which ideas such as the protection of children are (re)defined and how these redefinitions serve to draw attention away from the gendered elements of the crime. In drawing our attention to the problems, Foucault asks us to establish a critical relation to the present and to chip away at any certainties or claims to 'truth' (Arribas-Ayllon and Walkerdine, 2008). Dominant discourses privilege versions of a social reality, which will always prioritise existing power relations and social structures (Willig, 2015). Some discourses in relation to CSA have become so deep-rooted that it is difficult to envisage a concrete political challenge. However, it is within the very nature of discourse that counter-discourses such as the one outlined in this chapter can emerge.

Acknowledgements

I wish to thank my doctoral supervisor Dr Will Jackson for his excellent guidance, support and never wavering faith throughout this endeavour. I also wish to thank the European Group for the Study of Deviance and Social Control for this opportunity to share my research.

References

All Party Parliamentary Group on Child Protection and NSPCC (2014) *SEMINAR SERIES ON CHILD SEXUAL ABUSE: Recommendations for the Prevention of Child Sexual Abuse and Better Support for Victims* Available from: http://cdn.basw.co.uk/upload/basw_13644-2.pdf (accessed on 12th November, 2016)

Angelides, S. (2004) 'Feminism, Child Sexual Abuse, and the Erasure of Child Sexuality', *GLQ: A Journal of Lesbian and Gay Studies* Volume 10, No. 2 pp 141-177

Arribas-Ayllon, M. and Walkerdine, V. (2008) 'Foucauldian Discourse Analysis' pp91- 108 in Willig, C. and Stainton-Rogers, W. (eds) *The Sage Handbook of Qualitative Research in Psychology* London: SAGE

Ashe, M. (1987) 'Minds Opportunity: Birthing A Poststructuralist Feminist Jurisprudence' *Syracuse Law Review* Volume 38, No.4 pp 1129-1174

Atmore, C. (1998) 'Towards 2000: Child Sexual Abuse and the Media' pp 124 – 144 in Howe, A. (ed) *Sexed Crime in the News* Sydney: Federation Press

Ballinger, A. (2000) *Dead Women Walking: Executed Women in England and Wales 1900-1955* Dartmouth: Ashgate Publishing Ltd

Belknap, J (2014) *The Invisible Woman: Gender, Crime and Justice.* Fourth Edition USA: Cengage Learning

Bell, V. (2002) 'The Vigilant(e) Parent and the Paedophile: The News of the World Campaign' *Feminist Theory* Volume 3, No. 1 pp 83- 102

Belsey, C. (2002) *Poststructuralism: A Very Short Introduction* Oxford: Oxford University Press

Browne, V. (2014) 'The Persistence of Patriarchy: Operation Yewtree and the Return to 1970's Feminism' *Radical Philosophy No.* 118 pp 9-19

Children's Commissioner for England (2015) *Protecting Children from Harm: A Critical Assessment of Child Sexual Abuse in the Family Network in England and Priorities for Action* Available From: https://www.childrenscommissioner.gov.uk/sites/default/files/publications/P rotecting%20children%20from%20harm%20-%20full%20report.pdf (accessed on 9th September, 2016)

Cowburn, M. and Dominelli, L. (2001) 'Masking Hegemonic Masculinity: Reconstructing the Paedophile as the Dangerous Stranger' *British Journal of Social Work* Volume 31, No. 3 pp 399-414

Davidson, J. (2008) *Child Sexual Abuse: Media Representations and Government Reactions*, London: Routledge

Foucault, M. (1977) *Discipline and Punish: The Birth of the Prison* New York: Pantheon

From "Amused Tolerance to Outrage"

Foucault, M. (1981) 'The Order of Discourse' pp 48-78 in Young, R. (ed) *Untying the Text: A Post-structuralist Reader,* London: Routledge

Foucault, M. (1990) *The History of Sexuality: Volume 1: An Introduction* New York: Vintage Books

Foucault, M. (1991) 'Politics & the Study of Discourse' pp 53-72 in Burchell. G, Gordon, C. and Miller, P. (eds) *The Foucault Effect: Studies in Governmentality with Two Lectures and an Interview with Michel Foucault* Chicago: University of Chicago Press

Foucault, M. (2002) *Archaeology of Knowledge* London: Routledge Revivals

Freud, S. (1997) *The Interpretation of Dreams* Hertfordshire: Wordsworth Classics

Gallagher, B. (2014) Rolf Harris Guilty: But what has Operation Yewtree Really Taught us about Sexual Abuse *The Conversation* [online] 30th June 2014 Available From https://theconversation.com/rolf-harris-guilty-but-what-has-operation-yewtree-really-taught-us-about-sexual-abuse-28282 (accessed 25th November, 2016)

Gavey, N. (1989) 'Feminist Poststructuralism and Discourse Analysis' *Psychology of Women Quarterly* Volume, 13, No. 4 pp 459-475

Gordon, C. (ed) (1980) *Power/Knowledge: Selected Interviews and Other Writings 1972-1977 by Michel Foucault.* New York: Pantheon Books

Gray, D. and Watt, P. (2013) 'Giving Victims a Voice: A Joint MPS and NSPCC Report into Allegations of Sexual Abuse Made Against Jimmy Savile under Operation Yewtree' *NSPCC* Available From: https://www.nspcc.org.uk/globalassets/documents/research-reports/yewtree-report-giving-victims-voice-jimmy-savile.pdf (accessed on 20th March, 2016)

Greer, C. and Mclaughlin, E. (2013) 'Notes on a Scandal: The Jimmy Savile Case is all too Familiar' *The Conversation* [online] Available From: https://theconversation.com/notes-on-a-scandal-the-jimmy-savile-case-is-all-too-familiar-20379 (accessed on 25th November, 2016)

Hayes, S. (2014) *Sex, Love and Abuse: Discourses on Domestic Violence and Sexual Assault* Hampshire: Palgrave Macmillan

HM Government (2015) *Tackling Child Sexual Exploitation* Available From: https://www.gov.uk/government/uploads/system/uploads/attachment_data/file/408604/2903652_RotherhamResponse_acc2.pdf (accessed on 20th August, 2016)

Home Office (2010) *Call to End Violence Against Women and Girls*, London: Home Office

Home Office (2014) *Call to End Violence Against Women and Girls - Action Plan*, London: Home Office Available From: https://www.gov.uk/government/uploads/system/uploads/attachment_data/file/97901/action-plan-new-chapter.pdf (accessed 20th February, 2017)

Home Office (2015) *Working Together to Safeguard Children: A Guide to Inter-agency Working to Safeguard and Promote the Welfare of Children* Available From https://www.gov.uk/government/uploads/system/uploads/attachment_data /file/592101/Working_Together_to_Safeguard_Children_20170213.pdf (accessed 19th December, 2016)

HMSO (1967) *Sexual Offences Act 1967* Available From: http://www.legislation.gov.uk/ukpga/1967/60/pdfs/ukpga_19670060_en.pdf (accessed on 24th January, 2017)

Howe, A. (2008) *Sex Violence and Crime* Oxon: Routledge

IICSA (2016) *Investigating the Extent to Which Institutions have Failed to Protect Children from Sexual Abuse* 15th September 2016 Available From: https://www.iicsa.org.uk/ (accessed on 20th September, 2016)

Jackson, L. A. (2000) *Child Sexual Abuse in Victorian England* London: Routledge

Jackson, L. (2015) 'Child sexual abuse in England and Wales: prosecution and prevalence, 1918-1970' *History and Policy: Policy Papers* Available online at: http://www.historyandpolicy.org/policy-papers/papers/child-sexual-abuse-in-england-and-wales-prosecution-and-prevalence-1918-197 Accessed on: 12/04/2017

Jay, A. (2014) *Independent Inquiry into Child Sexual Exploitation in Rotherham 1997-2013* Available From: http://www.rotherham.gov.uk/downloads/file/1407/independent_inquiry_cs e_in_rotherham (accessed 16th January, 2016)

Jewkes, Y. and Wykes, M. (2012) 'Reconstructing the Sexual Abuse of Children: "Cyber-paeds", Panic and Power' *Sexualities*, Volume 15, No. 8 pp 934-952

Kitzinger, J. (2004) *Framing Abuse: Media Influence and Public Understanding of Sexual Violence Against Children* London: Pluto Press

Kitzinger, J. (2011) 'The 'Paedophile-in-the-Community' Protests: Press Reporting and Public Responses' pp 356-376 in Letherby, G. Williams, K. Birch, P. and Cain, M (eds) *Sex as Crime?* London: Routledge

Middleton, W. (2015) 'Tipping Points and the Accommodation of the Abuser: Ongoing Incestuous Abuse during Childhood' *International Journal for Crime, Justice and Social Democracy* Volume 4, No. 2 pp 4-17

Nava, M. (1988) 'Cleveland and the Press: Outrage and Anxiety in the Reporting of Child Sexual Abuse' *Feminist Review* No. 28, pp 103-120

Peci, A, Vieira, M. and Clegg S. (2009) 'Power, Discursive Practices and the Construction of the "Real"' *Electronic Journal of Knowledge Management* Volume 7, No. 3 pp 377 – 386

From "Amused Tolerance to Outrage"

Pilgrim, D. (2014) 'The Sexual Norms of the 1970s Now Look Like the Casual Rules of a Paedophile Playground' *The Conversation* [online] 11th July Available From https://theconversation.com/the-sexual-norms-of-the-1970s-now-look-like-the-casual-rules-of-a-paedophile-playground-28999 (accessed 21st January, 2017)

Reavey, P. and Warner, S. (2003) *New Feminist Stories of Child Sexual Abuse: Sexual Scripts and Dangerous Dialogues* London: Routledge

Richardson, S. and Bacon, H. (1991) *CSA: Whose Problem? Reflections from Cleveland.* Birmingham: Venture Press

Scott, S. (2001) Surviving Selves. Feminism and Contemporary Discourses of Child Sexual Abuse *Feminist Theory* Volume 2, No. 3 pp 349 - 361

Smart, C. (1976) *Women, Crime and Criminology: A Feminist Critique* London: Routledge and Keegan Paul

Smart, C. (1989) *Feminism and the Power of Law* London: Routledge

Smart, C. (1995) *Law, Crime and Sexuality: Essays in Feminism* London: SAGE

Smart, C. (1999) 'A History of Ambivalence and Conflict in the Discursive Construction of the Child Victim of Sexual Abuse'. *Journal of Legal Studies* Volume 8, No. 3 pp 391-409

Smart, C. (2000) 'Reconsidering the Recent History of Child Sexual Abuse 1910-1960' *Journal of Social Policy* Volume 29, No. 1 pp 55-71

Smart, C. (2016) 'Observations Through a Rear View Mirror: Revisiting Women, Crime and Criminology' *Critical Research Seminar: Centre for the Study of Crime, Criminalisation and Social Exclusion* Liverpool John Moores University, 16th March

The Sexual Violence Against Children and Vulnerable People National Group (SVACV), (2013) Available From: https://www.gov.uk/government/publications/sexual-violence-against-children-and-vulnerable-people-national-group (accessed on 3rd December, 2016)

Van Dijk, T. (1993) 'Principles of Critical Discourse Analysis' *Discourse and Society* Volume 4, No. 2 pp 249-283

Waitt, G. R. (2005) 'Doing Discourse Analysis' pp 163-191 in Hay, I. (ed) *Qualitative Research Methods in Human Geography* Oxford: Oxford University Press

Walklate, S. (2008) 'What is to be Done About Violence Against Women? Gender, Violence, Cosmopolitanism and the Law' *British Journal of Criminology* Volume 48, No. 1 pp 39-54

Warner, S. (2009). *Understanding the Effects of Child Sexual Abuse.* New York: Routledge

Weedon, C. (1997) *Feminist Practice and Poststructuralist Theory Second Edition* Oxford: Blackwell

Willig, C. (2015) 'Discourse Analysis' pp 160-185 in Smith. J. A (ed) (2015) *Qualitative Psychology: A Practical Guide to Research Methods* Third Edition London: SAGE

Woodak, R. and Myer, M. (2009) *Methods of Critical Discourse Analysis* London: SAGE

Extended Biography

Research

I began my current role as a Graduate Teaching Assistant (GTA) at Liverpool John Moores University (LJMU) in September 2015. Before this post, I undertook both my undergraduate degree and Masters by research at the University of Central Lancashire in Preston, England. My Masters research focussed upon the legal and media construction of criminal woman in 19th century England. Having chosen five case studies through analysis of the media reports from 1880-1890 I then undertook research into legal documentation including; judges notes, petitions, depositions and indictments pertaining to the five women. This research indicated that what is known about women criminals, not only as criminals but as women, plays an intrinsic role in determining how their crimes are constructed in both media and legal discourses. Recurring themes were present throughout the research, including double deviance, gender performance and ideals of femininity. These themes continue to play out within the contemporary Criminal Justice System through women as criminals and women as victims. My on-going PhD research is providing further evidence of this victimisation in relation to both men and women child-victims.

Following my MA research, I studied a Post-Graduate Teaching Certificate (PGCE) in Lifelong Learning through Teesside University. This course allowed me to undertake teaching practice within a further education setting. I undertook two years of teaching practice within both 16-18 and adult provision on courses such as Access to Education, Public Services and the PGCE. Having this experience has been invaluable within my current role.

Activism, Organisational Work and/or Professional Membership

Within my current role as GTA I have also been involved in the

From "Amused Tolerance to Outrage"

organisation and fulfilment of research seminars, lectures, conferences and events for the Centre of Crime, Criminalisation and Social Exclusion at LJMU alongside Professor Joe Sim and Dr Helen Monk. The centre itself has a vibrant research culture that produces interdisciplinary research and attracts international speakers. So far this academic year we have hosted critical lectures from Sheila Coleman of the Hillsborough Justice Campaign, Professor Carol Smart on 40 years since *Women Crime and Criminology* (1976) and Robert King and Albert Woodfox (2 of the Angola 3) as part of their *Freedom* tour. This experience allows for excellent networking within the field as well as building upon criminological and sociological knowledge and the skill of organising large-scale events.

Future Aspirations
My future aspirations post-PhD are to secure a teaching role and continue to engage in critical research with an overall aim for current research to have an impact on policy responses. The on-going IICSA (2016) will form the basis of post-doctoral research, the current institutional failings and very contestation over who should head this Inquiry leaves the future of responses to CSA in on-going uncertainty, already worthy of critical challenge.

Selected Works
As well as being heavily involved in all aspects of the Centre for the Study of Crime, Criminalisation, and Social Exclusion at LJMU I have also begun co-editing the collection of postgraduate research papers with a view to have this edited collection published in the summer of 2017 through both the centre and the European Group for the Study of Deviance and Social Control.

Contact Details
Twitter: @tucks1206
Academia.edu: https://ljmu.academia.edu/KatieTucker

24

Westminster's Narration of the Neoliberal Crisis: Rationalising the Irrational?

Holly White

Introduction

This chapter introduces my doctoral research, which draws on the work of Antonio Gramsci and Stuart Hall to analyse Westminster definers' narration of the 2007 onwards-neoliberal capitalist crisis. It centres on political elites' discursive strategies for maintaining hegemony. My thesis contributes a detailed analysis of elite narration of the General Election 2010, the Scottish Independence Referendum 2014, and the General Election 2015, including its aftermath of the Labour Leadership Election 2015.

This short chapter explains first, that Westminster elites operated to ensure that the crisis did not become a crisis *of* neoliberalism, and actually seized the opportunity presented by the neoliberal crisis to extend the project's reach and deepen its roots. Second, it argues that Westminster definers constructed a narrative that attempted to rationalise a response that empirical evidence and sound reasoning deems irrational but which has served the interests of private capital. Thirdly, the chapter presents a brief overview of some aspects of the research design, discussing the selection of what I term intense narration moments and its focus on the narration of challenges.

A *Neoliberal* 'Resolution' for a *Neoliberal* Crisis

The real existing neoliberal project, as opposed to neoliberal theory (see: Brenner and Theodore, 2002), caused a capitalist crisis. In particular, its generation of dramatic inequality, heavy dependence upon, and deregulation of, the finance industry, and the prioritisation of profit accumulation driven by narrow individualism, led to the financial system reaching the edge of collapse. Counter to neoliberal theory, unprecedented state intervention rescued finance capital, and the British economy, from disaster. The crisis provided seemingly undisputable evidence that the neoliberal project had failed. Rational 'evidence based' thinking it might have seemed, would lead to the death of the project. However, extraordinarily, Westminster elites, corporate elites, and financial elites, ensured it came back from crisis empowered and seemingly stronger. Remarkably, elites successfully defended the existing project, preventing a crisis *of* neoliberal capitalism[1] and what Gramsci (1988: 218) termed a "crisis of hegemony".

A capitalist crisis marks a "disruption" in the normalised functioning of capitalism (Clarke, 2010: 339). Such a crisis has the potential to render a form of capitalism, or even capitalism itself, intensely vulnerable. It may threaten "the legitimacy of political and economic order, the presumed social contract which underlies it and the distribution of power" (Gamble, 2009: 37). Crises may be "focussing events" (Birkland, 1998: 53), drawing attention to problematic actions that have been undertaken for many years, perhaps without much concern (Edelman, 1977). They can therefore, create contexts for restructuring or transforming political economic conditions (Gramsci, 1971). As Gramsci (1988: 208) recognised, capitalist crises create a "terrain more favourable for the dissemination of certain modes of thought, and certain ways of posing and resolving questions". Those seeking to maintain the existing order must defend it, particularly from those seeking to seize the opportunity for radical transformation.

Oppositional forces may organise to challenge the hegemonic project (Gramsci, 1971). A movement may engage in a "struggle to contest and disorganise an existing political formation" and to secure a level of "social authority sufficiently deep to conform society into a new historic project" (Hall, 1988: 7). An "oppositional movement" must have an "alternative vision" and significant power (Harvey, 2011: 227). A challenge must form a "powerful counter-veiling force" that "represents an organised majority or substantial minority" and "has a degree of legitimacy within the system or can win such a position through struggle" (Hall *et al*, 2013: 67). In such conditions, movements can form "counter-ideologies capable of challenging the overall hegemony of 'ruling ideas'" and may take "the

---

[1] A distinction is made between crises that lead to the end of a hegemonic bloc, or crises within a hegemonic bloc, or what Saad-Filho (2010: 242 emphasis added) respectively terms a "crisis *of* neoliberalism" and a "crisis *in* neoliberal capitalism".

transformation of society as a whole as their object" (Hall *et al*, 2013: 154).

Leaders whilst working to "defend the existing structure" and "overcome" contradictions and maintain hegemony (Gramsci, 1971 [1929-1935]: 400) do not necessarily seek to simply maintain the existing order. Rather, they may use the opportunity to deepen their project. As "neoliberal restructuring projects" are undertaken in particular national or local contexts a project may accommodate or inherit aspects of them, even if temporarily, if elites are to maintain consent (Brenner and Theodore, 2002: 349). The welfare state, for instance, could not be *completely* and *instantly* dismantled (see: Peck and Tickell, 2007). Rather it has been gradually 'reformed'. However, in a "state of exception" exceptional measures can be constructed as necessary (Agamben, 2005: 1) and it may become politically viable to elicit consent for the previously unacceptable (see: Edelman, 1977; Klein, 2007); the implementation of conditions can be accelerated. My thesis makes the argument that over the crisis period Westminster definers collectively constructed the National Health Service (NHS) as experiencing a crisis 'caused' by public inefficiencies. 'High' national debt and deficit were exaggerated to strengthen the framing of private capital as the 'resolution' to the failing public sector and therefore the crisis. This in turn has legitimised the next stage in the gradual privatisation of the NHS.

Westminster elites exploited the opportunity presented by the *neoliberal* capitalist crisis to extend *neoliberalism*. The financial crisis was "the alibi" David Cameron required for deepening neoliberal conditions and further shifting wealth and power "to the already rich and powerful" (Hall, 2011: 718, 721). Rather than addressing the structural causes of the crisis, elites used, what Gamble (2009: 66) terms, "strategic opening" to accelerate the erosion of resistant elements of social democratic capitalism and to roll out further neoliberal conditions.

An Irrational Response? Crisis 'Resolution' as a Class Project

Notwithstanding that deregulation of private capital was a key cause of the financial crisis, Westminster did not challenge the power of finance capital or seek fundamental reform of the finance industry. Private capital more widely indeed, was gifted further deregulation (see: Tombs, 2016). After the prioritisation of public and corporate profit accumulation, liberated by deregulation had brought banks to near disaster, they were rescued at public expense. They are currently in the process of being sold back to hedge funders, to date, at a loss (see: Treanor, 2015). Nationalisation was simply not discussed.

Whilst financial elites have largely escaped criminal justice punishment for their *role in the crisis,* welfare claimants are now subjected to actions more closely associated with the criminal justice system than the welfare system including: *trials* by private companies to determine 'fitness to work', harmful *sanctions* for perceived inactivity, and the provision of *free labour* for corporations. Rather than reducing power and wealth inequalities, Conservatives reduced labour power and cut welfare benefits, public sector pay, and local services. Neoliberal elites responded to a *privately generated* crisis with cuts to public spending and further privileges for the private sector. Whilst the interests of the powerful and wealthy have been protected, the vulnerable have become targets for blame, responses, and harms.

The political economic order is intrinsically harmful for those at the bottom of the class hierarchy, but responses to crisis have dramatically intensified harms. Largely as a result of falling real wages and benefit sanctions, delays, and changes, the Trussell Trust alone provided over one million three-day emergency food supplies in 2015/2016 (The Trussell Trust, 2016). Due to a lack of social housing, affordable homes, and expensive private rental costs, in 2016 more than 250,000 people were homeless in England (Richardson, 2016). Austerity has played a major role in the 9 per cent rise in death rate between June 2014 and June 2015 (Dorling, 2016). Before the crisis the suicide rate was falling however, since 2008 debt, unemployment, homelessness, and austerity appear to have contributed to an additional 1000 males committing suicide and up to 40,000 additional attempted male suicides (Gunnell *et al*, 2015). 'Benefit-related death' has come into existence, reflecting a major shift in the role and approach of the welfare system. A system created under social democratic capitalism *to protect the vulnerable* from economic harm has been 'reformed' to such an extent that it has *caused deaths of vulnerable persons*. Following a Freedom of Information request by Disability News Service, the DWP released 49 peer-reviewed reports on deaths following social security claims (see: Butler and Pring, 2016). Brian McArdle (see: Burns, 2012), Tim Salter (see: McVeigh, 2015), and Linda Wootton (see: Huffington Post UK, 2013) are three victims who died after Work Capability Assessments deemed them 'fit to work'. For Saad-Filho (2010: 244), "never in economic history has so much trouble and expense been rewarded with such effrontery".

If the neoliberal project is not viewed as a class project, but evaluated as a vehicle for successful economic functioning, defined as operating without crisis and benefitting the lives of the majority, then its resurrection seems completely irrational. If the crisis 'resolution' is not viewed as a process for furthering private capital's interests, but assessed by whether it addresses causes to prevent a repetition of the crisis, and moves the economy and the public out of crisis as swiftly as possible with minimal harm, then the choice of 'resolution' again appears irrational. As Davies (2016: 121, 122) suggests, there is "seeming irrationalism from above" and "a shift to unreason". "Increasingly it appears [...] that government are operating outside of the norms of judgement altogether" (ibid: 122). "Apparently impervious to evidence, evaluation or the merits of alternatives" neoliberal conditions, notably deregulation of private capital and austerity, "persist" (ibid: 121).

Westminster, possessing significant power to determine responses and to influence public sense making of the crisis, was for the most part ideologically unified, collectively constructing a narrative to maintain hegemony. As Tombs (2016) recognises, the political and popular framing of the crisis allowed neoliberal conditions to continue. Westminster identified false causes, and narrated flawed responses and challenges to rationalise a resolution that was irrational in terms of historic and contemporary evidence. They narrated the crisis to attain support for and acquiescence in a 'resolution' that maintains and deepens many of the conditions that caused the crisis, inflicts unnecessary harm particularly on the vulnerable, and major injustices, and prioritises the interests of private capital. In terms of class interest, the response might be seen as perfectly 'rational'.

An Overview of the Research Design

The idea for my doctoral research originated whilst volunteering for Citizens Advice, a charitable organisation providing advice on debt, welfare, and housing amongst other issues. I witnessed, and sought to help manage, the personal impact of, the harms intensified by responses to the crisis. Austerity policies meant more members of the public were requiring support whilst at the same time local authorities were experiencing cuts and legal aid was cut (see: Citizens Advice Bureau, 2011). This led to reductions in the bureau's funding and therefore less availability of experts and services at a time when they were needed the most. I became deeply concerned about the infliction of harms and the injustice of the burden of the crisis being carried by the most vulnerable. I sought to understand how Westminster definers' were justifying their crisis 'resolution' to attain public support and acquiescence.

My thesis contributes a critical analysis of Westminster's narration of crisis causes, responses and proposed responses, challenges from other political parties, and the narrative's development over the period of the crisis. When I began designing the research in 2013 there was no sign of an oppositional movement with an alternative vision that had the necessary power and legitimacy in the system to present a counter-hegemonic narrative at a national level, and therefore challenge the Westminster neoliberal project. However, as the crisis developed a number of challenges emerged that Westminster definers, concerned with protecting their 'resolution' and the wider neoliberal project sought to discursively counter. Countering challenges became an important element of the narration of the crisis that grew in significance as the crisis developed.

During the Scottish Independence Referendum 2014, the Scottish National Party (SNP) presented a challenge to Westminster's austerity project and called for a more socially just resolution. Whilst independence, patriotism and freedom from the perceived undemocratic domination of Westminster, were key arguments for independence, a 'socially just' alternative to austerity was *central the SNP's campaign* to the point that the core argument for independence was that it was a means for anti-austerity. This marked the first moment of the crisis in which Westminster were presented with a major challenge to their narrative that required discursive countering. Therefore, its analysis was key to understanding Westminster definer's narration of the crisis.

The SNP's 2014 challenge developed in the 2015 General Election with support from the Green Party and Plaid Cymru. Eventually in the aftermath of the 2015 General Election the consensus amongst Westminster elites started to publicly fracture. Challenging Conservatives, Liberal Democrats and New Labour's protection of the neoliberal project, Corbyn, supported by McDonnell, presented counter-hegemonic discourses challenging the limits Westminster had previously placed on debate. He reframed the crisis, recognising the injustice of harms and whose interests were served by the 'resolution', and called for an alternative political and economic order for the transformation of society.

From 2013 the United Kingdom Independence Party (UKIP) exerted a serious pressure on British politics that had major consequences. The party operated to channel blame for problems, largely caused by cuts in public spending, to immigration. This was a strategy for the nationalist pursuit of UK 'independence' from the European Union (EU). UKIP pressured Westminster elites for a 'tougher' response to immigration, framing the end of the free movement of immigrants from the EU as the path to restoring a Britain run in the interests of 'hardworking *British* taxpayers'. UKIP successfully attained the third highest votes in the 2015 General Election, reflecting a key change in Britain's political landscape, and Conservatives in particular moved right supporting the blaming of immigrants and committed to a referendum on UK membership of the European Union.

I developed the research to recognise the emergence and significance of these challenges and Westminster's countering of them became a key focus of the research. Within longitudinal analysis a focus is given to what I have termed intense narration moments. These occur when the public sphere becomes saturated with texts about a particular topic and public concern about the topic is heightened. I selected three intense narration moments to study: the General Election 2010, the Scottish Independence Referendum 2014, and the General Election 2015 and undertook detailed critical discourse analysis of over 180 texts, utilising Fairclough's (2000, 2003, 2009, 2010) framework.

I chose to analyse the two general elections because elections are moments when the public sphere is saturated with political elites' texts. These identify the key concerns of the period and the suggested responses. The crisis and possible responses were the central topics of both elections. Despite the intensity of narration during the elections and notwithstanding that they were such key moments in the narration of the neoliberal crisis there was not an analysis of them in the existing literature on crisis narration. Also, analysing two similar moments offered insights into the development of Westminster narration over the period of crisis. The 2015 General Election and aftermath was also a moment in which challenges were presented and discursively countered by Westminster.

I selected key texts disseminated directly to the public and texts produced through Westminster definer engagement with the mass media that had high audience figures, seeking to present a comprehensive analysis of the key texts produced by definers to influence public sense making. Texts were diverse, including radio interviews, televised election debates, budget statements, newspaper articles, The Andrew Marr Show interviews, manifestos and posters. I am currently in the final stages of my doctoral research and plan to explore the publication of my thesis in a single authored book, or the publication of the findings as case studies of the moments and a paper that discusses the narrative of crisis as a whole, particularly focussing on continuities, shifts, and changes.

Acknowledgements

I would like to thank Edge Hill University for funding the research and my supervisors, Dr Alana Barton, Dr Howard Davis, and Professor John Diamond for their continued support. I would also like to thank European Group members for their constructive feedback and encouragement over the last few years.

References

Agamben, G. (2005) *State of Exception* Trans by Attell, K. Chicago: University of Chicago

Birkland, T, A. (1998) 'Focusing Events, Mobilisation, and Agenda Setting' *Journal of Public Policy* Volume 18, No. 1, pp 53-74

Brenner, N. and Theodore, N. (2002) 'Cities and the Geographies of Actually Existing Neoliberalism' *Antipode* Volume 34, No. 3, pp 349-379

Burns, J. (2012) 'Atos Benefits Bullies Killed my Sick Dad, Says Devastated Kieran, 13' in *Daily Record* [online] 1st November Available from: www.dailyrecord.co.uk/news/scottish-news/atos-killed-my-dad-says-boy-1411100 (accessed 2nd March 2017)

Butler, P. and Pring, J. (2016) 'Suicides of Benefit Claimants Reveal DWP Flaws, Says Inquiry' *The Guardian* [online] 13th May Available from: www.theguardian.com/society/2016/may/13/suicides-of-benefit-claimants-reveal-dwp-flaws-says-inquiry (accessed 2nd March 2017)

Citizens Advice Bureau (2011) 'Cuts in CAB Funding Leaving Thousands with Nowhere to Turn for Help' [online] 6th September Available from: www.citizensadvice.org.uk/about-us/how-citizens-advice-works/media/press-releases/cuts-in-cab-funding-leaving-thousands-with-nowhere-to-turn-for-help/ (accessed 7th March, 2017)

Clarke, J. (2010) 'New New Deals: Reforming Welfare Again?' *Occasion: Interdisciplinary Studies in the Humanities* Volume 2, pp 1-13

Clarke, J. and Newman, J. (2012) 'The Alchemy of Austerity' *Critical Social Policy* Volume 32, No. 3, pp 299–319

Curtis, N. (2013) 'Thought Bubble: Neoliberalism and the Politics of Knowledge' *New in Formations: A Journal of Culture/ Theory/ Politics* Volume 80–81, pp 73-88

Davies, W. (2016) 'The New Neoliberalism' in *New Left Review* 101 September-October 2016

Dorling, D. (2016) 'Brexit: the Decision of a Divided Country' *The British Medical Journal* 354 doi: https://doi.org/10.1136/bmj.i3697

Edelman, M. (1977) *Political Language: Words that Succeed and Policies that Fail* New York: Academic Press

Fairclough, N. (2000) 'Dialogue in the Public Sphere' pp 170-184 in Sarangi, S. and Coulthard, M. (eds) *Discourse and Social Life* Essex: Pearson Education Limited

Fairclough, N. (2003) *Analysing Discourse: Textual Analysis for Social Research* London: Routledge

Fairclough, N. (2009) 'A Dialectical-relational Approach to Critical Discourse Analysis in Social Research' pp 162-186 in Wodak, R. and Meyer, M. (eds) *Methods of Critical Discourse Analysis* Second Edition London: SAGE

Fairclough, N. (2010) *Critical Discourse Analysis: The Critical Study of Language* Second Edition Oxon: Pearson Education Limited

Gamble, A. (2009) *The Spectre at the Feast: Capitalist Crisis and the Politics of Recession* Hampshire: Palgrave Macmillan

Gilbert, J. (2013) 'What Kind of Thing is Neoliberalism?' *New Formations: A Journal of Culture/ Theory/ Politics* Volume 80-81, pp 7-22

Gramsci, A. (1971) 'The Modern Prince' pp 313-441 in Nowell Smith, G. and Hoare, Q. (eds) *Selections from the Prison Notebooks of Antonio Gramsci* London: Lawrence and Wishart

Gramsci, A. (1988) 'Hegemony, Relations of Force, Historical Bloc' pp 189-221 in Forgacs D. (ed) *The Gramsci Reader: Selected Writings 1916- 1935* New York: New York University Press

Gunnell, D. Donovan, J. Barnes, M. Davies, R. Hawton, K. Kapur, N. Hollingworth, W. and Metcalfe, C. (2015) *The 2008 Global Financial Crisis: Effects on Mental Health and Suicide* Bristol: PolicyBristol

Hall, S. (1988) 'Introduction: Thatcherism and the Crisis of the Left' pp 1-16 in Hall, S. (ed) (1998) *The Hard Road to Renewal: Thatcherism and the Crisis of the Left* London: Verso

Hall, S. (2011) 'The Neoliberal Revolution' in *Cultural Studies* Volume 25, No. 6, pp 705-728

Hall, S. Critcher, C. Jefferson, T. Clarke, J. and Roberts, B. (1978) *Policing the Crisis: Mugging, the State, and Law and Order* Hampshire: Palgrave MacMillan

Hall, S. Critcher, C. Jefferson, T. Clarke, J. and Roberts, B. (2013 [1978]) *Policing the Crisis: Mugging, the State, and Law and Order* Hampshire: Palgrave MacMillan

Harvey, D. (2011) *The Enigma of Capital and the Crises of Capitalism* London: Profile Books

Huffington Post UK (2013) 'Atos Benefits Row: Transplant Patient Linda Wootton Dies After Being Judged Fit for Work' *The Huffington Post* [online] 28th May Available from: www.huffingtonpost.co.uk/2013/05/28/linda-wootton-dies-after-being-judged-fit-for-work_n_3346582.html (accessed 2nd March, 2017)

Klein, N. (2007) *The Shock Doctrine: The Rise of Disaster Capitalism* London: Penguin Books

McVeigh, K. (2015) 'DWP to Apologise to Woman Whose Brother Killed Himself After his Benefits Were Cut' *The Guardian* [online] 3rd December Available from: www.theguardian.com/society/2015/dec/03/dwp-apologise-linda-cooksey-tim-salter-benefits-cut (accessed 2nd March, 2017)

Peck, J. and Tickell, A. (2007) 'Conceptualising Neoliberalism, Thinking Thatcherism' pp 26-50 in Leitner, H. Peck, J. and Sheppard, E. (eds) (2007) *Contesting Neoliberalism: Urban Frontiers* New York: Guilford Press

Richardson, H. (2016) 'More Than 250,000 are Homeless in Britain - Shelter' *BBC News* [online] 1st December Available from: www.bbc.co.uk/news/education-38157410 (accessed 2nd March, 2017)

Saad-Filho, A. (2010) 'Crisis in Neoliberalism or Crisis of Neoliberalism' pp 242-259 in Panitich, L. Albo, G. Chibber, V. (eds) (2010) *The Crisis This Time* Pontypool: The Merlin Press

The Trussell Trust (2016) 'End of Year Stats' [online] 27th February Available from: www.trusselltrust.org/news-and-blog/latest-stats/end-year-stats/ (accessed 2nd March, 2017)

Tombs, S. (2016) *Social Protection After the Crisis: Regulation Without Enforcement* Bristol: Policy Press

Treanor, J. (2015) 'Lloyds v RBS – Two Banks with Different Problems and Very Different Results' *The Guardian [online]* 27th February Available from: www.theguardian.com/business/2015/feb/27/lloyds-v-rbs-two-banks-with-different-problems-and-very-different-results (accessed on 2nd March, 2017)

Extended Biography

Research

In 2013 I completed a BA (hons) degree in Criminology and Criminal Justice at Edge Hill University, UK. For my undergraduate dissertation, under the supervision of Dr Howard Davis, I researched the relationship between police and protestors, police strategies for attaining protesters' consent to conditions placed on protest, physical coercion of protestors and protestors' experiences, focussing on rights and harms. I conducted semi-structured interviews both with tactical advisors from several constabularies in the North West of England and protestors from anti-austerity, anti-war and environmental movements who organised protests in the North West. During my final year of my undergraduate degree, I was encouraged by my supervisor to apply for PhD funding. I was awarded funding for PhD study by Edge Hill University as part of a Graduate Teaching Assistant programme. I completed a Post-Graduate Certificate in Teaching in Higher Education in 2015, achieving a distinction and Fellowship of the Higher Education Academy. I am currently in the final stages of my PhD and work as an associate tutor teaching Criminology at the University of Chester and Edge Hill University.

Activism, Organisational Work and/or Professional Membership

I have worked with a number of charitable organisations in roles providing aid and advice and seeking social policy changes. I was a volunteer for the International Aid Trust collecting and distributing food and health parcels. I volunteered for the Citizens Advice Bureau as an assessor and social policy co-ordinator, collecting data for various campaigns most notably on the 'bedroom tax'. I am currently working with The Trussell Trust, a charity seeking to end UK hunger through food banks, research and raising awareness of causes.

I am a member of Edge Hill University's Power, Discourse and Harm research unit and in 2015 I was a member of the organising committee Cutting Edge, a multi-disciplinary annual postgraduate conference held at Edge Hill University. I am also a member of the European Group for the Study of Deviance and Social Control. In the early stages of PhD study, I presented an introduction to my research at the first European Group Postgraduate and Undergraduate Conference. The support, and engaging and open discussion, encouraged me to present at the 2014 annual conference and I have continued to present at each annual conference since, building a supportive network of friends and invigoration for the year ahead. Most recently, at the 2016 annual conference I presented some findings from my analysis of Westminster's narration of the Scottish Independence Referendum 2014.

Future Aspirations

I plan to develop my relationship and involvement with the advice and activist organisations I work with as well as the European Group, and continue to teach Criminology. I hope to disseminate my PhD research widely and continue researching in the area of elite narratives, public sense making and counter-hegemonic movements. In particular I plan to undertake a critical analysis of Westminster's narration of the intense narration moment of the European Union Membership Referendum 2016 and conduct interviews and focus groups to develop public sense making of crisis causes and responses, and the wider political and economic order.

Selected Works

White, H. (2014) *'Policing the Neoliberal Crisis: An Introduction'* Postgraduate Stream of the European Group for the Study of Deviance and Social Control Undergraduate Conference, Liverpool John Moores University, April 2014

White, H. (2014) 'Policing the Neoliberal Crisis: An Introduction to my PhD Research' *European Group for the Study of Deviance and Social Control: Summer Newsletter II*

White, H. (2014) *'On the Road to Genocide? A Critical Analysis of the Neoliberal Narration of Crisis'* European Group for the Study of Deviance and Social Control 42nd Annual Conference, Liverpool John Moores University, September 2014

White, H. (2015) *'Resisting the Hegemonic: Countering Elite Manufactured Knowledge and Ignorance'* European Group for the Study of Deviance and Social Control 43rd Annual Conference, University of Tartu in Tallinn, September 2015

White, H. (2016) *'Westminster and the Politics of ignorance: Discursive Repression of An Anti-austerity Opposition'* European Group for the Study of Deviance and Social Control 44th Annual Conference, University of Minho in Braga, September 2016

Contact Details

Email: hollywhite@live.co.uk
Twitter: @HollyWhiteCrim

25

'What Was it All For?': 21st Century Theatres of War and the Return to 'Post-Conflict' Life

Hannah Wilkinson

Introduction

This chapter draws on doctoral research currently being undertaken with former military personnel who have served in recent conflicts. The project seeks to explore the impact of serving in 21st century theatres of war, primarily Afghanistan and Iraq, on the return to 'post-conflict' life. Placing a rare criminological focus on those who do not obviously appear to fit the constructions of 'criminal' or 'victim', this research will uncover the voices of those who have not previously entered knowledge production. This chapter will begin by providing an insight into the growing body of criminological literature termed 'Criminology and War', highlighting several current gaps in knowledge. The chapter will then discuss how this research aims to narrow or close these gaps, followed by a brief discussion of the adoption of a Bourdieusian theoretical framework. The chapter will then conclude with a selection of emerging findings and will introduce the creation and development of the theoretical concept of 'combat capital'.

'Criminology and War'

Until recent years, the criminological voice has been curiously "silent" on the subject and realities of war (McGarry and Walklate, 2016: 2). Although war never fully left the agenda of criminology, the presence of critical discussions around former military personnel and their post-military experience have been considerably lacking. Concern and debate around the number of veterans in prison led to the production of the NAPO report (2009), *Ex-armed forces personnel and the criminal justice system*, which ushered an increased awareness and interest in the resettlement of British military personnel post-war (Murray, 2013; 2014). The Howard

League (2011) conducted one of the first large scale qualitative research projects looking at former armed service personnel in prison. The report examined the transition from the armed forces to civilian life, highlighting several difficulties faced by former armed service personnel. This included employment, housing, and finance and considered the relationship between recruits from disadvantaged backgrounds and their involvement in crime.

The "veteran offender" has since become a defined category of prisoner, subject to (albeit often unclear and contradictory) tailored modes of governance (Murray, 2013: 20). Although constructions of the veteran as 'offender' and 'criminal' have gained considerable attention, there is an equally important construction of the soldier and veteran as 'victim'. McGarry and Walklate (2011: 192) explored the contradictions and tensions between the constructions of 'soldier' and 'victim', suggesting that soldiers may "experience conflict in more 'common place' ways, whether unknowing of the extent of the harms they have encountered or facing barriers to the care they may require". They also call for the research to consider "what happens to soldiers after their service" (ibid: 911) and to explore the experiences of those "who may be on the fringes of the discipline [of criminology] but are nonetheless very much within its capacity to understand" (ibid: 913). What appears to currently be lacking in Criminology and War is research that occupies the space between the constructions of people with military experience as 'criminal' or as 'victim'. Or, in other words, the focus has primarily been on those considered or identified to be 'problematic', failing to capture the experiences and voices that exist between these two constructions.

A further 'gap' in the Criminology of War concerns the lack of critical engagement with the changing nature of war and the impact this might have on military personnel serving within such conflicts. Twenty-first century wars, unlike the vast majority of previous warfare, can be seen as ambiguous and uncertain in their very nature (Kilcullen, 2007). Based on ideologically driven motivations, the 'War on Terror' is fuelled by notions of unspecified 'risk' (Mythen, 2016), as well as unclear enemies, battlefields and definitions of 'victory'. Moreover, 21st century conflict is no longer fought solely by armed forces in designated combat zones. Instead, conflict spills over into the arenas of politics, economics, and the media, and into previously 'safe' civilian spaces.

Although total war in the 20th century embodied many of these same features, the nature of war was very different. Total war was fought against defined nations and their people, involving civilian societies, economies, and labour being redirected towards the war effort. The enemy's entire society and infrastructure were the targets of military operations, meaning the whole population felt the effects and presence of war, regardless of which side of the war they happened to be on (Metz, 2000). In contrast, 21st century war is fought against 'rogue' factions, 'bad' regimes and conflicting ideologies, of which the fallout rarely reaches the Western civilian population (Mythen, 2016: 50; Duyvesteyn and Angstrom, 2005: 110-111). The war in Afghanistan, for example, has been described as being more of a "spectator sport" for the West, due to the developments in technological communication and weaponry, allowing for visible precision killing from afar (Ignatieff, 2000 in Duyvesteyn and Angstrom, 2005: 17).

In addition to this, criminological literature regularly makes reference to the return to 'civilian life', or 'civvy street' (see: Treadwell, 2010*a*; 2010*b*; McGarry and Walklate, 2011; 2015), yet often fails to open a discussion around where this is, or what this means for those with military experience. Returning to civilian life is thus treated as a homogeneous experience, appearing (albeit unintentionally) to assume that the term and concept of 'civvy street' holds the same meaning for each person. This proves to be even more problematic when one considers the equally lacking discussion within Criminology and War of the differences in civilian life that distinguish late modernity from earlier periods (see: Beck, 1992; Young, 2007), resulting in an increasing sense of ontological insecurity.

Closing the Gap

This research will contribute towards closing the identified gaps in knowledge and will form part of the emerging field of Criminology and War. Those with military experience who are identified or constructed as 'problematic' have formed the foundations of research within this area. This research will therefore take a step back from previous criminological work and will instead focus on those not considered to be 'problematic'. As such, these individuals are not known to be involved with the criminal justice system and/or veteran organisations that support those who have had 'problematic' transitions back to civilian life. The majority of participants in the research are thus drawn from the informal networks of contacts who had been involved in earlier projects (see: Wilkinson, 2012) using a snowball sampling technique. However, to allow some form of comparison between 'problematic' and 'non-problematic' individuals with military experience, a small sub-sample of participants was drawn from a veteran housing organisation, which supports those leaving prison.

Considering the lack of focus within Criminology and War on the impact of 21st century conflicts, particularly on the experiential elements of serving in and leaving combat areas, this research seeks to explore first-hand accounts of those who have served in recent conflicts (e.g. Afghanistan and Iraq) and those who have subsequently left the military. Data for this project has been collected through a series of in-depth narrative interviews incorporating photo-elicitation – a method that uses visual images to prompt memories and reflexively shape the structure of the interview (Harper, 2002; Oliffe and Bottorff, 2007; Jenkings *et al*, 2008). Conducting the research in this way facilitates meaningful exploration of the life-course of the participant, as well as enabling discussion of life before, during and after military service. Moreover, this allows for a critical consideration of the fundamental nuances of both contemporary conflicts and late-modern societies.

An additional gap within the Criminology and War literature is the absence of an adequate theorisation of the return to 'post-conflict' life. This research therefore, questions the very term 'post-conflict' life and suggests that modern civilian societies are subject to a number of conflict-inducing forces. High-profile terrorist incidents have had profound political and emotional impacts on society (Zedner, 2009). This involves a shift in the public's sense of security and tolerance of governmental interference with their lives – including the role of the state in conducting surveillance, restricting travel, and generally minimising the "terrorist threat" (Mythen, 2014: 50). Those who left conflict areas prior to the 'war on terror' may have had reasonable expectation of returning to a civilian life that was free of existential threats. However, present-day civilian life may be experienced as a continuation of 'conflicts', which may include internal and/or subjective struggles. For instance, the perceived conflicts between 'ex-squaddie' and 'civvy' identities affected the lives of all research participants in some way.

A Bourdieusian Framework

This research draws on the work of Weston (2016), which utilises the conceptual 'thinking tools' of Bourdieu (1977) within the drug recovery sphere. Much of the sociological literature, as well as most policy and practice initiatives draw upon ideas of capital in an overwhelmingly positive light when attempting to explain the problems of disadvantaged groups. For instance, various forms of capital have been used extensively to theorise the pathways of recovery for problematic drug users (White, 2015; 2016), leading to the creation of the concept 'recovery capital' (Granfield and Cloud, 2001; Cloud & Granfield, 2009). Cloud and Granfield (2009: 1977) expanded their concept to include "*negative* recovery capital", although there still appears to be a lack of clarity on precisely *how* the notion of a deficiency or 'debt' of capital can affect transitions.

To resolve these problems, this research builds upon the work of Weston (2016) and applies a Bourdieusian theoretical framework to a critical engagement with the lived experience of leaving the military and returning to civilian life. Recently, Cooper *et al* (2016) have attempted to produce a similar framework which draws upon the idea of 'cultural competence' to account for positive and negative transitions from military to civilian life. However, this work does not appear to have been underpinned by the collection of empirical data. This places Cooper *et al*'s work somewhat at odds with the grounded approach which Bourdieu himself advocated[1].

Emerging Findings

Within the military, habitus ('disposition'), field ('social space') and doxa ('rules of the game') are usually very clear. All recruits pass through the same 12-week training programme to begin with, which immerses them in the military field, along with the expectations of the doxa. As such, a military habitus is formed. It is emerging that this habitus, and doxa, are further cemented through active service. 'Tom' (participant in current research), when talking about his time in Afghanistan, emphasised how exposure to combat had "changed" him and his comrades, often creating barriers to those outside the military, particularly to family and friends: "you've all experienced something that no one else can understand". The creation of barriers to those without military experience also seems to contribute towards low levels of 'help-seeking' behaviour. The intensification of a military habitus, arising from combat experience, therefore appears to be one of the contributing factors to problematic transitions from military to civilian life.

Combat zones and conflict areas can be thought of as a site where two or more fields overlap to create the 'battlefield'. There are certain boundaries, rules of engagement, practice, and rehearsed manoeuvres

---

[1] For more information on Bourdieu's thinking tools see: Grenfell (2012.).

and tactics, with various agents occupying different positions and ultimately, engaging in a struggle for power. Participants regularly discuss their combat experience as a point of no return in terms of their military identity and in addition, as no longer perceiving themselves as civilian. The experiences gained within combat and the tightening of social bonds to those with whom they served, create a strengthened habitus that, on return, does not always fit within a civilian field.

> yeah it changed me (pause) I mean you can't un-see or un-hear that shit. You can't undo it... When you've been in a position where your every move and decision can mean life or death (pause) for you and those around you, yeah that changes you ('Liam', research participant)

> bloody civvies, running around doing their pointless bollocks, worrying about the rat race. I can't do it
> ('Josh', research participant)

What might be being displayed in the narratives of former personnel within this research is 'hysteresis'; a potential mismatch between habitus and field, between identity and surroundings.

The battlefield is a unique area, usually only accessible to those fighting within it. This is where 'combat capital' is acquired, a resource comprised of, for instance, social, cultural and physical capital, combat experience, skills, and training (see: Wilkinson and RCPPA, 2016). When these, along with other things come together, they form a value. Which, depending on the context, can be more or less valuable – like currency. Combat capital aims to capture the relationships and networks that form as part of military service and culture, and the benefits and pitfalls this can create. Combat experience further strengthens combat capital and when used as a thinking tool, can allow us to make sense of the complex processes of returning from conflict and, to critically examine the ways in which leaving certain conflicts can be more or less valuable in terms of capital and reintegration.

Although still in development, the concept of combat capital is already proving useful for making sense of the lived experiences of those serving in recent conflicts and returning to 'civvy street'. In addition to the contribution combat capital is making towards the interpretation of research data, it has also informed and changed practice within an organisation in the voluntary sector, which supports former military personnel. This has been achieved through the development of a training programme delivered to staff, drawing on the findings and concept of combat capital emerging from this research.

Combat capital also appears to capture the differences in leaving 21st century conflict when compared with other research regarding previous conflicts (Leed, 1979; Figley and Leventman, 1980; Forrest *et al*, 2009). One participant of the current research, when discussing his service in Iraq and on the recent outcome of the Chilcot Report (2016), captured the essence of 21st century wars that are fought with ambiguous justifications and with no apparent means of achieving victory. He discussed the costs of war and the losses he had suffered personally, including divorce, costs to his health, employment, and financial losses, and the physical loss of life among his friends and colleagues whilst at war and in addition, at home, through suicide. Reflecting on all this, he simply asked 'what was it all for?'.

Acknowledgements

I would like to thank Keele University for funding the research and to my trio of supervisors, Ronnie, Evi and Sam, for their continued support and guidance. Thanks must also go to the many members of the European Group for the Study of Deviance and Social Control, who have always provided me with a wealth of encouragement, support and friendship.

References

Beck, U. (1992) *Risk Society: Towards a New Modernity* London: SAGE

Bourdieu, P. (1977 [1972]) *Outline of a Theory of Practice,* Nice, R. (trans.) Cambridge: Cambridge University Press. Originally published as *Esquisse d'une théorie de la pratique, précédé de trois études d'ethnologie Kabyle* Switzerland: Library Droz S.A

Chilcot, J. (2016) *The Iraq Inquiry.* London: Her Majesty's Stationary Office. (Referred to in-text as 'Chilcot Report')

Cloud, W. and Granfield, R. (2009) 'Conceptualizing Recovery Capital: Expansion of a Theoretical Construct' *Substance Use & Misuse* Volume 43, No. 1 pp 1971-1986

Cooper, L. Caddick, N. Godier, L. Cooper, A. and Fossey, M. (2016) 'Transition from the Military Into Civilian Life: An Exploration of Cultural Competence'.

Armed Forces & Society. DOY 10.1177/0095327X16675965. Published online ahead of print, 12th December, 2016.

Duyvesteyn, I. and Angstrom, J. (2005) *Rethinking the Nature of War* London: Frank Cass

Figley, C. R. and Leventman, S. (1980) *Strangers at Home: Vietnam Veterans Since the War* Praeger: New York

Forrest, A. Hageman, K. and Rendall, J. (2009) *Soldiers, Citizens and Civilians: Experiences and Perceptions of the Revolutionary and Napoleonic Wars, 1790-1820* Hampshire: Palgrave Macmillan

Granfield, R. and Cloud, W. (2001) 'Social Context and "Natural Recovery": the Role of Social Capital in the Resolution of Drug-Associated Problems' *Substance Use & Misuse* Volume 36, No. 11 pp 1543-1570

Grenfell, M. (2012) *Pierre Bourdieu: Key Concepts* Durham: Acumen

Harper, D. (2002) 'Talking About Pictures: A Case for Photo Elicitation' *Visual Studies* Volume 17, No. 1 pp 13-26

Howard League For Penal Reform (2011) *Report of the Inquiry into Former Armed Service Personnel in Prison.* London: Howard League (Referred to in the text as 'Howard League')

Jenkings, K. N., Woodward, R. and Winter, T. (2008) 'The Emergent Production of Analysis in Photo Elicitation: Pictures of Military Identity' *Forum: Qualitative Social Research* Volume 9, No. 3, Art. 30

Kilcullen, D. J. (2007) 'New Paradigms for 21st –Century Conflict' *Foreign Policy Agenda, eJournal USA* Volume 12, No. 5 pp 39-45

Leed, E. J. (1979) *No Man's Land: Combat and Identity in World War I'* London: Cambridge University Press

McGarry, R. and Walklate, S. (2011) 'The Soldier as Victim: Peering Through the Looking Glass' *British Journal of Criminology* Volume 51, No. 1 pp 900-917

McGarry, R. and Walklate, S. (2015) *Criminology and War: Transgressing the Border* London: Routledge

McGarry, R. and Walklate, S. (2016) *The Palgrave Handbook of Criminology and War* London: Palgrave Macmillan.

Metz, S. (2000) *Armed Conflict in the 21st Century: The Information Revolution and Post-Modern Warfare* US: Strategic Studies Institute

Murray, E. (2013) 'Post-Army Trouble: Veterans in the Criminal Justice System' *Criminal Justice Matters* Volume 94, No. 1 pp 20-21

Murray, E. (2014) 'Veteran Offenders in Cheshire: Making Sense of the 'Noise'' *Probation Journal* Volume 61, No. 3, pp 251-264

Mythen, G. (2014) *The Risk Society: Crime, Security and Justice* Basingstoke: Palgrave Macmillan.

'What Was it All For?'

Mythen, G. (2016) 'Terrorism and War: Interrogating Discourses of Risk and Security' in McGarry, R. and Walklate, S. (eds) *The Palgrave Handbook of Criminology and War* London: Palgrave

NAPO (2009) 'Armed Forces and the Criminal Justice System: A briefing from Napo the trade union and professional association for family court and probation staff.' London: Napo. Available From http://www.revolving-doors.org.uk/documents/napo-report-on-ex-forces-in-criminal-justice-systems/ (accessed 6th March, 2015)

Oliffe, J. L. and Bottorff, J. L. (2007) 'Further Than the Eye can See? Photo Elicitation and Research with Men' *Qualitative Health Research* Volume 17, No. 6 pp 850-858

Treadwell, J. (2010a) 'Counterblast: More than Casualties of War?' in *The Howard Journal* Volume 49, No. 1 pp 73-77.

Treadwell, J. (2010b) 'Are Today's Heroes Tomorrow's Prisoners?' *Criminology in Focus* Volume 5, No. 1 pp 8

Weston, S. (2016) 'The Everyday Work of the Drug Treatment Practitioner: The Influence and Constraints of a Risk-Based Agenda' *Critical Social Policy* Volume 36, No. 4 pp 511-530

White, W. L. (2015) 'From Trauma to Transformative Recovery' *Advances in Addiction and Recovery* Volume 3, No. 1 pp 28-30

White, W. L. (2016) 'Multiple Pathways and Styles of Addiction Recovery' *CCAR Multiple Pathways of Recovery Conference.* Groton, Connecticut (US) 2nd May 2016.

Wilkinson, H. R. (2012) *The Army: A Pathway to or From Crime?* Unpublished BA (Hons) Dissertation. Keele University

Wilkinson, H. R. and Reimagining Conflict: Pedagogy, Policy and Arts Group. (2016) *An Interview with Hannah Wilkinson, PhD Candidate, Keele University.* [Online Video]. 26th September 2016. Available from: https://www.ljmu.ac.uk/microsites/reimagining-conflict-pedagogy-policy-and-arts-group/projects [Accessed 27/03/2017] (Referred to in-text as 'Wilkinson and RCPPA, 2016)

Young, J. (2007) *The Vertigo of Late Modernity* London: SAGE

Zedner, L. (2009) *Security* London: Routledge

Extended Biography

Research

I am a third year PhD student in Criminology, within the school of Social Science and Public Policy at Keele University, in Staffordshire, UK. My doctoral research is supervised by Professor Ronnie Lippens, Dr Evi Girling and Dr Samantha Weston, and is funded by the Faculty of Humanities and Social Science. Prior to starting the PhD, I completed a Bachelor of Arts degree in Law and Criminology, and a Master of Arts degree in Criminology and Criminal Justice, both at Keele University. I am also a sessional teacher in Criminology and have contributed to the undergraduate and postgraduate programmes at Keele.

In addition to teaching and PhD responsibilities, I have worked as a research assistant on projects in the areas of drug prevention amongst young people and the prevention of child sexual exploitation, as well as working alongside the Reimaging Conflict: Pedagogy, Policy and Arts (RCPPA) Group. Most notably, I took part in the RCPPA project, 'Reimagine the Veteran', which involved creating a video about my research for an online platform, with the aim of bridging the gap between academic and public knowledge.

My research interests centre on the constructions and maintenance of identities, social networks and various forms of capital, particularly amongst those who have suffered harm as a result of their contact with state institutions. I have a strong interest in qualitative methods and have found the inclusion of visual methods, namely photo elicitation (also using items and objects) within my current research to be extremely insightful.

Activism, Organisational Work and/or Professional Membership

In addition to my doctoral studies, I have been engaged in the development of a training programme, 'Working With Former Military Personnel', for Fry Housing Trust, a charity providing housing for those with an offending history. The training has been successfully delivered to staff and aims to raise awareness of some of the issues that people with military experience might face, as well as best practices for staff, to improve their day-to-day interactions with this group. For further information about this training programme, please use the contact details

Selected Works

Wilkinson, H. R. and Weston, S. (2015) *'The 'Dark Side' of Social Capital for Marginalised Groups'* European Group for the Study of Deviance and Social Control 43rd Annual Conference. Tallinn, Estonia, August 2015

Wilkinson, H. R. (2016) 'Social Capital in No Man's Land: Exploring the experiences of former military personnel returning to civilian life' *Criminology, Criminal Justice and Ex-Military Communities: The Way Ahead?* University of Liverpool, June 2016

Wilkinson, H. R. and Reimagining Conflict: Pedagogy, Policy and Arts Group. (2016) *An Interview with Hannah Wilkinson, PhD Candidate, Keele University.* [Online Video]. 26th September 2016. Available from: https://www.ljmu.ac.uk/microsites/reimagining-conflict-pedagogy-policy-and-arts-group/projects

Wilkinson, H. R. (2016) *'"That's What my Life was worth, 600 fucking quid a month": The 'Invisible' Costs of Serving in 21st Century Conflict'* European Group for the Study of Deviance and Social Control 44th Annual Conference, University of Minho in Braga, Portugal, September 2016

Wilkinson, H. R. (2017) 'The Risks, Costs and Uncertainties of Serving in 21st Century Conflict and Transitioning to a 'Post-Conflict' Life: "What Was it All For?"' *Critical Approaches to Risk and Security: East, South, North and West.* International Sociological Association (ISA) Sociology of Risk and Uncertainty Thematic Group Mid-Term Conference, Singapore Institute of Technology, Singapore, April 2017

Contact Details

Email: h.r.wilkinson3@gmail.com
Twitter: @hrwilkinson1

26

Prison Theatre as Method: Focused Ethnography and Auto-ethnography in a Chinese Prison

Xiaoye Zhang

Introduction to Theatre and Prison

Prison theatre is a term that has been most widely used when referring to theatre-based work within the criminal justice system. It has also been referred to as 'theatre in prisons', 'theatre in prison and probation services', and has been an umbrella term that includes a wide variety of practices including: drama-based 'correctional' programmes, theatre productions with or by prisoners, interactive performances in prisons by specialised theatre companies, and some also include theatre work with at risk youth or ex-offenders.

Prison theatre, although defined by the name of the institution, is similar in many ways to other theatre practices with a certain community of people, as it is often categorised as one sub-category of applied theatre praxis. However, its engagement with the formal establishment and the political and judiciary powers also have been proven to be unique (McAvinchey, 2011; Thompson, 1998; Taylor *et al*, 2011). The practice itself began long before the term was coined. The earliest record of theatre production with/by prisoners was in 1789 by convicts who helped to found the British Colony of New South Wales (McAvinchey, 2011: 55). A much more recent and perhaps more relevant example would be the performance of *Waiting for Godot* by San Francisco Actor's Company at San Quentin Prison in 1956 (McCamish, 2004: 52).

Prisons theatre has been developing and maturing in the past thirty years in many countries including the USA, Germany, Italy, Russia, Lebanon, Israel, and the UK (McAvinchey, 2011; Balfour, 2004). Since the publication of the book *Shakespeare Comes to Broadmoor* in 1992, there has been a collection of books and articles dedicated to the field of prison theatre (Thompson, 1998; McAvinchey, 2011; Taylor *at el*, 2011). Nevertheless, almost all of which are outside of the criminological discipline. One of the few conceptualisations of prison theatre practices by a Criminologist came from Sylvie Frigon. In the book chapter about her collaboration with a French dance company and female prisoners, Frigon (2014) proposed a *'performative criminology'* [italic on original]. As stated by Merrill and Frigon (2015: 303) 'theatrical work allows for criminology as a field to be further developed directly by those we spend so much time researching and theorizing about'. Another case study of prison theatre work from a very different perspective was offered by Sarah Colvin on literary fiction and its relevance to Criminology through an analysis of the work of a German prison theatre company, aufBruch's. Colvin approached aufBruch's work mainly from a literary studies perspective with a considerable amount of references to Maruna's *Making Good* (2001) in terms of narrative identity.

One of the founding scholars and practitioners of prison theatre, Michael Balfour, tried to encompass all aspects of prison theatre work holistically, and suggested a way of conceptualising this with the use of desistance theories (Davey *et al*, 2014). The authors discussed prison theatre in relation to different aspects such as the desistance process, pro-social narrative, human capital, and community engagement. The above literature goes beyond assessing performing art's direct impact on the research subjects (restricted to offenders mostly), with more of a shift towards 'prison theatre as method' and a more dramaturgical and performative analysis of prison life, as well as a focus on the cultural study of the prison institute in its total complexity. Prison theatre as method no longer confines the creative process as situated within the 'what works' framework of offender rehabilitation research, instead it allies itself with the 'what helps' investigation in the desistance paradigm (McNeill, 2006). It recognises prison theatre's prospective capacity in engaging with rehabilitation on the four levels of personal, social, moral, and judicial as proposed by desistance researchers (Warr, 1998; Laub and Sampson, 2001; McNeil, 2012).

The Chinese Context

Prison theatre is an entirely new concept for the Chinese penal system, not because there are no performances inside Chinese prisons, but because prison theatre is much more than just any performances inside the barbed wire. As with the projects mentioned above, prison theatre involves partnership between multiple parties: prison bureau (and other policy making agencies), the specific prison, art organisations (or other types of organisations), project practitioners, and often an evaluator. Being an authoritarian one-party state, Chinese civil society has never been very strong and healthy in general. Chinese prisons as a concentrated arena of political power has been very closed and secretive until very recently, hence the ideal and practice of civil participation and collaboration which underpins prison theatre praxis is also a very new-born concept.

In 1979, the Ministry of Justice was founded, and in 1983 through 'reform through labour' prison affairs were handed over from the police department to the Ministry of Justice. It wasn't until 1994 that the current *People's Republic of China Prison Law* was issued. In 2002, changes were made by the Justice Department to make prisons in many provinces closer to the cities, so as to enhance civil engagement in rehabilitation, and better reentry. Relocations received a huge amount of state funding and were planned to be completed by 2010. 2003 was an important year as the *Notice on Further Enhancement of Legalising, Scientising and Socialising Prison Work* (司法部关于进一步推进监狱工作法制化、科学化、社会化建设的意见，司发[2003]21号) was issued, and was thereafter referred to as "Three –ize" (三化), and appeared continuously in official discourse until today.

I am aware that "socialisation" in the English literature refers to the process of acquiring social skills and relationships as a child grows up (Maccoby and Martin, 1983). It can also point to the process of one being socially influenced by the culture of a particular group, such as the socialisation of new prisoners into the prison subculture, often referred to as 'prisonization' (Thomas, 1977). In both areas of research, the agent within the socialisation process is the individual human being. However, in the context mentioned above, the phrase "socialisation of prison" has the institution as the agent of socialisation, and in the Chinese discourse it refers to the increasing involvement of social organisation within the prison walls, as well as the selective opening up to the public about prison. This socialisation process of prison has also been described by a Chinese prison scholar as "the mutual opening" (Song, 2016: 28), which also advocates for prison resources to be more open for social engagement, especially in research and legal aspects. A phrase that describes the process more precisely might be 'restoration of the social prison', stressing the social role that prisons should take on more for the purpose of crime reduction, which also echoes with the restorative justice model.

Access to the Research Setting: A Chinese Prison

Research access into Chinese prisons has never been easy, it is strictly impossible for foreign scholars to conduct research in Chinese prisons in person due to the prison policies, therefore most English literature on the Chinese penal system come from research into historical materials, especially around the end of Qing dynasty and during Republic China era, and at most until the beginning of post-Mao era (Dikötter, 2002; Dutton, 1992; Kiely, 2014). Among Chinese scholars who have conducted research in Chinese prisons, the majority of them are survey or questionnaire based studies, partly because ethnography, fieldwork, participant observation and other qualitative in-depth methods require much more access and collaborative effort than is available.

In the first half of 2014, I spent five months approaching, negotiating and waiting to access to a Chinese prison for a practice-led research project on prison theatre workshop for my MA dissertation (project completion in August). I applied and began my PhD study in September 2015 knowing very clearly that I wanted to continue prison theatre practice and research. In February 2016, through a theatre producer friend's casual conversation with a friend of hers, I was introduced to the Performing Arts Centre of city A (PACA), as they were looking for a person with the relevant background to join them for a "Theatre Goes Inside" project. The head of the Education Department of the centre then connected me to W.X, who was the initiator and organiser of this project. I soon learnt that W.X is a professional actor, and two years ago he served a 9 months' sentence, half of which was in Prison B. Now he wishes to return to that prison and start a theatre group with the support, and in the name of, the state-owned PACA.

From February onwards, we started to exchange messages, emails and phone calls about our partnership. W.X was planning to start off the project in May, but the process was far messier and longer than he expected (before he reached me he had already spent a year working on getting two organisations together). Having settled all matters with the art centre, the prison and my institution on the collaboration, I finally moved to city A from Hong Kong and planned to be there full-time for six months. Before I moved there I only visited him and the prison officers once in person, they warned me about being careful with the publicity of my writing and told me that I had to restrict my research on this theatre project, not expanding it into their management or structural aspects.

Focused Ethnography Overview

By the time I moved from Hong Kong to city A, it had become clear that this would be a research with an ethnographic/grounded theory approach. However, it was also clear that this study would not be able to follow a typical immersive ethnographic method either, as my access to the prison was still very limited, and therefore a focused ethnographic approach would suit best, which is less immersed than an Anthropological ethnographic tradition and centres around selected elements in one's own society (Knoblauch, 2005). My fixed hours in the prison were every Wednesday from 8:30am until 4pm, and in about 60% of the weeks I would have one or two extra days there for viewing documents, or interviewing prisoners and officers. During the last two weeks, I spent almost every day there. My time spent in the prison was very 'focused' indeed, as I wasn't allowed to spend time in the cell block, factory-workshops, nor prisoner canteens, it was not going to qualify as a 'proper' ethnography for the study of life in the prison community. Therefore, my study is a prison theatre as method case study of the socialisation processes of Chinese prison today.

Auto-ethnography

Auto-ethnography, the researcher's autobiographical refection and its connections with the wider context, was an unavoidable and essential part of my research. This is not only because my participation required constant reflexivity, but also because the high level of sensitivity required complicated role management which was demanding throughout the whole process. The self-reflection can also be placed within a broader context relevant to the overall research in terms of the contemporary prison as a dynamic field of interaction between the past and the future, between conservative and liberal ideologies, and between closeness and openness. Below is a brief collection of my roles and identities during my fieldwork period, and how they were perceived by the other parties, and how they influenced and informed me as well.

PhD student
I am certain that the student identity had placed me under a certain protective colour which gave a certain sense of ease to the prison authorities. The student identity also implies a 'still a learner' status, which is important for any researchers as it presents an invitation for the

research participants or informants to 'teach' you. I often came across the impression that many people do not place a big difference between PhD student and Doctors, this also manifested in the prison as I was referred to as 'Dr. Zhang' by both prison officers and prisoners. Being a 'Dr.' also brings about contradicting effects: on the one hand, academic scholarship is highly regarded in China, but at the same time there is also a strong distain to the armchair academics. As one midlevel prison official advised me: "What you are missing is actually doing the job. There are many prison 'experts' who have no idea what's going on!". I was invited by him to join the prison work force upon my PhD completion on multiple occasions. This also reflected a complex relationship between the political leaders and the intellectuals, as I have often placed my observation of the prison in the context of the party history.

Researcher (who writes in English)
Being the first outside researcher prison B has ever had (as I was told), I was received quite well by the officers of the Education and Correction department with whom I worked closely with at all times. However, most of the times when I met with a more senior official, I would be warned that prison is still a very sensitive area, and that they knew the world was watching China's human rights records, and "prison is the frontline of this fight". Nevertheless, I was allowed access, given a certificate of appointment as the academic consultant for prison theatre programme, and finished my six-month engagement there including audio taped interviews with officers and prisoners. This is also an indicator of the changing climate in Chinese prisons in the past few years as part of the mutual opening process.

PACA Project consultant
This role was to a certain extent conflicted with my role as a researcher of the project, but the extent to which it worked against/for my research depended on how I managed the relationship and collaboration creatively. To be concise, in the six-month period of time I went through roughly four stages: Participant Observation (low level participation), Participatory Action Research/Practice-led Research (high level participation), Participant Observation (medium level participation), and in the final two weeks, back to low level participant observation.

Prison B theatre correctional programme academic consultant
I was handed a thick red velvet textured "Letter of Appointment" as academic consultant on the theatre correctional programme, at an official conference in front of the whole 2000+ prison population. The uneasiness I felt when my overseas affiliating institutions were announced loudly across the big hall was particularly interesting. I was not given any actual tasks to complete, but because of my newly acquired identity within the prison I was spared from signing a formal contract of confidentiality, but only a "letter of intent of confidentiality". According to my partners from PACA (two of them have also received such a certificate), it was merely a symbolic gesture of appreciation since the prison was not paying for the most part.

Workshop facilitator
From the beginning of the third month until the end of the last month, I was facilitating the weekly theatre workshops mostly on my own because my partners were too busy with their commercial performances. During which time, I designed and led various activities, and had interesting feedback that helped my understanding of the culture inside. Another interesting discovery also arose from this period of intensive frontline participation: a comparison between the facilitation between W.X and I, and most importantly how the prisoners and officers received us differently. This leads to a rich case study of a comparative model of engagement which also echoes with the "prison theatre learnt" and "prison theatre found" comparison (or "Western" versus "Chinese characteristics") at large.

Conclusion

The above presented material is an important but small part of my PhD thesis, which I hope to complete by autumn 2018. The self-reflection used in the auto-ethnography has documented my personal experience of getting access into a Chinese prison, which for too many researchers is an impossible mission. The dilemma arose from conflict and identity confusion within my role and was examined with respect to the political and penal culture of China. As far as I understand, this was the first 'research Chinese-prison-break' achieved by a female doctoral student trained in London and Hong Kong. I hope this piece of study would contribute to the "Three –ize" in the development of rehabilitative and restorative services in Chinese prisons.

Zhang

Acknowledgements

My sincere gratitude to my PhD supervisor Prof. T Wing Lo and the Department of Applied Social Science at City University of Hong Kong for providing me with this platform and financing my research. I would like to thank my colleagues and research participants at PACA and Prison B for making everything happen. I also extend my sincere thanks to the European Group for the Study of Deviance and Social Control for inspiring ideas and exciting opportunities.

References

Balfour, M. (2004) *Theatre in prison: Theory and practice* Intellect Books

Cox, M. (1992) *Shakespeare Comes to Broadmoor: The Actors are Come Hither: the Performance of Tragedy in a Secure Psychiatric Hospital.* Jessica Kingsley Publishers.

Dikötter, F. (2002) The Promise of Repentance. Prison Reform in Modern China. *British Journal of Criminology* Volume 42, No.2 pp 240-249

Davey, L. Day, A. and Balfour, M. (2015) Performing desistance: how might theories of desistance from crime help us understand the possibilities of prison theatre? *International journal of offender therapy and comparative criminology* Volume 58, No.9 pp 798-809

Dutton, M.R. (1992) *Policing and punishment in China: from patriarchy to" the people"* (Vol. 141). Cambridge: Cambridge University Press

Frigon, S. (2014) *When prison blossoms into art: Dance in prison as an embodied critical creative performative criminology* Ashgate Publishing: London

Kiely, J. (2014) *The Compelling Ideal: Thought Reform and the Prison in China, 1901-1956* Connecticut: Yale University Press

Knoblauch, H. (2005) Focused ethnography, *Forum: qualitative sozialforschung/forum: qualitative social research*, Volume 6, No.3 p 1

Laub, J.H. and Sampson, R.J. (2001) Understanding desistance from crime *Crime and Justice* Volume 28, pp 1-69

Laub, J.H. Nagin, D.S. and Sampson, R.J. (1998) Trajectories of change in criminal offending: Good marriages and the desistance process, *American Sociological Review*, Volume 63, No.2 pp 225-238

Maccoby, E.E. and Martin, J.A. (1983) Socialization in the context of the family: Parent-child interaction in Mussen, P.H. (1983) *Handbook of child psychology: formerly Carmichael's Manual of child psychology*

Maruna, S. (2001) *Making good: How ex-convicts reform and rebuild their lives* American Psychological Association

Merrill, E. and Frigon, S. (2015) Performative Criminology and the "State of Play" for Theatre with Criminalized Women *Societies* Volume 5, No.2 pp 295-313

McAvinchey, C. (2011) *Theatre & prison* Palgrave Macmillan.

McCamish, M.D. (2004) *The Theatre of Prison: Power and Resistance, Family and the Production of Illegality, Starring the California Department of Corrections* (Doctoral dissertation, California Institute of Integral Studies).

McNeill, F. (2012) Four forms of 'offender' rehabilitation: Towards an interdisciplinary perspective. *Legal and Criminological Psychology*, Volume 17, No.1, pp 18-36

McNeill, F. (2006) A desistance paradigm for offender management. *Criminology & Criminal Justice*, Volume 6, No.1 pp 39-62

Song, L. (2016) Predicament of Prison and the Mutual Opening Strategies (监 狱 的 困 境 及 双 向 开 放 策 略). *Journal of Henan Judicial and Police Vocational College (河 南 司 法 警 官 职 业 学 院 学 报)* no.1, pp. 23-29

Taylor, J. Dworin, J. Buell, B. Sepinuck, T. Palidofsky, M. Tofteland, C. McCabe-Juhnke, J. Jinks, J. Lajoie, S. Dowling, A. and Trounstine, J. (2011) *Performing New Lives: Prison Theatre* London: Jessica Kingsley Publishers.

Thomas, C.W. (1977) Theoretical perspectives on prisonization: A comparison of the importation and deprivation models *Journal of Criminal Law and Criminology*, Volume 68, No. 1 pp 135 - 145

Thompson, J. (ed) (1998). *Prison theatre: perspectives and practices*. London: Jessica Kingsley Publishers

Warr, M. (1998) "Life-course transitions and desistance from crime" *Criminology* Volume 36, No.2 pp 183-216

Extended Biography

Research

I obtained my Bachelor of Arts in English from Nanjing Normal University Taizhou College in 2010, and a Master of Arts in Applied Theatre from Goldsmith College, University of London in 2014. After graduating from Goldsmith, I returned to Beijing and worked as project coordinator for the 6th Nanluoguxiang International Performing Arts Festival from January to August 2015, just before I enrolled in the PhD programme at City University of Hong Kong in September 2015. For my MA dissertation, I returned to China and attempted to find a prison to experiment on offering theatre workshops to prisoners. After four months, I finally obtained access and assistance to work in a male adult prison in Beijing with two groups of pre-release unit prisoners, aged between 20-60 and all within three months of their release date. 25 hours of workshops in total were carried out with each group.

I am currently in continuous collaboration with a state-owned performing arts centre and a local prison through their theatre project, where I have carried out focused ethnographic work for 6 months as discussed in the main section of this chapter. However, the research will be an ongoing project, and currently this project aims to cover theatre work with prison officers as well, which I am also enthusiastic to research. The collaboration invoked and continues to gather a variety of materials and observations on different aspects of prison study: offender rehabilitation, narratives of offenders, officer anxieties, identity and politics, and much more. I am also working with other groups under applied theatre praxis outside of the criminal justice system, and reflecting on this practice through research and writing.

I have two main areas of research: one is around prison, and the other is around the practice of the Theatre of the Oppressed in the Chinese context, currently with a focus on gender-related oppression. Both the practices and research originated during my MA study at Goldsmith, where I uncovered Prison Theatre for the first time and immediately knew that this is what I wanted to devote myself to. Theatre of the oppressed can be said to be one of the fundamental rocks of applied theatre, which is a system of theatrical practices originating in Brazil in the 1970s as a form "language", a means and a space for self-cultivation, sharing, and empowerment of oppressed individuals and groups. A 'rehearsal for revolution', or put mildly, rehearsal for life. It expects and aims for a performative efficacy of transforming reality as its 'end point'. Having learnt and experienced prison theatre and theatre of the oppressed in the British context, it was only natural for me to want to experiment and develop these concepts and praxis in my own cultural, social and political soil. The desire of doing so was also coupled with a need to better navigate the socialist China in its various conflicting forms, and to participate through theatre with a focus on the punishment and rehabilitation of the criminalised.

I have just finished a Chinese language draft of a piece of practice-led research on gender and forum theatre (theatre of the oppressed), and will be working on an English version for academic publication. I will also start to work on a collection of prisoner autobiographies with a narrative criminological approach, the preliminary findings are due to be presented at the Second Narrative Criminology Symposium in June this year in Oslo, with a formal written publication to follow afterwards. I have also applied to participate in a research project organised by the Research Institute of Crime Prevention under the Criminal Justice Department of China on the socialisation (opening up) of prison's correctional work. The most recent research proposal I am involved in is a collective research project on a comparative study of present prison managerial predicaments and solutions in mainland China, Taiwan and Hong Kong, which will hopefully result in a book.

Activism, Organisational Work and/or Professional Membership
During my years of working with theatre festival and project-based collaborations, I have worked with several LGBT groups and Non-Governmental Organisations (NGOs) in China (including translation work during my college years). I have also been officially appointed by one prison as their academic consultant on theatre in rehabilitation. Another movement which I used to be very involved in was the Camphill Community Movement, as I spent three years after college graduation living and working in one of the Camphill Communities for young adults in England: http://www.mountcamphill.org I have given talks and interviews about my experience there and how the community live and thrive with its residents of various needs in China.

Future Aspirations
In the coming years, apart from finishing my PhD thesis and the aforementioned research projects, I wish in particular to turn to three other areas of research: women's prison in China, Chinese prison officers, and comparative studies of prisons in mainland China, Taiwan, and Hong Kong.

Selected Works
Correction Collaborated: A Case Study of Theatre Project by X Prison and Local Performing Arts Centre. *Journal of Crime and Corrections Research* (in Chinese), 2017 (In progress)

A Play Within a Play: A Pilot Study of Prison Theatre Workshop in a Beijing Adult Male Prison (English). Conference presentation at Cultural Typhoon, Tokyo, Japan, 2016

Prison Theatre: Rehearsing for a Better Future (Chinese). *New Script Magazine,* 2016(5)

Article about Forum Theatre as Practice for a sociological imagination (in Chinese):https://mp.weixin.qq.com/s?__biz=MzI1ODQ4OTYzMA==&mid=2247483666&idx=1&sn=55557b60f6938ce3006540f4a4d0244e&scene=0#wechat_redirect

Article about practice-led research of forum workshop and public performances on gender-based oppression in two cities in China (in Chinese):https://mp.weixin.qq.com/s?__biz=MzI1ODQ4OTYzMA==&mid=2247483758&idx=1&sn=0927f467801839b93e0fc379f7051d3f&scene=0#wechat_redirect

Contact Details
Email: zxy.light@gmail.com
Academia.edu: https://cityu-hk.academia.edu/ZhangYe

Available from

Press

http://www.egpress.org/

Voices of Resistance
Edited by: *Kym Atkinson, Antoinette R. Huber and Katie Tucker*
A collection of postgraduate essays exploring subjugated knowledge and the challenge it represents to the criminal justice system.

Cadenza: A Professional Autobiography
Thomas Mathiesen (with the assistance of Snorre Smàri Mathiesen)
The English translation of Mathiesen's important account of his career as a public intellectual and activist

Women Crime and Criminology: A Celebration
Edited by: *Helen Monk and Joe Sim*
Includes contributions from Frances Heidensohn, Richard Collier and Carol Smart as well as an introduction by Helen Monk and Joe Sim.

Beyond Criminal Justice
Edited by: *J.M. Moore, Bill Rolston, David Scott and Mike Tomlinson*
An Anthology of Abolitionist Papers presented to conferences of the European Group for the Study of Deviance and Social Control.

Emancipatory Politics and Praxis
David Scott (with Emma Bell, Joanna Gilmore, Helena Gosling, J M Moore and Faith Spear)
An anthology of essays written for the European Group for the Study of Deviance and Social Control, 2013-16

Penal Abolitionism
Edited by: *Andrea Beckman, J.M. Moore and Azrini Wahidin*
Papers from the Penal Law, Abolition and Anarchism Conference Volume I

Justice, Power and Resistance
The Journal of the European Group for the Study of Deviance and Social Control.
For details of volumes published and subscriptions please visit
http://www.egpress.org/content/justice-power-and-resistance

Made in the USA
Columbia, SC
11 October 2017